YANKEE KINGDOM
VERMONT AND NEW HAMPSHIRE

REGIONS OF AMERICA

A series of books that depict our natural regions, their history, development and character.

Edited by Carl Carmer

YANKEE KINGDOM

VERMONT AND NEW HAMPSHIRE

UPDATED EDITION

RALPH NADING HILL

Illustrations by George Daly

A REGIONS OF AMERICA BOOK

HARPER & ROW, PUBLISHERS

NEW YORK, EVANSTON, SAN FRANCISCO, LONDON

Map by Jean Tremblay

For Lura B. Cummings

CONTENTS

ACKNOWLEDGMENTS

The generous help and encouragement of the following persons is gratefully acknowledged. Dr. Seymour T. D. Bassett, Mr. William Beardsley, Mr. Allan J. Bertrand, Mr. Harrison A. Brann, Mrs. Dorothy Brodie, Mr. Carl Carmer, Mr. John Clement, Mr. John De Courcy, Dr. John S. Dickey, Miss Julie Eidesheim, Professor Allen R. Foley, Mr. Philip Guyol, Mr. Walter Hard, Jr., Captain B. J. Harral, Professor Herbert W. Hill, Governor Phillip H. Hoff, Dr. Ernest M. Hopkins, Professor John Huden, Mr. Edward Connery Lathem, Mr. Marcus A. McCorison, Mrs. Joyce McLaughlin, Miss Fannie Rothman, Miss Mary L. Roy, Mr. Glenn B. Skillin, Miss Dorothy M. Vaughan, and Mr. M. S. Wyeth, Jr.

R. N. H.

I

PROLOGUE

The happy union of the four seasons with the mountain and valley country has been put asunder. In *A Study of History* Arnold Toynbee has declared that New Hampshire is north of "the optimum climatic area" and that Maine is merely the habitat of "woodmen and watermen and hunters." Except as an offshoot of New York, Vermont is not mentioned. "...when we speak of New England and the part it has played in American history," says this distinguished assessor of civilizations, "we are really thinking of only three of its five little states—of Massachusetts, Connecticut and Rhode Island." Since this book is written in admiration of Vermont and New Hampshire, the chronicler of the excellent state of Maine must fend for himself, and should make rewarding work of it.

If you are to accept Vermont as a part of New England, Mr. Toynbee, there are in all *six* states. And if your readers are to accept the phrase "optimum climatic area" for what it seems to mean, they must ask how it is possible to draw a line boldly through an area and assert that everything to the south is optimum and everything to the north more or less minimum. For if optimum areas are those where people respond most vigorously to their background of climate and geography, and you do not include New Hampshire and Vermont among them, then, Mr. Toynbee, your theory does not hold water.

Our winters are hard, no denying that, and back in the sheep-raising days they used to joke about our special breed with pointed noses that evolved from eating grass between the stones. But the word "Yankee," which during recent wars at least has come to mean all Americans, has a unique significance when applied to the spare, silent and frugal people of the three northernmost New England states. In field and factory, in the councils of the nation during peace and war, the people of Vermont and New Hampshire, whether as a result of geography and climate, optimum or otherwise, have shown spirit and character that have marked American institutions permanently and irrevocably. They have done so to a degree that is all out of proportion to their numbers and to the size of their homeland.

Through the years the number of native-born Vermonters in *Who's Who in America* has been astonishingly high; indeed, in

3

at least one year, Mr. Toynbee, there were more per capita than from any other state. This sinfully provincial statistic is offered in defense, not so much of a state as of a region which you believe to be the preserve of woodmen, watermen, hunters and tourists. We do have a good many visitors, but how does it happen that so many of those who think are not only touring but moving to these minimum states from such optimum places as New York City? It is true that an enormous emigration to other parts of the country has held the populations of these states nearly stationary but this can be traced as much or more to the ambition and vitality of the emigrants, and their need for room to grow, as to the harsh disciplines of life on the vertical pastures of the White and Green Mountains. Of course, by the time these emigrants "escaped" the disciplines of the upland farm they had already become disciplined; they had developed an impelling physical and intellectual force that enabled them to deal effectively with any environment. The people of the more "optimum" areas found them useful in fighting their wars, founding their religions, their colleges and businesses, establishing and editing their newspapers, building and running their railroads.

From your statement implying that nothing important ever happened in the New England northcountry, one must conclude that your *Study of History* is no study of our history, at least. You are concerned with the rise and collapse of whole civilizations. It may surprise you that nowhere in the United States is the democratic ideal more fully embodied in government and in the life of the people than in these two tiny American states tucked away up east under the Canadian border. According to Viscount James Bryce, a former ambassador to the United States from your native England:

> You men of northern Vermont and northern New Hampshire, living among its rocks and mountains in a region which may be called the Switzerland of America—you are the people here who have had hearts full of love of freedom which exists in mountain people, and who have the indomitable spirit and the unconquerable will which we always associate with the lake and mountain lands of the Alps and Scotland.

Consider also the words of one who became a more or less permanent tourist, Sinclair Lewis: "If you happen still to have faith in
Democracy, you will rejoice that for at least a few years there will
be refuge for that quaint doctrine in this odd, beautiful, tight-
lipped, cautiously humorous state." He happened to be referring to
Vermont, but a good many things you can say about Vermont go
for New Hampshire, and vice versa. They are "yoke-fellows in the
sap-yoke of old in many marches," says Robert Frost, whom you
Englishmen consider America's foremost contemporary poet and
whose life has been spent in, and much of whose poetry is about,
this less than "optimum" land.

It is noble country from the Isles of Shoals and the tidal inlets
of the Piscataqua 200 miles west over the mountains to glimmering
Champlain. The whole is rich in human experience and in meaning
not only because, in the words of de Tocqueville, it is here that
"democracy finds a more judicious choice than it does elsewhere,"
but because in the wild tempo of the present day it is one of the
truly civilized places in which to live.

Traveling north through the Champlain valley not long ago
two men fell to discussing what one of them called the "myth" of
Vermont. "You are talking of a Vermont that once was, but no
longer is," declared the driver.

"Look around you," answered his friend, a native of the Green
Mountains. "What makes you think this is any less beautiful than
it was a hundred years ago?" He waved toward the gentle green
hills and the lake bathed in sunshine and the blue Adirondacks
beyond.

"Right here, yes. But Burlington and Rutland are no more the
old Vermont than Manchester and Nashua are the old New
Hampshire. All right, I'll grant that the small towns are pretty
much the same. What I'm talking about is the people—all the
stories about the old-time Yankee. I'll bet five dollars that the
proprietor of the next store we come to is a French Canadian."

"Take you up," said the Vermonter, defenseless for the moment
and annoyed at being pinned down to a bet that wouldn't necessarily prove anything.

They entered a small general store not far up the road. At first as they gazed across the miscellany of merchandise they could see no one. But then, way up back, they saw an elderly man standing at a wall-type telephone. He had been listening since they entered but now he straightened up and in unmistakable accents announced to the party on the line: "We don't deliver, and that's *final!*"

The Vermonter at the door held out his hand to receive the $5 that his friend had already extracted from his wallet.

The legendary New Hampshire and Vermont Yankee—independent, frugal, laconic, somewhat austere (but, as Charles Edward Crane says, with recesses of beauty, like the chambered Nautilus)—is still present in flesh and spirit. He has made some concessions to the twentieth century but his individuality has not yet been eroded away. And the character of a countryside that Bernard DeVoto said is every American's second home remains largely the same. The valley towns, white and serene, seem to have become a universal symbol of nostalgia—of belonging somewhere, even to those who have seen only pictures of them reproduced on calendars. The reason is, perhaps, that the people of a rootless age find something admirable about a slice of hillcountry that has resisted being made over into the latest fashionable image.

During the past few years there have been symptoms of a tremendously renewed interest in the American heritage. This may be because we are now old enough as a nation to look back at our beginnings with real perspective and appreciation, but there is a deeper reason, a psychological one. If we do not know where we are going today, it is at least reassuring to know where we have come from. It is comforting to sense our kinship with the pioneers whose burdens were far heavier than ours but who nevertheless seemed to know where *they* were going.

A country without history and a people without tradition are a country and a people without character. Vermont and New Hampshire are, in this respect, abundantly rich. To their heritage of history, to their mountains and valleys, and to the four seasons, northcountry Yankees must owe their survival as rugged individuals in a suburban age of "togetherness."

II

WHITE STRANGERS
IN THE SHADOWS

During the late sixteen-hundreds a New Hampshire minister was berating his congregation for lacking the piety of their ancestors, whereupon one of his parishioners said: "Sir, you entirely mistake the matter; our ancestors did not come here on account of their religion, but to fish and trade." It is clear that Portsmouth was not Plymouth Rock nor Jamestown and that the people who first dwelt there—at Strawberry Bank on the rim of the deep harbor—were Pilgrims only in the sense that they were the first to come—in 1623.

The explorers were the earliest traders, although sometimes they came just for adventure or glory. Forty voyages to our shores before the coming of the Pilgrims are recorded and probably there were many more that we know nothing about, even before the hallowed date of 1492. Cabot came in 1498 and Corterreal in 1501. In 1524 Verrazzano sailed the New England coast and, says Parkman, surveyed "ill-pleased the surf-beaten rocks, the pine tree and the fir, the shadows and the gloom of mighty forests." Over three quarters of a century later, near the end of the reign of Queen Elizabeth, a member of Bartholomew Gosnold's crew wrote of going upon the unknown coast of Maine and New Hampshire and of seeing land full of "faire" trees and a Baske-shallop full of naked Indians "of tall stature, broad and grim visage, of blacke swarthe complexion, their eye-browes painted white."

The next year, 1603, two small ships named the *Speedwell* and the *Discoverer*, carrying a crew of 43, including a youth "who played homely airs upon the gitterne" and two great mastiffs, Foole and Gallant, sailed up the lower Piscataqua into the great forests behind New Hampshire's coastline. Discoverer Martin Pring found "Deere, Beares, Wolves, Lucernes [lynxes] and Dogges with sharp noses," but no one with whom to trade his cargo of clothing, spades and axes, "scissors and chissels," bells, beads, bugles and looking glasses, thimbles and needles. The cod fishing was excellent, better than at Newfoundland, thought Pring, and he imagined the possibilities of trading in furs.

The most durable of the explorers was Samuel de Champlain, a native of the port of Brouage, sometime soldier in Brittany, captain in the French Navy, adventurer in the West Indies, Mexico and

9

Panama, observer of the desolate St. Lawrence, mapmaker of the harbors and headlands of the New England coast, of the Isles of Shoals, guardians of Portsmouth, and of the harbor itself. His character, says Parkman, "belonged partly to the past, partly to the present. The crusader, the romance-loving explorer, the curious knowledge-seeking traveller, the practical navigator, all claimed their share in him." This dauntless adventurer (who took as his bride a child of twelve) wrote that he "delighted marvelously in these enterprises." Though his companions fell victim to scurvy or the cold, spring found Champlain always alive and optimistic about his search for a route to the Indies.

It was in 1605 that he had navigated the Maine and New Hampshire coast and had seen, far to the west, the peaks of the White Mountains. He had spent the next two winters in North America and returned to France only to embark again, in 1608, with Sieur de Monts. On April 18 his ship left the Brittany port of Honfleur and stood for the Grand Banks, Gaspé and the long St. Lawrence that Jacques Cartier had navigated many decades before. In the fall a young Algonquin chief from the river Ottawa begged him to lead an expedition against the Iroquois, the warriors of the Five Nations, and the following spring, 1609, the 43-year-old Champlain resolved to do so.

At the mouth of the River of the Iroquois, now the Richelieu, which drains the great lake bordering western Vermont into the St. Lawrence, Champlain's boisterous allies paused to hunt, to feast—and to quarrel. Three quarters of them withdrew, but with the remainder, 60 warriors in 24 canoes, Champlain pressed forward. With each dip of the paddles his pinnace passed silently up an aisle of green until he came to swift rapids. Here a portage through the forest brought him again to quiet water and the southward voyage was resumed. Certainly in all Champlain's travels there had been no such majesty as that now unveiled in the distance.

At first the lake had seemed no more than a river, but then great islands, heavy with foliage and game, had passed, and now in mid-July, beyond a promontory (Cumberland Head) that had withheld a longer view, the water widened grandly to reveal at its far limits tiers of blue mountains both east and west. Scarcely knowing what to put down in his journal, Champlain wrote that the Indians had given him the snout of a garfish which is "wonderfully cunning in that when it wishes to catch birds, it goes into the rushes or reeds that border the lake in several places. The result is that when the birds come and light on its snout, mistaking it for a stump of wood, the fish is so cunning that, shutting its half-open mouth, it pulls them by their feet under water."

The Indians asserted that the lake went to meet the [Green] mountains [by way of rivers] to the east. Champlain described finding a grove of chestnuts, which probably placed him on the banks of the Winooski River, where settlers later found such trees. The fireflies astonished him. One night he dreamed of an Iroquois drowning in the lake. Seizing upon this as a happy omen, his Algonquin scouts told him he would meet his enemies to the west at the foot of the [Adirondack] mountains. To the south the lake still disappeared beyond the horizon, but as the days passed it narrowed and the bays and points and rocky escarpments to the west and east drew nearer. Danger, too, was close at hand and the Indians insisted that they travel at night.

On the evening of July 29 Champlain came to a cape on the western shore which some historians believe to have been the promontory below what was to become Fort Ticonderoga. Others declare that it was Crown Point, ten miles to the north, later the site of two other great fortresses, where the lake is so narrow that a shout on the New York shore may be heard in Vermont. Here or near here on this fateful night three and a half centuries ago, Iroquois cries and shouts pierced the dark. The enemy, quickly paddling to the west shore, threw up a barricade and ambassadors from them again appeared out of the night in two elm-bark canoes. According to Champlain, they wanted to know whether his Indians would fight

> and these replied that they had no other desire, but for the moment nothing could be seen and that it was necessary to wait for daylight in order to distinguish one another. They said that as soon as the sun should rise, they would attack us, and to this our Indians agreed.

Both nations of Indians passed the night screaming insults, the Iroquois on land and the Algonquins in their canoes lashed together offshore. Early in the dawn battle lines were drawn up and Champlain's war party could see that they were outnumbered three to one, for there were about two hundred Iroquois.

> They came slowly to meet us with a gravity and calm which I admired; and at their head were 3 chiefs. Our Indians likewise advanced . . . and told me that those who had the 3 big plumes were the chiefs . . . and I was to do what I could to kill them. . . . I marched on until I was within some 30 yards from the enemy, who as soon as they caught sight of me halted and gazed at me and I at them. When I saw them make a move to draw their bows upon us, I took aim with my arquebus and shot straight at one of the three chiefs, and with this shot 2 fell to the ground and one of their companions was wounded who died thereof a little later . . . as soon as our people saw this shot so favorable for them, they began to shout so loudly that one could not have heared it thunder, and meanwhile the arrows flew thick on both sides. The Iroquois were much astounded although they were provided with shields made of cotton thread woven together and wood, which were proof against their arrows . . . seeing their chiefs dead, they lost courage and took to flight . . . into the depths of the forest, wither I pursued them and laid low still more of them. Our Indians also killed several and took 10 or 12 prisoners.

Pursuing his explorations after the battle, Champlain scouted to the south the outlet of Lake George which drains into Champlain at Ticonderoga. The fact that he did this immediately after his victory lends credence to the belief that Ticonderoga was the scene of his encounter with the Iroquois. Guy Coolidge says, however, that the discoverer, returning northward, paused at Chimney Point on the Vermont shore directly opposite Crown Point and there gave his name to the lake. That night his Indians bivouacked at the mouth of Otter Creek, some ten miles north, to torture their prisoners. It is a ghastly story that he painted, and one rarely told, although a more graphic account of Indian battle temperament is nowhere to be found.

> . . . the Indians, towards evening, took one of the prisoners, to whom they made a harangue on the cruelties which he and his friends without any restraint had practiced upon them, and that similarly he should resign himself, to receive as much, and they ordered him to sing, if he had the heart. He did so, but it was a very sad song to hear.

Meanwhile our Indians kindled the fire, and when it was well lighted, each took a brand and burned this poor wretch a little at a time in order to make him suffer the greater torment. Sometimes they would leave off, throwing water on his back. Then they tore out his nails and applied fire to the ends of his fingers. . . . Afterwards they scalped him and caused a certain kind of gum to drop very hot upon the crown of his head. Then they pierced his arms near the wrists and with sticks pulled and tore out his sinews by main force, and when they saw that they could not get them out, they cut them off. This poor wretch uttered strange cries, and I felt pity at seeing him treated this way. Still he bore it so firmly that sometimes one would have said he felt scarcely any pain. They begged me repeatedly to take fire and do like them. I pointed out to them that we did not commit such cruelties, but that we killed people outright, and that if they wished me to shoot him with the arquebus, I should be glad to do so. They said no, for he would not feel any pain. I went away from them as if angry at seeing them practice so much cruelty on his body.

When they saw that I was not pleased, they called me back and told me to give him a shot with the arquebus. I did so, without his perceiving anything, and with one shot caused him to escape all the tortures he would have suffered.

2

History applauds the discoverer who kept journals and sometimes exaggerated his accomplishments. But what claim is to be made for the mysterious people who built the stone tower at Newport, Rhode Island—if indeed they did—and for the Bretons and Basques who were known to be fishing in Newfoundland and Nova Scotia during the fifteen-hundreds and probably strayed to the coast of New Hampshire?

The pages of history, prior to the lucid journal of Champlain, are unfortunately blank. Was the Indian population once large? What of the ancient residents of prehistory, the so-called "red paint people" whose skeletons, crumbling upon contact with the air, have been found in a sitting position facing east? In each case the sand around them was noticeably red, or reddish brown. From the evidence unearthed, chiefly stone objects varying according to their period, the timetable of Indian occupation seems to have run as follows: a pre-Algonquin and/or Eskimo culture extending from a date prior to 2000 B.C. to perhaps A.D. 1300. From 1300 to 1790 the recent Algonquin tribes, each speaking a different dialect, were wholly confined to New England and Canada. For a time their Mohegan brothers controlled Lakes Champlain and George, but the Mohawks ruled these waters when Champlain arrived. Without the security provided by his arquebus the Algonquins might never have accompanied him up the lake, for they feared the Mohawk and other tribes of the Long House as much as they hated them.

The more recent Algonquin inhabitants of New Hampshire and Vermont were the Abnakis, Pennacooks and Pocumtucs and other tribes, who scattered evidence of their occupation along the shores of lakes and streams, in valleys and on the mountains, to which they gave euphonious names. They tapped the sugar maples and raised corn on the intervales. That they had villages on the Missisquoi near Lake Champlain, on the Connecticut, at St. Francis and at other scattered places, there is no question; but their numbers, whether large or small, and the dates of their settlements, will always remain in doubt. There are references to a vicious plague which fell upon them before the Pilgrims arrived. "They died in heaps," says Thomas Morton in *New English Canaan*, "and the living that were to shift for themselves would run away and let them dy, and let their carkases ly above the ground without buriall. For in a place where many inhabited, there had been but one left alive to tell what became of the rest."

The Abnakis were using the heavily wooded area of future Vermont as a hunting preserve as late as 1749, when Peter Kalm, the Swedish naturalist, visited Lake Champlain!

> We often saw Indians in bark canoes close to the shore, which was, however, not inhabited; for the Indians come here only to catch sturgeons, wherewith this lake abounds, and which we often saw leaping in the air. These Indians lead a very singular life. At one time of the year they live upon the small store of maize, beans and melons, which they have planted; during another period, or about this time, their food is fish, without bread or any other meat; and another season they eat nothing but stags, roes, beavers, and so forth, which they shoot in the woods and rivers. They, however, enjoy long life, perfect health, and are more able to undergo hard-

ships than other people. They sing and dance, are joyful and always content; and would not for a great deal, exchange their manner of life for that which is preferred in Europe.

The Europeans were quick to seize upon the hostility between Iroquois and Algonquin and to make use of it in their war for empire. It has often been said that the Iroquois was the enemy of New France from the moment Champlain fired his arquebus, but the alignment of the Iroquois with the British and the Algonquin with the French was owing as much to the fur trade. A brisk commerce in beaver pelts developed first with the Dutch, then with the British. Gradually, as the supply dwindled in the Adirondacks and the Iroquois trappers worked north, they collided with the Algonquins and French. To protect the treasures of his northern forests and those of the rich Ohio valley, the King of France sent troops to Canada. Thus the broad trough of water leading from the heart of New France to the heart of New England and New York became a caldron of war.

Champlain's discovery was a critical event in colonial history— and one of the first. When he looked west upon the coast of New Hampshire and then east upon the Green Mountains from the lake he claimed for France, New Amsterdam did not exist. Henry Hudson's *Half-Moon* had not yet sailed the broad river to the south, nor had Captain John Smith yet explored the Massachusetts coast. Jamestown was only two years old. The Spanish were in Florida and New Mexico but the only settlements in the north, aged three and one, respectively, were Champlain's own—the infant Port Royal and Quebec.

III

THE BEGINNINGS
OF EMPIRE

As the portal of a heavily forested land settled largely during the middle or late seventeen-hundreds, the old town of wood and brick with the "rich red rust on the gables looking seaward" somehow seems incongruous. Despite a disastrous fire which in 1813 destroyed many of the houses built in the late sixteen- and early seventeen-hundreds, Portsmouth, like Salem, Newburyport and Charlestown, still has an air of great antiquity.

It was indeed long ago—over three and a quarter centuries— when a tiny ship anchored near the mouth of the Piscataqua at Odiorne's Point with a cargo of settlers, of guns and powder, beaver spears, sailcloth, pitch and tar, rope, fishlines and nets, blacksmith tools, seeds, iron kettles, and clothing. David Thompson, leader of the expedition, had come as the agent of Captain John Mason, who had received a land grant from King James I through the Council of New England and had formed a trading organization called the Laconia Company, or Merchant Adventurers Beyond the Seas. A former governor of Newfoundland, Mason was a partner of Sir Ferdinando Gorges, with whom he eventually held title to an immense but vaguely defined tract of land between the Merrimack and Kennebec Rivers and extending clear to the Great Lakes. Mason planned an offshore fishing industry, as well as a fur-trading post, since he thought that the River Piscataqua rose in Lake Champlain. After two years David Thompson, his agent, departed and settled on an island in Boston Harbor. Mason sent another expedition but because of the interval when no one lived at Portsmouth, Edward and William Hilton may have made the first permanent settlement in New Hampshire at Dover Point. In 1638 two ministers founded Exeter and Hampton. For four decades these lonely communities were the only villages in what is now New Hampshire.

We know that the people burned the trees and made potash, obtained furs of the beaver, otter, fox and raccoon from the Indians, and fished. At the Portsmouth communities of Strawberry Bank and Little Harbor there were, in 1632, 24 cows and 34 other "neat" cattle, 92 sheep, 27 goats, 64 hogs and 21 horses and colts. Three years later thirteen large shallops were in trade along the coast. In his *Annals of Portsmouth* Adams mentions an order of the general court in 1635 that a Negro brought back from Guinea as a slave be sent home. The drinking of healths, a "heathenish" practice, was prohibited by law in 1649, and the wearing of long hair by men was roundly condemned:

> Foreasmuch as the wearing of long hair, after the manner of ruffians and barbarous Indians, has begun to invade New England, contrary to the rule of God's word, which says it is a shame for men to wear long hair. . . . We, the Magistrates, who have subscribed this paper . . . do declare and manifest our dislike and detestation against the wearing of such long hair . . . whereby men do deform themselves and offend sober and modest men, and do corrupt good manners. . . .

In 1656 Goodwife Walford, New Hampshire's only alleged witch, was hailed into court on a complaint of Susannah Trimmings, who testified:

> As I was going home on Sunday night, the 30th of March, I heard a rustling in the woods, which I supposed to be occasioned by swine, and presently there appeared a woman, whom I apprehended to be old Goodwife Walford. She asked me to lend her a pound of cotton; I told her I had but 2 pounds in the house, and I would not spare any to my mother. She said I had better have done it, for I was going on a great journey . . . She then left me, and I was struck as with a clap of fire on the back; and she vanished toward the waterside . . . in the shape of a cat. She had on her head a white linen hood, tied under her chin, and her waistcoat and petticoat were red, with an old green apron, and a black hat upon her head.

Mrs. Trimmings' husband, Oliver, then testified that

> my wife came home in a sad condition. She passed by me with her child in her arms, laid the child on the bed, sat down on the chest, and leaned upon her elbow. Three times I asked her how she did. She could not speak. I took her in my arms, and held her up, and repeated the question. She forced breath, and something stopped in her throat, as if it would have stopped her breath. I unlaced her clothes, and soon she spake, and said, "Lord have mercy upon me, this wicked woman will kill me." I asked her what woman. She said Goodwife Walford. I tried to pursuade her it was only her weakness. She told me no, and related as above, that her back was a flame of

fire, and her lower parts were . . . numb and without feeling. I pinched her, and she felt not. She continued that night, and the day and night following, very ill, and is still bad of her limbs and complains still daily of it.

Agnes Puddington testified that

on the 11th of April, the wife of W. Evans came to her house, and lay there all night; and a little after sunset the deponent saw a yellowish cat; and Mrs. E. said she was followed by a cat, wherever she went. John came and saw a cat in the garden—took down his gun to shoot her; the cat got up on a tree, and the gun would not take fire, and afterward the cock would not stand. She afterwards saw cats—the yellow vanished away on the plain ground. She could not tell which way they went.

In 1662 the selectmen of Portsmouth voted that a "cage" or some other device be invented in which to put people who slept or took tobacco on Sunday, and that whoever killed a wolf should "nayle" its head on the meetinghouse, and have five pounds for his "paynes."

The mast trade with England was flourishing in 1665 and shipbuilding was going "gallently" on. In 1671 the New Hampshire ports exported 500 tons of fish, ten shiploads of masts and several thousand fur pelts, and imported at least 2,000 tons of salt and 300 casks of wine and brandy. The will drawn up in 1680 by Richard Cutt, the wealthiest man in the colony, shows that he left his wife his dwelling house, bakehouse, brewhouse, barn, log warehouse and wharfing, garden and orchard; and other property to his daughter.

For over a century and a quarter the settlers of the Piscataqua and of the great salt bay inside the coast could never be sure that dawn would not bring a marauding band of Indians out of the woods to their back doors, although much of the time they traded with them peaceably. In an attack on Dover in 1689 its most prominent citizen, Major Richard Waldron, who the Indians thought had betrayed them some thirteen years before, suffered a violent death. Nearly a hundred people perished in a French-inspired attack by two hundred Indians on Oyster River in 1684. At different times and places individuals and small groups were ambushed, like the renowned Hannah Dustan, who in March, 1697, with a young boy and her baby's nurse (the baby had been killed),

slew their Indian captors on an island at the mouth of the Pennacook, escaped in a canoe and returned forty miles to Haverhill,
Mrs. Dustan's home.

It is unfortunate that more is not known of the temper of the
times and of the people in their hard new country, but they could
scarcely be expected to have set down their reminiscences, even
in their old age, when the work of every hand was required for
survival. The early historians considered military and political
events, and particularly the everlasting intrigues of Mason and his
heirs and assigns, the principal materials of history. In the struggle
for empire it was the homesteaders who eventually triumphed over
the landholders of Portsmouth in their powdered wigs, and through
them, the provincial government and the King of England.
Democracy won. Neither the valleys of northern New England
nor the people who lived in them were suited for the life of the
manor.

Unable to unite in a central government of their own and too few
to protect themselves (there were only 209 voters in all of Portsmouth, Dover, Hampton and Exeter as late as 1679), the people
of the four towns were taken over by Massachusetts in 1641. Thirty-
eight years later New Hampshire became a separate province, an
event that the settlers did not applaud since it was the handiwork
of Robert Tufton Mason, heir to landholder John Mason. Claiming
that Massachusetts had been illegally granting New Hampshire
lands when the four towns were under its jurisdiction, Mason
succeeded in persuading King Charles II to give New Hampshire
a separate government, and in getting the new governor and council
to help him try to drive squatters off his lands. He failed (as did
his heirs) because the government also contained an assembly of
the people which always frustrated his designs.

In 1691 the Masons gave up and sold their claims to one Samuel
Allen for £2,750. Although the King made Allen governor and
commander in chief, he could not control his lands either because
of the people's juries and the Assembly, their only defense against
the landlords. New Hampshire and Massachusetts had the same
governor from 1698 to 1741, but from then until the Revolution
the controversial Benning Wentworth, followed by his very able

and respected nephew John, governed New Hampshire as a separate province.

All during these many decades the ghost of John Mason still stalked the hinterlands. After Mason's heirs sold out to Samuel Allen, they again claimed and, through a technicality, received title to the lands of New Hampshire. Their prospects were immensely brightened when it seemed certain that the empty wilderness of the Green Mountains might be theirs for the granting. Rather than try to enforce their claims, however, they sold out to a group of twelve residents of New Hampshire, most of whom were related to or in league with the Governors Wentworth. The so-called Masonian proprietors henceforth granted the land, reserving tracts in each township for themselves.

After the first settlement at Portsmouth nearly a century and a half elapsed before the population of New Hampshire reached 50,000. One reason was that the settlers did not want to buy land and then find that they did not have clear title to it. Then, of course, there were many absentee grantees with no idea of settling the land but bent on holding it for speculation. Finally, through nearly two centuries, there was war and the threat of war, particularly in the Champlain valley. The Jesuit priests, bold followers of their pioneering countryman, were the first to suffer the tortures of savages whom they tried futilely to convert to belief in the word of God. In 1666 the French built a small fort at Isle La Motte in northern Lake Champlain near what is now the border between Vermont and Canada. Two years later the first bishop of Quebec, Monsignor de Laval, journeyed to this bleak outpost in a canoe and held a service for the soldiers. To the south the great forests on the shores were as wild and still as when Champlain had seen them fifty-nine years before. The King of France authorized laying out the land in sections called seigneuries, and the seigneurs were to colonize them but made less than halfhearted attempts to do so. Early in the eighteenth century one seigneur said that he had been trying to find farmers for his land but had not succeeded. If he could find some, he said, he was ready to furnish them with axes and picks. If the French had shown as much vigor in settling the land as the British did elsewhere in New England, the fortunes of this great valley might have been different.

The next settlement in Vermont was not French, but British. In 1690 Captain Jacobus de Warm, leading an expedition from Albany against the French, built at Chimney Point a small fortlike trading post, a wall of which may stand today as part of a brick house that was serving as a tavern during the Revolution. Since neither de Warm nor the French at Isle La Motte remained long, a stout fort of yellow pine on the Connecticut River near the southeast corner of Vermont is considered to have been the state's first permanent settlement (although it was then in Massachusetts). Named after William Dummer, lieutenant governor of the Bay Colony, this bastion of the inland frontier was built in 1724, the year that John Lovewell, the professional Indian fighter of Dunstable, himself fell victim to redmen at Ossipee Lake.

Like those of a large log house, the timbers of Fort Dummer were locked together at the corners. The one-hundred-eighty-foot-long fort was nearly square, its rear wall serving also as a wall of several houses within. Lieutenant Timothy Dwight, founder of an illustrious family of educators, built the fort and, as its first commander, carried such unlimited responsibilities as that of father-confessor to the Indians, with whom Massachusetts was trying to keep on good terms.

> I have given them [the Indians] a dram this morning, [Dwight despaired in a letter to Colonel Stoddard], and they have been here this hour begging for more, and they daily call upon me for shirts, pipes, bullets and powder, flints and many other things; and the Court have granted all but powder, and they don't send it, and I cannot discourse with them, and they are mad at me for that; and unless the country will provide stores and inform me I may dispose thereof to them, I cannot live here, if it be possible to avoid it.

To which Colonel Stoddard replied on August 6, 1724:

> I am sensible of the trouble you meet with from the humors of the natives. Your best way is, when you have a supply of liquor, to give them ordinarily a good dram each, in a day. And you may tell them for me, that we give them drink for their comfort, not to un-man them, or make beasts of them; and that if they will not be content with what we give them, they shall have none at all.

The waters behind Vernon Dam now cover what was once a busy crossroads on the northern frontier. Here came scouts for supplies before they entered the forests, Indians seeking a better price for their furs than they could obtain from the French, and a homely procession of settlers bound for the rich bottom lands of the upper Connecticut.

In 1740 three Massachusetts families ventured thirty miles further north and began a settlement at Charlestown, the site of Number 4, the important fort with the prosaic name. The frontier knew no bolder people than those who defied the enemy in the woods by tilling fields sometimes far from the stockade. The story of how John Kilburn and his family managed to repel some four hundred Indians (whose red legs his son and hired hand had discovered standing "as thick as grasshoppers" among the alders) has always been a spellbinder. Now that the seacoast and the valley of the Merrimack were theirs, nothing, it seemed, could stop these dauntless settlers farming in the shadow of the majestic pines along the Connecticut.

IV

FOOTPRINTS
ON A WARPATH

There had been a watermelon and flip party for the neighbors at James Johnson's log house on the evening of August 29, 1754. Everyone had retired at midnight, wrote Miriam Johnson, "except a spruce young spark who tarried to keep company" with her sister. Now that her husband had returned from his three months' trading trip to Connecticut, the worry and strain of living 100 rods distant from Fort Number 4 without his protection were over.

But the next morning between daybreak and sunrise the Indians, "fixed horribly for war, rushed furiously in." One caught hold of Mrs. Johnson, another pulled her sister out of bed, four were tying up Johnson, his hired man and a neighbor named Labarree, who had just arrived for a day's work. As shots of warning rang from the fort, they were already on the march, or "munch," as the Indians put it. Mrs. Johnson, faint and trembling, had lost a shoe and her small children were crying but the Indians would not stop for three miles for fear that a party from the fort was in pursuit. She might have been able to get on with her bleeding feet and scratched legs had she not been pregnant. While the captives were forcing down what breakfast was available, Old Scoggin, a horse belonging to Phineas Stevens, fortunately wandered that way and Mrs. Johnson, wearing Labarree's stockings and a pair of moccasins, was now able to ride.

They went six or eight miles that day and took lodging "with the sky for a covering and the ground for a pillow." Up before sunrise, with only some water gruel for breakfast, they marched sorrowfully on for an hour or two when a "keener distress was added to my multiplied afflictions;—I was taken with the pangs of childbirth." The Indians thoughtfully constructed a booth near a brook and about ten o'clock, with her husband and sister in attendance, a daughter was born. When the Indian who, having first seen Mrs. Johnson in the raid, saw the baby he clapped his hands exclaiming: "Two monies for me," meaning the reward he would get from the French on delivering up his prisoners. The child was dressed in clothes taken in the raid. Mrs. Johnson was allowed to rest that day while the Indians made a litter on which to carry her.

On the following morning the sad procession was under way again with Labarree, Farnsworth, the hired man, and Johnson alternately supporting the mother and baby on the litter. Johnson's six-year-old son and his sister-in-law rode Scoggin and two Indians carried his small daughters on their backs. When, after two miles, the litter bearers became exhausted, Mrs. Johnson's Indian said that if she could ride the horse she could proceed, but must otherwise be left behind. "Here I observed marks of pity on his [her Indian's] countenance, but this might arise from the fear of losing his two monies." Although every step of the horse seemed almost to end her life, Mrs. Johnson did ride all that day, as well as the fourth and fifth, with only a brief rest at the end of each hour. Beyond the height of land on a river that joins Otter Creek to flow into Lake Champlain their food ran out. Since no fish were to be caught, nor game to be found, the Indians began looking speculatively at the horse. Poor Scoggins! They led him off and shot him, and soon he was roasting on the coals. "To use the term politeness in the management of this repast may be thought a burlesque, yet their offering the prisoners the best part of the horse certainly bordered on civility; an epicure could not have catered nicer slices, nor in that situation served them up with more neatness." The Indians gorged themselves and so did the children, who became sick. Mrs. Johnson greatly relished the broth, seasoned with roots, that was prepared for her.

She was certain that the sixth day of the march would be her last, since she still could not walk. When she dropped from fatigue and her son saw an Indian lift his hatchet over her head, he cried, "Ma'am, do go, for they will kill you!" Somehow Mrs. Johnson did struggle forward, first supported and then carried by her husband in a pack saddle made from the bark of a tree. On the sixth day she had to wade across a beaver pond, which weakened her grievously. The Indians luckily found a bear which they had killed and cleaned on their way to Number 4. Although the fatigue of the captives was now such that it seemed beyond the power of food to revive them, the bear meat did so measurably. Two more days they staggered forward on bloody feet until, on the sunny morning of the ninth day, the Indians announced they would reach Lake Champlain before nightfall.

"Those who languished with sickness, fatigue or despair, now marched forward with alacrity. . . . About the middle of the afternoon the waters of the lake were seen . . . the hour I sat on the shore of Lake Champlain was one of the happiest I ever experienced." The next morning they arrived by canoe at a great rock on the far shore. While meat, bread and green corn, borrowed from a Frenchman who lived nearby, were prepared, the Indians insisted that the captives sing and join in a war dance. As Mrs. Johnson took a few awkward and grotesque steps she was required to chant "danna witchee natchepung" which was "very painful and offensive."

At Crown Point they were treated with civility. Mrs. Johnson was put to bed and given a nurse and the French commander saw to it that her children were decently clothed. Four days after their arrival, however, the Indians led the captives to a boat and the entire party set sail for St. Johns, far to the north. It happened that a canoe going in the opposite direction came alongside and Mr. Johnson was able to ask one of its passengers, bound for Albany, that a message be put in the Boston papers assuring the friends of the captives that they were all alive.

The journey down the lake and through the River Richelieu to the St. Lawrence and then to St. Francis was accomplished with more discomfort than hardship. On their arrival a "cloud of savages" ran toward the shore, daubed the captives with bright paint and required them to run the gantlet, although the Indians merely touched them on the shoulder as they passed. Mrs. Johnson went to live with the family of her original captor, the son-in-law of the grand sachem. While he was wealthier than most of the others and could afford better fare, she could scarcely countenance the messy disorder of the dirt floor of his wigwam. "Indians threw themselves down . . . in a manner that more resembled cows in a shed than human beings." They made fun of her as she tried to fall on her knees, and then sit back on her heels, Indian fashion, to eat. She was, however, ceremoniously adopted into the family and soon grew very fond of her helper, Sebatis, the young son of her master. But no sooner had she begun to accustom herself to the primitive life than Mr. Johnson was led away to Montreal to be sold, as were her two daughters, her sister, and Labarree. One day her six-year-old son came running to her, his face swollen with tears, exclaiming that the Indians were going to take him into the woods to hunt. As his master pulled him away, the child was crying, "Ma'am, I shall never see you again!"

"The keenness of my pangs," wrote Mrs. Johnson, "almost obliged me to wish that I had never been a mother. 'Farewell, Sylvanus,' said I, 'God will preserve you.' "

Despite the shock and horror of seeing a raiding party bring in a string of English scalps for display, Mrs. Johnson could not help being grateful for the curious contradictions of nature and custom that enabled this most barbaric people to be, at the same time, most civilized. She testified that they never treated her cruelly, but rather with patience and understanding. "Can it be said of civilized conquerors that they, in the main, are willing to share with their prisoners the last ration of food when famine stares them in the face? Do they ever adopt an enemy, and salute him by the tender name of brother?"

In November Mrs. Johnson received a letter from her husband asking her to encourage the Indians to bring her to Montreal to be sold, as he had made arrangements that would be satisfactory to them. This happily took place. All the Johnsons, except Sylvanus and the baby, were lodged with important or well-to-do families in Montreal, including that of the mayor. Having received permission from the government to go to New England and raise the money for the redemption of his family (who in effect were held as hostages until his return), Johnson, after a difficult trip, appealed to the governors of Massachusetts and New Hampshire for funds. The legislature of the latter finally granted him £150 sterling, but he was not allowed to return with the money on the grounds that conditions on the frontier were now too dangerous. Thus his parole lapsed and in Montreal things went very hard with his family. When he finally arrived, the specie he brought for their redemption was refused, a new governor had taken office, and the army of Dieskau, having arrived from France, was preparing to invade the Champlain valley.

Thus new and perhaps greater misfortunes than their march through the wilderness befell the prisoners. While her sister and eldest child (who had been adopted by three old maids named Jaisson) remained in Montreal, Mrs. Johnson, her husband, and their two youngest children (they had heard nothing of poor Sylvanus) were brought to Quebec and thrown into a filthy jail. "In the corner sat a poor being half dead with smallpox. In another were some lousy blankets and straw. In the center, a few dirty dishes . . . we were supported by small pieces of meat each day, stewed with some rusty crusts of bread." On the fifteenth day in jail Mrs. Johnson contracted smallpox, which soon infected the whole family, including the baby, whom they called Captive. No sooner had they recovered from this than Mrs. Johnson was again taken desperately ill with a month-long fever. Winter, in the meantime, had descended upon the drafty prison and the misery of cold was added to that of hunger. Through the help of a friend and a letter to the governor, the family were removed at last to the much-superior civil prison, where they remained all the next summer and fall. In December, 1756, Mrs. Johnson had a baby who lived but a few hours. This winter of misfortune also brought news that her father had been killed by Indians and a brother had struggled into the fort with a spear sticking out of his thigh. Again, illness and melancholy struck Mrs. Johnson.

Finally, in 1757, came bright, scarcely believable news. An exchange of prisoners had been arranged between England and France and the Johnsons were to be freed in June. Was it possible that fate, which had singled out this one New Hampshire family for so much suffering, had relented? It had not. Just three days before their departure word arrived that Mr. Johnson would not be allowed to go. Thus in the most pathetic leave-taking ("Mr. Johnson took me by the hand. Our tears imposed silence . . .") the mother, her two youngest children, and her sister set sail for England.

After much delay and disappointment in that country Mrs. Johnson at last obtained passage for America and on December 10, 1757, she had the "supreme felicity" of again touching native soil. The mayor of New York procured lodging for her and here Mrs. Johnson heard the heavenly news that her husband had been released. The grand reunion took place at two o'clock on the morning of January 1, 1758. Happy New Year? Their pleasure was so intense that she could not describe it.

But the New Year was to bring the greatest sorrow of all. Not long after they returned to their home at Fort Number 4, still the northern outpost, Mr. Johnson joined the army in Abercrombie's

assault on Ticonderoga, and was killed. "Humanity will weep with
me," wrote Mrs. Johnson. "The cup of sorrow was now replete with
bitter drops. All my former miseries were lost in the affliction of a
widow." But it was some consolation to hear that Sylvanus was
still alive although "sick of scald" at Northampton.

> I hastened to the place and found him in a deplorable situation;
> he was brought there by Major Putnam, afterwards General Put-
> nam, with Mrs. Howe and her family, who had returned from
> captivity. . . . It was 4 years since I had seen him. He was then 11
> years old; during his absence he had entirely forgotten the English
> language, spoke a little broken French, but was perfect in Indian.
> He had been with them in their hunting excursions, and suffered
> numerous hardships—he could brandish a tommahawk or bend the
> bow, but these habits wore off by degrees.

In October, 1759, Mrs. Johnson moved from Lancaster back to
Charlestown. The sight of her old home near the fort at the edge
of the wilderness "afforded a strange mixture of joy and grief," for
Robert Rogers returned that year from St. Francis bringing with
him a young Indian boy whom he had spared in his raid upon the
Indian village.

Upon seeing Mrs. Johnson the boy cried, "My God! My God!
Here is my sister!" It was her little "brother" Sebatis (Rogers
called him Billy) who used to tend the cows for her when she was
a prisoner at St. Francis.

> He was transported to see me and declared that he was still my
> brother and I must be his sister. Poor fellow! The fortune of war had
> left him without a single relation, but with his country's enemies
> he could find one who too sensibly felt his miseries. I felt the purest
> pleasure in administering to his comfort.

Mrs. Johnson wrote that her family would always remember Sebatis
with affection. He "had a high sense of honor and good behaviour,
he was affable, good natured and polite."

In the summer of 1760 Mrs. Johnson's brother-in-law and
neighbor, Joseph Willard, was captured by Indians and with his
wife and five children suffered the same hardships on much the
same route that the Johnsons had traveled six years before. Two
of the Willard children succumbed. Arriving in Montreal just

before the French surrendered, this family returned home after four months and brought Susanna Johnson with them. She had received an excellent education from the Misses Jaisson with whom she had stayed in Montreal. She spoke nothing but French and did not know her mother. They had been separated for six years—years that convinced Mrs. Johnson "that the passions of men are as various as their complexions."

In 1762 Mrs. Johnson married Mr. John Hastings of Charlestown and by him had seven more children, five of whom died in infancy. As an old woman she could count thirty-eight grandchildren and twenty-eight great-grandchildren. She wrote that, although she had drunk so largely from the cup of sorrow, yet she had had her share of happiness. Now the savages were driven beyond the lakes and her country had no enemies. The gloomy wilderness had vanished and the thrifty farm smiled in its stead.

> My daughter, Captive, still keeps the dress she appeared in when brought to my bedside by the French nurse at the [Crown Point] hospital; and often refreshes my memory with the past scenes, when showing it to her children. . . .
>
> My aged mother, before her death, could say to me, arise daughter and go to thy daughter, for thy daughter's daughter has got a daughter; a command which few mothers can make and be obeyed.

2

Like Dummer and Number 4, Robert Rogers was a bulwark of the frontier. There has never been a more fearless scout and Indian fighter. Historians cluck because his personal habits were bad, because he was allegedly involved in shady transactions as commander of the trading post of Michilimackinac, and because he went to the British in the Revolution. But how is one to cure a dog that has tasted blood from running sheep? What is one to expect of a man who year in and year out must fight and kill while the army paymaster all but ignores him? If physical bravado is found in an individual, especially in a war, he is not likely to bother with nice distinctions between right and wrong afterwards. Rogers had too much adventure and excitement in the woods to settle down and wear a powdered wig after the shooting was over.

His father moved from Methuen, Massachusetts, into the woods of

Dunbarton, New Hampshire, in 1739 when Robert was only eight, so he knew all about Indians by the time he had grown to six feet and was ready for war. He was in his late twenties at the height of French power in America, and at the height of his own abilities and reputation as a scout, bold, untiring, sensible, as the disarmingly matter-of-fact entries in his journals show. In 1756 he and his Rangers were annoying and killing what French and Indians they could in southern Lake Champlain and reporting intelligence about the French.

July 7. Rogers reported sighting a 40-ton schooner and thirty other boats en route to Canada. In the evening, 15 miles farther down the lake, he learned that a schooner was at anchor about a mile from his camp. Ordering his men to lighten their boats, he prepared to launch an attack against the schooner but was prevented from doing so by two lighters coming up the lake.

> . . . these we fired upon, then hailed them, and offered them quarters if they would come ashore; but they hastily pushed towards the opposite shore, where we pursued and intercepted them; we found their number to be twelve, three of which were killed by our fire, and two wounded, one . . . in such a manner that he soon died. We sunk and destroyed their vessels and cargoes, which, consisted chiefly of wheat and flour, wine and brandy; some few casks of the latter we carefully concealed. . . .
>
> These prisoners upon examination reported: That a great number of regular troops and militia were assembling at Chamblee, and destined for Carillon, or Ticonderoga . . . that a party of 300 French and 20 Indians, had already set out to intercept our convoys of provisions between Albany and Lake George; that 60 livres was the reward for an English scalp, and that the prisoners were sold in Canada for 50 Crowns each; that their prospect of an harvest was encouraging but that the smallpox made great havoc amongst the inhabitants.

The military scene on Lake Champlain in the bright sunset of French colonial power and on the eve of Rogers' remarkable expedition against the St. Francis seemed to the British dark and unavailing. Britain had conquered Canada in 1629, only to return it to France five years later in the treaty of Saint-Germain. During the next century and a quarter one frightful attack after another from north to south and south to north even in the dead of winter over the frozen lake kept both sides in fear and under arms. There was the French Governor Courcelles's hopeless expedition in 1666 when 400 men on snowshoes with 25-pound packs set out in January on a 300-mile trek to attack the Mohawks and very nearly froze to death. The following September 1,200 Frenchmen and Indians in shining regalia embarked from Fort Sainte-Anne in 300 light boats and bark canoes but could not find the Mohawks to the south.

Lachine, an outpost settlement of Montreal, fell in 1689 before the onslaught of 200 Iroquois, who as a measure of defiance ate some of their prisoners. In 1690 the Count of Frontenac fitted out a winter expedition against Albany but his 44 men and 96 Indians attacked Schenectady instead, burning the town and massacring or capturing 140 of the inhabitants. In retaliation that same year Captain John Schuyler fell upon the settlements south of Montreal and the next year a force of British and Iroquois under Peter Schuyler met the French and Algonquins in the first battle in America, it is said, in which these four nations were opposed.

Little wonder that the Champlain valley remained largely unsettled until after the American Revolution. Through the gate to the country, as the lake was called by the Indians, were to pass many more ragged, sick and freezing armies. In midwinter, 1693, Frontenac, determining to put an end to British raids, sent 600 French and Indians over the ice of the lakes to destroy the Mohawks. Finding them absent, they instead demolished their villages. The story of the return of the French force to Montreal, and the British pursuit under Schuyler, is one of a blizzard, starvation, of the eating of boiled moccasins by the white soldiers and dead prisoners by the Indians.

In the Champlain valley one could scarcely have told that the first French and Indian War, that of King William, had ended, and that the second, Queen Anne's, had begun. In 1704 the French struck at Deerfield by way of the Winooski valley in Vermont and the Connecticut River. The ghastly march of the prisoners through the forests has been told by many, but never more graphically than by the Rev. John Williams, who survived it. In 1709 and 1711 two attempts of the British to invade the Champlain valley failed because of bungling commanders and the watchful Governor Vaudreuil of Canada who sent 1,500 men up the lake to defend it.

The Treaty of Utrecht in 1713 merely slowed preparations for the convulsive struggle that was coming between France and England.

The French decided that stone and mortar, as well as men, were required if they were to become the real masters of the northern gateway, and in 1731 they built a stockade called Frederic at the lake's narrowest point. Strengthened in 1734 and vastly improved in 1742, the star-shaped redoubt was a bold obstruction to British designs against Canada. From 1731 to 1759, 243 baptisms, 31 marriages, and 198 deaths were recorded at the fort and the village around it on both sides of the lake. Peter Kalm, the Swedish traveler, left the best description of Frederic, for he saw it in 1749 when it was virtually new.

> The fort is built on a rock, consisting of black lime slates. . . . On the easten part . . . is a high tower . . . provided with very thick and substantial walls, and well stored with cannon from the bottom almost to the very top; and the Governor lives in the tower. In the terre-plein of the fort is a well-built little church, and houses of stone for the officers and soldiers. . . .
>
> The soldiers enjoy such advantages here as they are not allowed in every part of the world. . . . They get every day a pound and a half of wheat bread. They likewise get plenty of peas, bacon, and salt meat in plenty. Sometimes they kill oxen and other cattle, the flesh of which is distributed among the soldiers. All the officers kept cows, at the expense of the King, and the milk they gave was more than sufficient to supply them. The soldiers had each a small garden without the fort. . . . Some of them had built summer houses in them and planted all kinds of pot herbs . . . and as the lake close by was full of fish, and the woods abounded with birds and animals, those amongst them who choose to be diligent may live extremely well, and like a lord in regard to food. . . . When this is considered, it is not surprising to find the men are very fresh, well fed, strong, and lively here.

Directly opposite, on the Vermont side of the water at Chimney Point, the French strengthened the old outpost of the Dutchman, de Warm, and built a stone windmill to grind grain to make bread for the soldiers across the way. The mortar in Frederic was scarcely dry before the guns of empire boomed again, this time in King George's War from 1744 to 1748. Again the English in their wooden villages to the south arose to the hair-raising war whoop, the glint of the scalping knife and the flickering red torch. Again a treaty—Aix-la-Chapelle—a brief, false stillness before France and England once more dipped the wilderness in the blood of the Seven Years' War. In 1755 the first of the great armies, a brilliant pageant numbering some 3,500 men, sailed up Lake Champlain under command of the Baron de Dieskau to prevent the vain and militarily inept Sir William Johnson from taking Crown Point. This Dieskau did, although the Battle of Lake George cost him dearly in dead and wounded.

Advertising at court what he thought was a great victory, Sir William won a title and a handsome reward for prowess that not he, but his junior officers, had shown. Actually Britain had gained little or nothing. The Champlain valley belonged more securely to the French than ever, for south of St. Frederic on the bluff between Lake George and Lake Champlain they were building another and greater fort, that which they called Carillon. To the Indians, however, this was the place between the waters—Ticonderoga—a ringing and fateful name in American history.

Thus the scales of empire were tipped on the side of France when Rogers, the hardy scout from New Hampshire, and his Rangers took to the shores of the lakes with their flintlocks. It is curious that of all the exploits of the noted generals and their armies during the French and Indian Wars, those of Rogers are the best known. Perhaps it is because there is less scope and confusion and more narrative in his adventures, as there is in the legend of Duncan Campbell and the Black Watch at Ticonderoga, or the murder of Jane McCrea in the Revolution. Certainly the proportions of Rogers' deeds were as symbolic of the American frontier as those of the man himself. He has been described as being as big as a moose with a face almost as plain, massive of shoulders and arms, yet slim of hips and legs, sure-footed and silent in his travels through the forests as a catamount.

August, 1756. Rogers had captured a Frenchman, his wife and daughter and had conducted them to Fort William Henry on Lake George for interrogation. The man reported that there were 4,000 troops at Ticonderoga and that the French had 150 boats on Lake Champlain, 35 of them constantly plying between Ticonderoga and Lower Quebec. He declared that provisions and equipment had recently arrived at Frontenac to reinforce Montcalm's army of 5,000 men.

January 21, 1757. A fierce fight with the Indians in the woods near Lake George. About sunset a bullet passed through Rogers' hand. To stop the flow of blood one of the Rangers cut off Rogers' queue and bound his wrist. Meanwhile the enemy were using "many arts," from flattery to severity, to induce him to surrender, promising that he and his men would be treated with kindness should he do so. The Rangers held their ground, but when they arrived at Fort William Henry two days later their ranks had thinned to 48 effective men.

It was with great difficulty that Rogers found recruits, for he had been unable to obtain money due the Rangers for their services during the winter of 1755. To his pleas for funds General Abercrombie replied that since the services in question were rendered prior to the time he took command he could not authorize payment for them. Rogers was therefore obliged to pay the men out of his own pocket as the result of lawsuits they brought against him.

March 5, 1757. Rogers was taken ill with smallpox and confined to his bed for over five weeks.

August 9, 1757. Through the cowardice of his Majesty's General Daniel Webb, Fort William Henry had fallen to the Marquis de Montcalm, leaving Fort Edward the only remaining outpost of the British on this frontier. A few days before the fort was besieged Rogers' brother, Richard, had died of smallpox. Such was the enemy's cruelty and rage after their conquest that they disinterred him, as they did many others, and removed his scalp for the bounty. The Indians paid heavily for their avarice. The infection began to spread to them and many died on their return to Canada.

March 13, 1758. Greatly outnumbered at Lake George, the Rangers fought their most desperate battle with the Indians.

> . . . I fired a gun, as a signal for a general discharge upon them . . . which killed above 40. . . . I now imagined the enemy totally defeated . . . but we soon found our mistake, and that the party we had attacked were only their advanced guard, their main body coming up consisting of 600 more . . . upon which I ordered our people to retreat to their own ground, which we gained at the expense of 50 men killed; the remainder I rallied, and drew up in pretty good

order, where they fought with such intrepidity and bravery as obliged the enemy . . . to retreat a second time; but we not being in condition to pursue them, they rallied again, and recovered their ground, and warmly pushed us in front and both wings. . . . About this time we discovered 200 Indians going up the mountain on our right . . . to prevent which I sent Lt. Philips, with eighteen men, to gain the first possession, and beat them back; which he did.

As his situation grew more desperate Rogers advised some of his men, who were recent volunteers and not trained fighters, to withdraw.

I had before this desired these gentlemen to retire, offering them a Sergeant to conduct them, that as they were not used to snowshoes, and were quite unacquainted with the woods, they would have no chance of escaping the enemy, in case we should be broke and put to flight, which I very much suspected. They at first seemed to accept the offer, and began to retire; but seeing us so closely beset, they undauntedly returned to our assistance.

Rogers and his more experienced men made good their escape but the members of the hapless detachment (after surrendering on the promise of fair treatment) were tied to trees and literally hacked to pieces. Lieutenant Philips, contrary to accounts that he was hanged with the others, managed to free one hand, to open his knife with his teeth and cut himself loose, to escape, to live to a great age and die a pauper. His wife joined the Shakers at Canterbury, New Hampshire, but Philips said he "could not dance and would not join."

Although the good William Pitt gravely erred in choosing the sickly, slow-witted James Abercrombie as the general to crush the French in the Champlain valley, his army might yet have won the day had it not been for the bullet that carried away his junior in command, young General George Augustus Lord Howe, "the noblest Englishman that has appeared in my time," according to General Wolfe, "and the best soldier in the British Army."

Giving the impression that he was an ordinary man among ordinary soldiers was Howe's most unusual, indeed extraordinary achievement and the army worshiped him for it. No dusty British manuals for him here in the wilderness, no rigid ideas about massive formations, no stuffiness, no condescension about the peasants in arms. He went with Rogers to learn how the Rangers fought and must inevitably have carried the army over the walls of Ticonderoga—if he had lived.

Moving the largest European army ever assembled in America to the head of Lake George by way of the Hudson River and Fort Edward in hundreds of bateaux, wagons and carts, with thousands of barrels of provisions, thousands of tents, and tens of thousands of arms had been a frightful burden for the frail Abercrombie. Early on the morning of July 5, 1758, 15,000 men were afloat on southern Lake George in 900 bateaux, 135 whaleboats, and two floating batteries, presenting, according to witnesses, a fantastic spectacle. Rogers and his green-clad Rangers were in the vanguard; there were just under 6,000 British regulars in red (the Black Watch regiment in kilts), thousands of provincial farmers and townsmen in blue, and a host of fiercely painted Iroquois. Bayonets flashed, bugles and bagpipes blew, drums rolled. It was a vast Oriental rug floating north—"a tropical garden in bloom," writes Lamb.

At Sabbath Day Point the army paused to regroup and there Lord Howe and John Stark, a New Hampshire lieutenant in the Rangers, were seen lying on a bearskin talking strategy. In the darkness the army embarked again and the next morning, in the woods north of the lake, it was much closer to doom. Rogers was in the vanguard. Lord Howe, Israel Putnam, and 200 Rangers were leading the main column some distance behind. Astonished, frightened and lost, a French force of 350 men, while trying to gain the safety of the fort, collided with Lord Howe's men. A brief skirmish, a few shots, and Howe fell. Howe was dead! Paralysis seized the King's legions. Like a centipede without a nervous system the army began to trip over itself. Shots rang through the trees. The French? Who knew? In the forest darkness and panic reigned.

The next morning orders came to return to the landing place. At length the army, heavy in heart, again started for Ticonderoga, beneath whose walls the great Montcalm, his army outnumbered three to one, had built a breastwork of logs and an abattis of trees with the stripped branches facing the enemy. As Abercrombie's legions lumbered forward, his Indians took seats in a kind of spectators' gallery on the safe slopes of Mount Defiance. From his headquarters in the rear the General gave orders to charge this impossible entanglement with bayonets. "Then," remembered a wounded Ranger, "out of the woods behind us issued the heavy red masses of the British troops advancing in battle array with purpose to storm with the bayonette." How they died that day, wave after wave of red before the fire from behind those pickets!

And the Lord of Inverawe, Duncan Campbell of the brave and dying Black Watch, learned too late the meaning of the strange, half-forgotten curse of the ghost of his murdered cousin: "Farewell, Inverawe! Farewell, until we meet at Ticonderoga!"

> And far from the hills of heather,
> Far from the isles of the sea
> He sleeps in the place of the name
> As it was doomed to be.*

In his journal Major Rogers wrote of the rout and retreat of his Majesty's splendid army with notable economy and understatement: "We toiled with repeated attacks for four hours, being greatly embarassed by the trees that were felled by the enemy without their breastwork, when the General thought proper to order a retreat, directing me to bring up the rear, which I did in the dusk of the evening."

It was the methodical Lord Jeffrey Amherst, who, replacing Abercrombie in the Champlain valley, sent Rogers the following year into the forests of Vermont and Lower Quebec against the St. Francis on the most frightful mission of this, or perhaps any, colonial war.

> You are this night to . . . proceed to Misisquoy Bay, from whence you will march and attack the enemy's settlements on the south-side of the river St. Lawrence, in such a manner as you shall judge most effectual to disgrace the enemy, and for the success and honor of his Majesty's arms.
>
> Remember the barbarities that have been committed by the enemy's Indian scoundrels on every occasion, where they have had an opportunity of shewing their infamous cruelties on the King's subjects. . . . Take your revenge, but don't forget that tho' those villains have dastardly and promiscuously murdered the women and children of all ages, it is my order that no women or children are killed or hurt.

*Robert Louis Stevenson.

October 5, 1759. Rogers had reached St. Francis after twenty-two grueling days by boat and on foot. A bag of powder had blown up during a bivouac on the shore of Otter Creek and a number of injured men had to be sent back. Nine days had been spent wading through a dismal spruce bog north of Missisquoi Bay.

From a tree, Rogers at last viewed his target three miles away. Whether he and his 142 officers and men could themselves escape with their lives the village of St. Francis was theirs. Stealing to the outskirts of the settlement and observing the Indians "in a high frolick or dance" (a drunken celebration of a chief's wedding), Rogers returned to his men, marched them to within 500 rods of the settlement, stripped them of their packs, formed them for attack and, a half hour before sunrise, struck. So silently did they pour over the stockade, so fast and savagely did they kill (when they saw 700 English scalps waving from poles), that 200 Indians were dead by seven o'clock, including those they burned in their fifty houses and those shot or sunk in their boats as they tried to escape. Storming into the wooden chapel the Rangers saw, among other treasures, golden candlesticks, a solid silver image of the Virgin, and a knot of Indians behind the altar. A wild fight raged. There were gunshots and the thuds of tomahawks. In a few minutes all the Indians and one Ranger were dead; the gold and silver were safely outside, and flames were crackling over the altar. Until the belfry burned the bell slowly tolled, they say, and then with a clang plunged into the ruins.

Of the twenty women and children who remained Rogers decided to release fifteen and to take five—two Indian boys and three girls—with him. He also took five English captives of the St. Francis. In the three buildings left standing was corn which would help keep the Rangers alive during the terrible days ahead. Since 300 French and Indians had captured their boats and supplies and another enemy force was somewhere up the St. Francis River, the only possible escape was on foot through the forests to Fort Number 4, some 150 miles to the southeast on the Connecticut River.

Having sent Lieutenant McMullen to General Amherst to request that supplies be sent to the mouth of the Ammonoosuc River at the end of the Cohase Intervales (Barnet, Vermont), Rogers only hoped that he could outmarch both his pursuers and starvation and reach this place alive. A cruel trek of eight days merely brought them to

Lake Memphremagog. Since their provisions already were low, Rogers, considering that in this case, at least, there was greater safety in fewer numbers and better chances to obtain game, divided his party into small groups. Each was to forage for itself and to try to reach the rendezvous by a different route. One of the detachments, overtaken by 200 French and Indians, was annihilated.

In his journal Rogers wrote that it was hardly possible to describe the suffering of those who were able to make their way through swamps and over mountains to the Connecticut River intervales at Cohase; or their consternation when they found that no supplies awaited them there. For, although the scout whom Rogers had sent to General Amherst had arrived safely at Crown Point, and General Amherst had dispatched an officer carrying supplies to the meeting place with instructions to wait as long as there was any hope of Rogers' return, the officer "being an indolent fellow, tarried at the place but 2 days, when he returned, taking all the provisions back with him, about 2 hours before our arrival. Finding a fresh fire burning in his camp, I fired guns to bring him back, which guns he heard, but would not return, supposing we were an enemy."

So weak were the Rangers and so depressed that they were almost resigned to death by starvation. That fate was in store for the men who were too fatigued to go farther, but Rogers, with Captain Ogden and one other Ranger and Billy, the Indian boy, managed to build a raft of dry pine trees and set themselves afloat downstream. On the second day of their voyage they barely escaped being dashed to pieces when their raft was shattered on the rocks below the falls of the White River.

> . . . while Captain Ogden and the Ranger hunted for red squirrels for a refreshment . . . I attempted the forming of a new raft for our further conveyance. Being not able to cut down trees, I burnt them down, and then burnt them off at proper lengths. This was our third day's work after leaving our companions. The next day we got our materials together, and compleated our raft, and floated with the stream again until we came to Wattockquitchey Falls, which were about 50 yards in length; here we landed, and by a weath [withe] made of hazel bushes, Captain Ogden held the raft, till I went to the bottom, prepared to swim in and board it when it came down, and if possible paddle it ashore, this being our only resource

for life, as we were not able to make a third raft in case we had lost this. I had the good fortune to succeed, and the next morning we embarked and floated down the stream to within a small distance of No. 4, where we found some men cutting off timber, who gave us the first relief, and assisted us to the Fort.

Allowing himself a scant two days to recuperate, Rogers struggled back up the Connecticut with a relief party carrying provisions in canoes. Fearing that some of the lost and starving Rangers had straggled deep into New Hampshire, he sent supplies also to Suncook and Pennacook on the Merrimack. Hope at length waned and he had to report to General Amherst that since leaving St. Francis he had lost three officers and 46 sergeants and privates. Those unfortunates, dead and dying, were scattered through the wilderness of northern New Hampshire and Vermont. A farmer pulling a birch stump south of Lake Memphremagog in 1861 is said to have found the golden candlesticks buried by the Rangers in their flight. Sergeant Bradley and eight others apparently hid some of the remaining treasure of the St. Francis—gold, jewelry and wampum—at the mouth of Cow Brook (North Littleton, New Hampshire). Neither this nor the silver image has ever been found, but the bones of Sergeant Bradley, identified by his leather queue ribbon, were discovered the following summer.

On December 1 Rogers (many, indeed, thought it was the ghost of Rogers) returned to General Amherst's new fort at Crown Point, which he had left by whaleboat on September 13 for almost certain oblivion. His destruction of St. Francis became legendary. Throughout the colonies it was regarded as a symbol of the rising power of the British in the north. Political intrigue and corruption in the Quebec government and lack of military support from France had reduced Montcalm to near helplessness, and when General Amherst advanced down Lake George with a strong new army the French, with only 2,300 men to defend Ticonderoga, knew that the jig was up. At eleven o'clock at night on July 26, 1759, a thundering roar echoed in the Vermont hills across the water as great chunks of the proud fort plummeted into the lake. The French were blowing up their own works and leaving the Champlain valley forever.

Amherst, to the contrary, was building and repairing forts as he advanced—Fort George at the foot of that lake, Ticonderoga, and now Crown Point, which cost England the enormous sum of $10 million. From Fort Number 4 on the Connecticut through the Vermont wilderness to Chimney Point directly across the way, he planned a military highway to link the Champlain valley with New Hampshire and southeastern New England. On October 16 Major John Hawkes and Captain Stark, with 250 men, were turned loose in the forests west of Chimney Point with 250 axes, a grindstone and a supply of biscuits. The next spring Lieutenant Colonel John Goffe, also of New Hampshire, with 800 men cut the remaining 26 miles from the Connecticut River side.

There seemed to be no stopping the colonists now. The British planned to reduce Montreal by approaching it from three directions: up the St. Lawrence from Quebec and down it from Lake Ontario, and north from Lake Champlain. During the summer of 1759 Amherst was so preoccupied with his fort building that he failed to advance until October, when cold weather was at hand and it was too late. Within a few months the superb General Wolfe had scaled the heights of Abraham. Even as he and Montcalm (the great last hope of France) lay dying on the battlefield, the British flag rose over Montreal and all Canada.

As if he had not fought and suffered enough, Major Rogers had the misfortune to accompany Colonel William Haviland, Amherst's spiteful and cowardly brigadier, on the expedition to reduce what was left of the French in northern Lake Champlain and the Richelieu River. After drawing a plan of his march to St. Francis for General Amherst he had recruited more men, and on his way to Crown Point in February, 1760, was ambushed by sixty Indians who killed five of his men and took four prisoners. In June Rogers was off again down the lake with 250 men to Isle aux Noix, where he waged a stubborn fight against a superior force of French and Indians. Sending back his wounded and burying his dead, he marched farther north and through a clever stratagem destroyed the fort and settlement of St. Thérèse.

It was Rogers, once again, who in August with 600 Rangers did the work of a small army in putting the last enemy force of 1,500 to flight out of St. Johns. Haviland, with most of his troops, remained safely behind until the shooting was over. In his memoirs John Stark declared that Haviland was the same man who had sent Rogers out in March, 1758, with a small force when he knew a superior one awaited him. "He was one of the many British officers who were meanly jealous of the daring achievements of their brave American comrades, but for whose . . . arduous services all the British armies sent to America during the Seven Years' War, would have affected little towards the conquest of Canada." There was, in truth, scarcely a campaign in this war, or series of wars, that was not a compound of unsavory politics, of blundering bad judgment on the part of commanders, of jealousy, vanity and jostling for rank or power. In view of the fighting that was always going on in the back yards of Europe it was, of course, prodigiously difficult to send fully equipped armies to fight three thousand miles away and, with communications so difficult, to keep abreast of strategy or to remove inept commanders.

The English won because it was their policy to colonize America and not merely to drain it of its riches, as France and Spain tried to do. America's fields, villages and industries, not to mention the thousands of provincial volunteers, were a bulwark for his Majesty's troops. But even the colonials, fighting for their homes, were far from above reproach. If their terms of enlistment ended in the middle of a campaign they would merely pick up and start for home. The success of the British therefore depended upon the professional soldiers who trained the provincials, regulars, and even the generals to fight in the woods. Among them the Rangers were pre-eminent. Rogers of New Hampshire, a veteran of more fighting than perhaps any other single individual in the war, had this to say in his journal of the colonials' good fortune:

> Thus at length at the end of the 5th campaign, Montreal and the whole country of Canada was given up, and became subject to the King of Great Britain; a conquest perhaps of the greatest importance that is to be met with in the British annals, whether we consider the prodigious extent of country we are hereby made masters of, the vast addition it must make to trade and navigation, or the security it must afford the northern provinces.

The major returned from a long sortie into the west to marry, in June, 1761, a beautiful daughter of a spoiled—or at least rich, mannered and complacent—society in Portsmouth. She was Elizabeth, the daughter of the Anglican minister, Arthur Browne. This was the gentleman who a year previously had married old Governor Benning Wentworth to his servant girl, Martha Hilton, much to the dismay of Portsmouth society, if to the delight of poets and folklorists of a later generation. By becoming a legend on the frontier Rogers had compensated for not being one of the elite, and Portsmouth could take much more pride in this marriage. The lovely Elizabeth wore yellow satin and lace (the same gown in which she appears in a portrait by Joseph Blackburn) and went in style to live in Concord, where she was waited upon by three servants, including Billy, the Indian boy whom Rogers had brought back from his raid on St. Francis.

The marriage was ill-advised because the major could not settle down.

His subsequent wanderings were as eventful as those of the French wars, the difference being that his prestige did not keep pace with his adventures. To what extent the pathetic circumstances of his later life were owing to his enemies and fate and to what extent to his weaknesses is still a question. There is no doubt that he was gravely misrepresented and evilly treated by powerful enemies like General Thomas Gage and Sir William Johnson, and by the government in failing to pay him what was due for his war services. On the other hand, there is much to suggest that he was an opportunist, sometimes an amoral one. Certainly Rogers' strengths were magnificent and his weaknesses, under the circumstances, no more than human.

On his scout to take possession of the western forts at the end of the war his imagination had been stirred profoundly by a country rich with game, and rivers so full of salmon that with a torch and spear one could fill a canoe with them in half an hour. He thought Toronto would make a good place for a factory. In the place that was to become Cleveland he smoked the peace pipe with the illustrious Chief Pontiac. In 1765 he went to England and obtained an appointment from the King as commander of the frontier post of Michilimackinac, and with his wife he journeyed the 1,300 miles to that place in the following year. Soon there were rumors that he was engaged with the Indians in dark schemes to enrich himself and betray his government. General Gage and Sir William Johnson managed to have him put in irons in 1768 on trumped-up charges, but in Montreal, where he was taken for trial, he was found innocent. At this critical point in the

major's fortunes the selfish Elizabeth, who had expected to live with
as much glitter out West as she had in Portsmouth, sued for divorce
on the grounds of infidelity.

In 1769 Rogers, humiliated and abandoned, appeared in Africa and
fought two battles under the Dey of Algiers. He spent the next
six years in England, where he published his journals, with a companion volume called A Concise View of North America, and where

> a mail coach in which he was a passenger, was stopped by a highway-
> man on Hunslow Heath. The robber, thrusting a pistol through the
> coach window, demanded the purses and watches of the occupants.
> While others were taking out their valuables, the bold American
> stranger suddenly seized the man by the collar by main strength,
> drew him through the window and ordered the coachman to drive
> on. The captive was an old offender for whose apprehension a
> reward of 50 pounds sterling had been offered by the government.

Since he was a retired officer in the British Army on half pay, he was
looked upon as a Tory when he returned to America on the eve of the
Revolution in 1775. On December 2 of that year Eleazar Wheelock,
founder of the New Hampshire Indian college in Hanover, wrote
General Washington:

> On the 13th . . . the famous Major Robert Rogers came to my
> house from a tavern in the neighborhood, where he called for re-
> freshments. I had never seen him before. He was in but ordinary
> habit, for one of his character. He treated me with great respect:
> said he had come from London in July, and had spent 20 days with
> the Congress in Philadelphia . . . had been offered and urged to take
> a Commission in favor of the Colonies; but, as he was on half pay
> from the Crown, he'd thought proper not to accept it; that he had
> fought two battles in Algiers under the Dey . . . that Lord Dart-
> mouth, and many other noblemen had spoken of it . . . [Rogers sug-
> gested to Wheelock that he might gain much wealth for the College
> in England.] He went to aforesaid tavern, and tarried all night: the
> next morning told the landlord he was out of money, and could not
> pay his reckoning—which was about 3 shillings, but would pay him
> on his return, which would be within about 3 months, and went on
> his way to Lime; since which I have heard nothing from him. But
> yesterday, 2 soldiers . . . on their return from Montreal, informed me
> that our officers were assured by a Frenchman, a Captain in the
> Artillery, whom they had taken captive, that Major Rogers was

second in command under General Carlton; and that he had lately been in Indian habit through our encampments at St. John's, and had given the plan of them to the General; and suppose that he made his escape with the Indians.

While it appeared that the report of the latter incident was untrue, Washington not only felt that Rogers' conduct "should be attended with some degree of vigilance" but saw to it that it was.

Although Rogers declared, "I love North America; it is my native country, and that of my family, and I intend to spend the evening of my days in it," it was whispered that a man who had been involved in counterfeiting during the French wars and who had behaved so badly at Michilimackinac was now offering his services to both sides. In February, 1776, Rogers' name appeared with 23 others on a petition for a grant of 23,000 acres on the east side of Lake Champlain (now Burlington) to be called Rogerston. None of the magnificent country for which he had so bravely fought was to become his. Confined in jail as a poor security risk while Congress was considering the Declaration of Independence, he escaped to join the British as commandant of the Queen's American Rangers. While serving on Long Island he narrowly escaped being taken by his American countrymen.

In 1781, when returning from Quebec on a recruiting mission, he was not so fortunate and was again lodged in jail. Divorced by Elizabeth and almost forgotten by old friends and foes alike, he returned to England, where he remained the rest of his intemperate and debt-ridden life.

During his declining years in London flashes of memory must have returned him now and then to the terror and excitement of his youth, to good and bad, but withal to his best days in the pungent forests of the Champlain valley, and to the nights of bitter clear cold described by Whittier:

> Robert Rawlin!—Frosts were falling
> When the Ranger's horn was calling
> Through the woods to Canada. . .

V

THE LAST
OF THE WENTWORTHS

John Wentworth was yet another example of the right man at the wrong time, whereas his uncle Benning, who had governed New Hampshire for the previous twenty-five years, from 1741 to 1766, had been, if not the wrong man, a luckier one at the right time. His career ended before the Americans declared open season on royal governors.

Although they had been among the earliest settlers in New Hampshire the Wentworths had not been born to the colors. The original Wentworth in America had been William, a follower of John Wheelwright, the outspoken Puritan minister and refugee from Massachusetts, who had founded the town of Exeter. William's seafaring grandson, John, had become lieutenant governor in 1717 and it was he, apparently, who began to apply to himself the precept of kings: God and my right. He joined the Church of England and lived grandly and so it was logical that Benning, the eldest of his sixteen children, should do likewise on his accession to the governorship. Benning was not an evil man. He was, according to Belknap, neither brilliant nor contemptible but rather an honest, if calculating merchant and, to those he considered important and wellborn, an engaging host. As he had no patience with opposition, his temper, particularly during an attack of gout, was violent.

In military matters he did rather well by his province during the French and Indian Wars but is claimed to have been too sharp a speculator when he became preoccupied with land in the New Hampshire Grants. How much too sharp is a question. As compared with George Washington's transactions, for example, Wentworth's appear quite modest; as contrasted with the immense half-million acre tracts that were being parceled out in manorial New York, his holdings were meager. It is true that he acquired for himself at no cost perhaps 70,000 acres. It is true that he collected fees for every grant he made to others, but there were the expenses of surveying mapmaking and recording to be deducted from each fee. It is also true that he parceled out tracts to his family and friends. Mark Hunking Wentworth, his brother, received 37 lots, Theodore Atkinson, his father-in-law, 57 lots in as many towns, Theodore Atkinson, Jr., 16 lots, and so on. The Governor thought that those in power (his relatives) should be people of property. By dividing the spoils he was assuring their loyalty and as well a tight succession of Wentworths to the governorship. When word of his misbehavior reached the ears of the King's ministers his punishment was merely an order that he resign. The fact that he was let off so easily lends credence to the theory that it was not thirst for land but politics at home and in England that were responsible for his resignation. When he took office in 1741 during the latter part of the reign of George II, a Liberal government was dictating English colonial policy, one which favored the small landholders of New England. This was followed by George III's Tory government, which supported the manorial system of New York. New York desired the land of the Green Mountains: the King in Council supported that government in its claims. Wentworth had no recourse but to resign.

While his second marriage, that to his maid, Martha Hilton, was for years the subject of riotous gossip in Portsmouth, it might not have survived as the most significant event of his career were it not for *Tales of a Wayside Inn*, in which it appears as a classic of the rags-to-riches theme.

> Yet scarce a guest perceived that she was there,
> Until the Governor, rising from his chair,
> Played slightly with his ruffles, then looked down,
> And said unto the Reverend Arthur Browne:
> "This is my birthday: it shall likewise be
> My wedding-day; and you shall marry me!"
> The listening guests were greatly mystified,
> None more so than the Rector, who replied:
> "Marry you? Yes, that were a pleasant task,
> Your Excellency; but to whom? I ask."
> The Governor answered: "To this lady here";
> And beckoned Martha Hilton to draw near.
> She came and stood, all blushes, at his side.
> The Rector paused. The impatient Governor cried:
> "This is the lady; do you hesitate?
> Then I command you as Chief Magistrate."
> The Rector read the service loud and clear:
> "Dearly beloved, we are gathered here,"
> And so on to the end. At his command
> On the fourth finger of her fair left hand
> The Governor placed the ring; and that was all:
> Martha was Lady Wentworth of the Hall!

For Wentworth's nephew John, who took office as governor in 1766 at the age of twenty-nine, the important fact about his uncle's marriage was that Martha Hilton inherited not only the old man's money but Wentworth Hall, the mansion by the sea whose gables and rambling rooms still breathe of the eighteenth century, of lace and satin and white wine. Even without his uncle's estate John Wentworth was in no real danger of poverty. Mark Hunking Wentworth, his father, was one of the group of twelve Masonian Proprietors to whom the original land patents of the state had descended. He also had done very well in getting out masts for the Royal Navy, and in the West Indies trade. His gambrel-roofed home in Portsmouth bespoke position, pride and prosperity. In 1751, at fourteen, his son was enrolled near the top of the list of freshmen at Harvard. Social position, not the alphabet, then determined one's rank and one's privileges in the class. If young Wentworth's instincts, despite his background, had not been democratic, he would scarcely have been a close friend of one John Adams, a farmer's son whose name under other circumstances might well have begun with Z, so far was it down the list.

After college John went to work for his father and in 1763 sailed for England to represent the Wentworth enterprises there. An engaging and good-looking American with the right friends had no difficulty finding favor in aristocratic circles. If Wentworth's three years in England were gay, apparently they were not frivolous, for he earnestly opposed the Stamp Act, then under consideration, and otherwise took an enlightened interest in the relationship between Britain and her colonies. In 1766 the King appointed him governor of New Hampshire and surveyor general of his Majesty's woods in North America. In the same year Oxford University bestowed upon him an honorary degree. The proud recipient of all these distinctions started for America to take the reins from Uncle Benning and to retrieve, if possible, the prestige of the Wentworths.

The young governor's tour of his Majesty's woods from south to north on his way to Portsmouth was punctuated heavily with calls upon the first families of the various provinces. He indulged in cards with the Byrds at their splendid mansion in Jamestown, visited the Randolphs of Virginia, where he purchased two pairs of thoroughbreds, and the William Bayards of Weehawken, New Jersey. When word was received that he had sailed from New York to Boston lavish plans for his home-coming went forward in Portsmouth. At the New Hampshire boundary he was greeted by a delegation of officials and "two troops of horse" and was escorted to the capital through lines of the military who presented their arms. The booming of cannon reverberated from William and Mary, the fort in the harbor. There were volleys of cheers and of muskets and a public banquet.

He was popular from the first. Though he continued to indulge in extravagant tastes and to seek the company of polite society, he loved the woods and felt his responsibilities to the Merrimack valley settlers from Massachusetts and to the people in homespun from Connecticut who lived along the banks of the broad, placid river beyond the mountains. In the years before the Revolution the problems of royal government in New Hampshire were such as to tax the ingenuity of the most resourceful executive, since the attitudes of the people in the three areas all differed. While the settled inhabitants of the coast were accustomed to royal governors and what John Adams called "the pomps and vanities and ceremonies of that little world, Portsmouth," the people of the Merrimack traded to the south with Boston and had Boston feelings. The people of the Connecticut valley, in accordance with the very liberal charter of the province from which they had come, were independent. Wentworth planned to conquer geography by linking Portsmouth and the outlying valleys with roads. Thus were the fresh-water communities of Hanover, Charlestown, Boscawen, Wolfeborough, Lancaster, and Northumberland united with the coast at Durham and Portsmouth. That Wentworth did not succeed in gathering together the frayed ends of geography and politics was no reflection on his efforts. His roads did spur settlement and create a feeling of solidarity since the militia, which he insisted that New Hampshire maintain, could now reach the frontier with dispatch. As Mayo points out in his enthusiastic biography of Wentworth, the fact that the very militia he created turned against him and seized power in the early days of the Revolution was more the result of fate and the harsh policies of Great Britain than anything the governor did. Like Louis XVI, he was the pawn of circumstance.

In trying to carry out his duties as surveyor general and protector of the great pines marked for masts in his Majesty's fleet, he was frequently at odds with the local woodsmen. And he caused much resentment by retrieving lands which his uncle had willed to Martha Hilton and which he thought were rightfully his. When he revoked the grants to such unsettled tracts east of the Connecticut and regranted them to others, including himself, the foundations of his office shook violently; indeed he almost lost his commission, but the Privy Council finally vindicated him. He appears also to have been somewhat hypocritical in his attitude toward the lands in the New Hampshire Grants west of the Connecticut River. At first he supported the settlers who had received grants there from his uncle, but when the King decided in 1764 that the area beyond the river belonged to New York Wentworth appealed (in vain) to the New York Governor to keep him in mind when making any new grants. Thus in one sense he was selling the New Hampshire settlers down the river, and in another was merely obeying the decision of the King and trying to increase his holdings in the only possible legal way. So far as officeholders are concerned it is too easy to apply twentieth-century standards of morality to the eighteenth century, when everyone was speculating in land. Officials were not prevented from acquiring land so long as they did so with propriety and in accordance with the King's desire that granted land should be settled and not speculated upon. Perhaps if John Wentworth had had his uncle's opportunities, temptation might have carried him too far; but he did not have them and his energies found release in endeavors more worth while to the people.

His help in establishing Dartmouth College in 1769 was certainly one of the landmarks of his career, although it pleased him little that Eleazar Wheelock, founder of the school for Indians in the wilderness at Hanover, had no regard for the Church of England. An evangelist of the George Whitefield stripe, Wheelock spent much of his life trying to educate the Indians and sending them back to their tribes as teachers and missionaries. He thought that if half the money spent on forts were devoted to making Christians out of the Indians war might be avoided; even if it were not, the Protestants might at least match such efforts on the part of France and the Jesuit priests. Apparently the British nobility thought so too, for Wheelock's good friend, Nathaniel Whitaker, and Samson Occum, his prize pupil, raised large sums in England for the new school in Hanover, where ex-Governor Benning Wentworth had provided 500 acres of land. In 1770 Wheelock moved there to start afresh, followed shortly by his wife in a carriage, thirty students on foot, including two Indians who refused to drive the cows, and his nephew driving a baggage wagon containing, among other items, a barrel of rum (although not the 500 gallons as claimed in the late Richard Hovey's Dartmouth song.)

> I housed my stuff [wrote the 59-year-old preacher], with my wife, and the females of my family. in my hutt—my sons and students made booths and beds of hemlock bows, and in this situation we continued about a month , . . when I removed with my family into my house. And though the season had been cold, with storms of rain and snow . . . yet by the pure mercy of God the scene changed for the better in every respect.

Unfortunately the redskins found the Muses little more to their liking in the wilderness than they had in Wheelock's former school in Connecticut. Strangers to discipline and study, friends of drink and passion, they fell, with few exceptions, by the wayside. Many of the exceptions, sent out as missionaries, returned to the wild ways of their tribes. What Wheelock did, of course, accomplish, with the help of John Wentworth, a guest at the first commencement in 1771, was the founding of one of New England's great colleges for students of every color.

In his book entitled *Eleazar Wheelock* James Dow McCallum brings the founder's vexations vividly in focus:

> What shall be done with the body of Joshua Tilden found frozen on the road one day in January? Certify to the coroner that you have removed the body and he will probably be satisfied. Directions for rafting logs down the Connecticut. Orders for grass, rum, beef. Wheelock is accused of inhospitality at the college commencement of 1773; he denies the charge, adds that his wife has been ill, the cook drunk, and besides the college has only one tablecloth.

John Crane, physician, begins a defense of himself before Wheelock: "Since I have lately been accused of malpractice in the obstetricate art by a number of good old mischief-making matrons at the bar of whose shallow understanding contrary to scripture truth and humanity my character has been arraigned tried judged and condemned without my cognizance. . . ."

"Some misdemeanor," writes McCallum, "perhaps that of the students in Lebanon, causes Wheelock to write that 'the Old Serpent has waked up lately and acts like himself yet. I hope he will bite his tongue and become speechless by and by'. . . . Members of the freshman and sophomore classes wish to be allowed 'to spend certain leisure hours allotted to us for the relaxation of our minds, in such sort as stepping the minuette and learning to use the sword. . . .'"

Opposing outlooks on religion strained the friendship of Wheelock and the Governor in the cause of higher education for New Hampshire. The first settlers, unlike those of Massachusetts, had no particular quarrel with the Church of England, for they had come to trade. When New Hampshire temporarily became a part of Massachusetts in 1641 and zealots of the latter province found a Church of England minister preaching in Portsmouth, they indignantly removed him. Although as time passed New Hampshire began to fill up with Massachusetts Congregationalists and Connecticut freethinkers, the Anglican church returned to Portsmouth during the time of Queen Anne and flourished as the official creed of the Governor and fifty or sixty wealthy satellite families. In Queen's Chapel Wentworth's pew was "raised a little above the rest and surmounted by a heavy wooden canopy which bore the Royal arms and festoons of red plush." The Governor, in view of the heavy financial support Dartmouth had received from England, wanted it to be a Church of England college with the Bishop of London on the board of trustees. Wheelock engaged in tooth-and-nail opposition for five years until the Revolution solved his problem. Yet the northcountry college derives from the stormy co-operation of these two men. The Governor had to respect the different political and economic outlook of the Connecticut River people, and as a moderate did not care to antagonize Wheelock, their spokesman. One hundred miles of woods separated the worlds of Hanover and Portsmouth. Certainly if Dartmouth had been situated on the golden coast its history would have been different.

While the people of the capital were not by any means all royalists, their institutions were bound with the fetters of colonial government. The population of Portsmouth was rather like that of a modern duchy, with a benign, if rich, hierarchy superimposed, like gold leaf over pine, on a population of merchants, shopkeepers and artisans. Until the War of 1812 the port was everything. Inside the small-paned windows of their countingrooms overlooking the river, wrote Thomas Bailey Aldrich, "used to stand portly merchants in knee breeches and silver shoe-buckles and plain-colored coats with ruffles at the wrists, waiting for their ships to come up the Narrows; the cries of stevedores and the chants of sailors at the windlass used to echo along the shore where all is silence now."

Twenty or thirty ships at once were often loading cargoes for England or the West Indies: lumber, pork, beef, pigs, mules, oxen, horses, sheep and geese; or unloading rum, sugar, coffee and molasses. The Piscataqua was busy with small craft carrying oysters, lobsters, and fish of all kinds to the market on Spring Hill. The streets crowding the waterfront were narrow and most of the houses, even of the rich, were of wood. There was a hotel, a customhouse and post office and an assembly house for dramatic offerings. A town crier carrying an oversized bell announced the events of the day to a polyglot population which in 1764 contained 124 male and 63 female slaves.

Apparently John Wentworth had no such servants. When he sailed from England to take office he brought a number of Yorkshire footmen whom he installed in his bachelor's hall on Portsmouth's Pleasant Street, a 2½-story house tastefully decorated with fine furniture from Boston. Discovering the advantages of becoming freemen, some of the Yorkshiremen withdrew and Wentworth was soon writing an English friend to find him two footmen "that can play well on a French horn . . . or one of them . . . on a violin." He offered them free passage on one of his Majesty's mast-carrying ships, to clothe them in his livery and, at the end of five years' service, to give them each 100 acres of good land. The Governor's stable was well stocked with horses and an assortment of glittering carriages and when he went on an official trip it was in state in an elegant coach accompanied by eight servants. In ordering a sulky from Philadelphia he specified "steel springs, with wheels at least 4 inches lower than our good friend Mr. Foxcroft's, to be painted the lightest straw color and gilt moldings, with my crest and cypher (as on the seal of this letter) enclosed in a plain oval without the least ornament, and rather in a small compass." The man who might one day be seen in a splendid carriage and the next in a sulky behind a fast trotter, on the third might gallop happily into the woods to live the hardy life of a surveyor.

His best friend was his cousin, Michael Wentworth, a retired British colonel with whom he enjoyed horses, cards and music. When Benning Wentworth died, leaving all his money to Martha Hilton, Michael Wentworth saw a means of recouping his fortunes. He married her, went to live in Wentworth Hall, spent her fortune, and on his deathbed is said to have announced: "I have had my cake and ate it." History does not have much to say about the relationship between the Governor and his cousin after he obtained by marriage money that might otherwise have been the Governor's.

There seems to have been a parallel between the slightly incestuous blood lines of British royalty and the Wentworths. The secretary of the province, Theodore Atkinson, Jr., whose mother was a sister of the Governor's father, had married Frances, the daughter of another uncle of his and of the governor's—Samuel Wentworth, a rich Boston merchant. The Governor, Atkinson and his bride were all first cousins. Her delicate features—she was one of America's loveliest women— have, with those of John Wentworth, descended to posterity on canvases by John Copley. It is at least a tradition that Mrs. Atkinson had once had great affection for John, but during his absence in England she had married Atkinson. Wentworth's return kindled old feelings and, according to local rumor, nocturnal signals were exchanged between her window and the Governor's.

In any case the 33-year-old Atkinson fell sick of consumption and died. The beautiful widow of twenty-four wore black at the funeral service conducted by the Rev. Arthur Browne (father-in-law of Robert Rogers) but, according to Charles Brewster, immediately shed her mourning robes. Ten days after the funeral, on November 11, 1769, Browne married Mrs. Atkinson to the 32-year-old governor and in his excitement after the ceremony fell down the front steps of Queen's Chapel and broke his arm. "The Day is spent in innocent mirth" read a dispatch to Boston. "The colours of the Shipping in the Harbor are displayed—all the Bells are ringing and the cannon roaring—in a word Joy sits smiling in every Countenance. . . . Happy, thrice happy the Ruler! . . ."

For over a year the Governor had been lavishing funds on his summer residence at Lake Wentworth; in the months and years following his marriage he spent much of his energy making it the

perfect country seat. In October, 1770, his wife wrote to Mrs. Woodbury Langdon in Portsmouth:

> I get but very little of my governor's company. He loves to be
> going about and sometimes (except at meales) I don't see him an
> hour in a day. . . . I tell the Governor he is unlucky in a wife hav-
> ing so timid a disposition, and he so resolute. For you know he
> would attempt, and effect if possible, to ride over the tops of the
> trees on Moose Mountain, while poor I even tremble at passing
> through a road cut at the foot of it. . . .

Frances could never adjust to country living, although her life in the
country could scarcely have been called primitive. The house was 104
feet long and 42 feet wide, the stable over half as large and another
barn even larger. There were saw- and gristmills, blacksmith, joiner
and cabinetmaker's shops, a smokehouse, a dairy and a garden walled
with stone on three sides as well as boats and a boat landing, since
the whole fronted on a landscaped arm of the lake. The Governor
was interested in "any curiosities" as he wrote, "natural or artificial."
He brought in English pheasants to see how they would get on,
stocked a pond with a thriving species of cod. His interest in im-
proving the country, in welcoming settlers—even giving them land
near his plantation—saved him from the onus of a dilettante indulging in idle diversions.

For six years the Governor and his lady remained childless—if
three nieces and a nephew of a deceased brother were not to be
counted. The Governor took great pride in providing for their education. He felt that there were not three nicer girls in America, and
as for the nephew: "He has grown into a fine youth, and is soon to
return to me to attend instructions in mathematics, French, fencing
and dancing to qualify him for the navy which is his passion, and
wherein, I dare say, he will make a good figure. . . ." On January 20,
1775, Frances Wentworth bore the Governor a son. It was as if a
prince had been born, for here was the heir to continue the Wentworth succession.

But ill winds were blowing through Wentworth Manor and all the
great houses of colonial governors. Among them there was perhaps
none who less deserved the buffeting of the next months, none more

reasonable or who tried harder for honorable compromise than New Hampshire's last royal governor. The first rupture with the British had of course been the Stamp Act, which the newly appointed governer had opposed strenuously. George Meserve, his Majesty's agent for distributing stamps in New Hampshire, had swung in effigy in Portsmouth's Hay-Market. On November 1, 1765, the day the act went into effect, ships in the harbor carried their colors at half-mast. A funeral procession bearing a coffin with the inscription "Liberty— aged 145" passed through the streets. The repeal of the tax in 1766 was accompanied by ringing bells, roaring guns and fireworks—the whole being conducted, according to Nathaniel Adams, "with decorum, sobriety and innocent mirth."

In 1774 Portsmouth citizens fought the importation of duty-carrying tea and might have dumped it in the ocean had it not been for the Governor's diplomacy. Though sympathetic toward his countrymen he was nevertheless bound to uphold the King's decrees. His sentiments during these very anxious years were revealed in a letter to a friend:

> These Americans have been very wrong, but any dispassionate observer would honestly say that those who have made them so are more culpable. I mean the execution—not the Acts themselves, they are not for me to consider. Nor would they have been effectually opposed had they civilly and with tolerable decency and good humor been presented instead of crammed down harshly and with contempt.

In a letter to the Marquis of Rockingham the Governor declared:

> I sincerely wish I could think the Colonies . . . were likely to get back to their old ground. The contrary seems to me to be daily obtaining, and I really think that unless there are some means found to allay their apprehensions and jealousies, and to invigorate the powers of government in its first principals, these colonies will forever be the cause of difficulty and trouble to Great Britain.

It is at least conceivable that New Hampshire's last royal governor might have been the first republican one, so great was his popularity even in these times, had he not secretly agreed to send carpenters to Boston to help build barracks for his Majesty's troops. When the people learned of this they turned their backs on him. They seized the guns in the ancient harbor fort, William and Mary, and elected delegates to the First Continental Congress.

In 1775, during the twilight months of colonialism, the British fleet still controlled the harbor at Portsmouth and the Governor, now virtually powerless, but still in residence "in vain strove almost to death," as he wrote, "to prevent the oncoming hurricane." When the King's warship *Scarborough* intercepted two vessels bringing needed food and supplies to the town, Wentworth appeared on board to plead that they be allowed to land and discharge their cargoes. They were instead sent to provision the British fleet in Boston. When a force of six or seven hundred angry citizens appeared with guns to try to drive the *Scarborough* out of the harbor, the captain began seizing the crews of in- and outbound fishing schooners and impressing them into his own service. The Governor interceded and the prisoners were released. Since he was still the agent of the King's government his position gradually became untenable, even dangerous; in June he had to leave his splendid home and move his wife and infant son to the tumbling walls of Fort William and Mary. It was miserably damp and bleak there even in summer but the *Scarborough*'s guns afforded protection and the Governor held on tenaciously. "I will not complain," he wrote, "because it would be a poignant censure upon a people I love and forgive. For truely I can say with the poet in his *Lear*, 'I am a man more sinned against than sinning.'"

In August the bumbling captain of the *Scarborough* became involved with the people of Portsmouth in a shooting incident which the Governor could not moderate. Since all communication with the town was severed and it was necessary for the *Scarborough* to sail for Boston for provisions, the only choice was flight. On August 23 he left his beloved town by the sea forever. In September he did see it again in the distance when he landed at Gosport on the Isles of Shoals to proclaim a meeting of the Assembly, but the Revolution had begun.

In January his wife and son sailed from Boston for England. The Governor went briefly to Nova Scotia, then Long Island, but as it became clear that the war would be long and perhaps disastrous to Britain and that there was no possibility of his returning to New

Hampshire, he too sailed for England in February, 1778. The great house at Lake Wentworth remained standing until it burned in 1820. The Governor's lands, his home at Portsmouth and most of his possessions, along with those of other loyalists, were sold at auction to pay the expenses of the militia and the state government. The people turned over his furniture and paintings, however, to his father, Mark Hunking Wentworth, who remained with the Revolutionists.

For sixteen years New Hampshire's first citizen in exile remained more or less a man without a country. In 1792 he became acting governor of Nova Scotia, where he died at the advanced age of eighty-three, not the least bitter about the cruel twist of fate that had turned him out of his homeland.

> I do most cordially wish the most extensive, great and permanent blessings to the United States, and of course rejoice at the establishment of their federal Constitution as a probable means of their happiness. If there is anything partial in my heart . . . it is that New Hampshire, my native country, may arise to be among the most brilliant members of the Confederation. . . . For this object nothing appeared to me too much. My whole heart and fortune were devoted to it.

VI

LORDS OF THE GATEWAY

Concerning the capture of Fort Ticonderoga by Ethan Allen and Benedict Arnold more ink seems to have flowed than blood on the battlefield of Saratoga. Presumably this is because the daring coup on May 10, 1775, was one of the first events of the Revolution, because possession of the fort was of profound importance to any army invading America from the north and because of the interesting circumstances under which two of the war's foremost extroverts contrived to subordinate their egos to the common cause. Allen has fared much better under history's pitiless floodlight than the unfortunate Arnold, whose treachery must always overshadow his gallantry early in the war.

The idea of surprising the British garrison in the crumbling fort first occurred to Allen. As the leader of the settlers streaming into the New Hampshire Grants from Connecticut after the French and Indian Wars, Ethan and his brother Ira realized after the Battle of Lexington that unless Ticonderoga and Crown Point were to be seized Vermont would become the first hostage of any invading British army. Arnold, for the broader reason, that the British would try to isolate all New England by seizing the Hudson and Champlain valleys, received a commission from the Provincial Congress of Massachusetts to accomplish what his rival had already set out to do by the time he reached Vermont.

Gersham Beach, a blacksmith from Shoreham, had on Allen's orders made an astonishing journey to rouse the freemen of Rutland, Pittsford, Brandon, Middlebury and Whiting and to summon them to a meeting in Castleton. It is a matter of history that Beach covered 60 miles over wooded terrain in 24 hours, a feat that rather dwarfs Paul Revere's ride. When Arnold arrived at Castleton the gathered yeomen would scarcely listen to his headstrong argument that he should lead the expedition. He persisted in his claims, even in the darkness as the 83 Green Mountain Boys readied themselves to embark from Hand's Cove, Shoreham, on the Vermont shore nearly opposite the fort.

Presently it was agreed that, although Ethan would command, Arnold might march at his side and to that extent share the honors. The rest is well enough known. Historians have unraveled and scrutinized every small and frayed detail—whether Ethan did in fact demand the surrender of the fort from its commander "In the name of the Great Jehovah, and the Continental Congress" (he appears to have said just that, and not something more profane); whether it was British Lieutenant Feltham or the commander, Captain Delaplace, who had not had time to put on his breeches (it appears to have been the latter). The great though dilapidated fortress had in any case fallen to a band of rough farmers from Vermont and, as Ethan wrote: "The sun seemed to rise that morning [May 10] with a superior lustre; and Ticonderoga and all its dependencies smiled on its conquerors, who tossed about the flowing bowl and wished success to Congress, and the liberty and freedom of America." The flowing bowl "for the refreshment of the fatigued soldiery," as Ethan put it, seems to have been at least as important as the captured rifles, cannon and military stores and on this subject William Cullen Bryant rekindled the spirit of the day:

> Fill up the bowl from the brook that glides,
> Where the fireflies light the break;
> A ruddier juice the Briton hides
> In his fortress by the Lake.

The shocked representatives in Philadelphia were not prepared militarily or psychologically for such aggression and in order to stamp their approval on this *fait accompli* they resolved that the action was necessary to forestall what they understood was a British plot to invade the northern region. They directed that the captors take an inventory of the articles seized so that these might be "safely returned when the restoration of the former harmony between Britain and the Colonies so ardently wished for by the latter, shall render it prudent and consistent with the overruling law of self-preservation."

Meanwhile Allen and his aides had swept the lake clean of the British. They captured the garrison at Crown Point and the settlement of an ardent colonial, Philip Skene, at the southernmost point of navigation. Arnold seized a list of British troops in the northern department and, proceeding to St. Johns in a schooner taken at Skenesborough (Whitehall) he forced the surrender of the garrison there and all the remaining British boats. During succeeding weeks the dispute between the two commanders over their authority grew quite serious. It subsided only when Arnold resigned his command in disgust on June 24 and returned to Connecticut. "The unhappy controversy between the officers at Ticonderoga relative to the command," General Philip Schuyler wrote the Continental Congress, "has, I am informed, thrown everything into vast confusion. Troops have been dismissed, others refuse to serve if this or that man command. . . . I shall hurry up there . . . that I may attempt discipline amongst them."

A much greater cause for alarm, at least for the settlers of the Champlain valley and New England, was Congress's decision to abandon Ticonderoga and all Lake Champlain and to transport the captured military stores to the head of Lake George. Allen and others protested hotly, and the fort was not abandoned. Its capture had consequences far different, though scarcely less important, from those Ethan had dreamed. Without the artillery he had seized, Washington probably would not have been able to drive the British out of Boston. In a prodigious feat accomplished by a former bookseller, Henry Knox, 59 guns great and small were dragged over the snowbound Berkshires by steaming oxen deep in the winter of 1776. When this artillery was brought in to Dorchester Heights, his Majesty's forces moved out.

The conviction that Montreal and Canada could be taken without much trouble, if it were done before the British were able to set the wheels of their ponderous military machine in motion, had long possessed Ethan Allen and indeed many other New Englanders. Much of their energy and blood had flowed in the wars against the French. They thought they had as much right as the British to Canada, particularly to the St. Lawrence basin, so often a gateway of invasion against them. Ethan coveted Canada and wanted to invade it. Perhaps it was because of a dispute over this very matter with the Green Mountain Boys that he had been replaced as their leader by Seth Warner, whom apparently he could not convince of the wisdom of an attack on Montreal. In the hope that Congress would authorize such an invasion he journeyed to Philadelphia to assure the legislators that now was the time, since Montreal's troops were besieged to the south at St. Johns by General Montgomery.

At length, in the fall of 1775, Ethan resolved to storm the French citadel himself, and might actually have done it with a small force if one John Brown, who with his men had agreed solemnly to take part in the raid, had lived up to his agreement. Instead of Montreal it was Ethan who was taken and he departed for England in chains, thus depriving the remaining chapters of the war in the northern department of the colorful language of its most original character.

Among the figures who played critical roles in the dispute of the following months was, of course, Benedict Arnold, whose real nature, despite all that has been written about him, remains indistinct. According to Jared Sparks, this spoiled and unstable son of a prominent New England family had an "innate love of mischief" and "an obduracy of conscience, a cruelty of disposition, an irritability of temper and a reckless indifference to the good or ill opinion of others. . . . One of his earliest amusements was the robbing of birds' nests, and it was his custom to maim and mangle birds in sight of the old ones, that he might be diverted by their cries." Written in an era when Arnold's name was synonymous with everything hateful in human nature, this report is biased and without apparent basis in fact. In *The Traitor and the Spy* James Thomas Flexner cites Arnold's statement to a patriot leader that "his courage was acquired and that he was a coward until he was fifteen years old." Although he became quarrelsome and aggressive after that, his adversaries were always larger boys, not those who were his inferiors in feats of strength. At sixteen he ran away to enlist with the colonials but soon returned home with a stomachful of the French War. He was an apothecary and a bookseller for a while and at an early age went to sea as a kind of merchant-navigator who sailed his own sloops at great profit.

During the early years of an unsatisfactory marriage which failed to provide him with the large helpings of praise, the sympathy and understanding he craved, three sons were born. From time to time rumors of drunkenness and philandering at various ports where his ship called reached his wife, and for a while they parted. But life at the outbreak of the Revolution was beginning to suit him as well as his fine house in New Haven and the scarlet coat and ruffled shirt he wore as captain of the New Haven company of Governor's Foot Guard. From then on he had enough action and excitement, but never, it seems, enough glory. If one is to judge his career and abilities as his contemporaries viewed them, he emerges as a brilliant tactician, a fearless and, to his men, inspiring fighter whose sensitive pride gave rise to fits of pompousness, of brooding and despondency. The difference between Arnold and, for example, John Stark of New Hampshire, whose great services also were overlooked when the politicians handed out promotions, was that Stark bitterly took his medicine and returned to the colors, while Arnold went over to the enemy.

His record in the northcountry, however, was all good. When Congress finally decided upon a campaign against Canada in the fall of 1775, Arnold, having rejoined the war, helped save his army from complete disaster. To the spirited Richard Montgomery and to such of his durable regimental commanders as Seth Warner, new leader of the Green Mountain Boys, St. Johns had capitulated and Montreal was also theirs. Quebec, however, and its ally, the bitter cold, proved overwhelming. On the last day of 1775 General Montgomery died in the arms of Captain Aaron Burr; and the disabled Arnold, who had led his gaunt troops through the forests and icy rivers of Maine to the cliffs of Quebec, was carried from the field. That winter in the American camp outside the walls of the city was one of the most harrowing in American military annals. The soldiers were cold, wet and hungry. Two thousand one hundred of them were victims of smallpox at one time, leaving merely 900 to carry on the siege.

Spring brought relief only from the cold. Arriving in Montreal early in May, 1776, after a rigorous journey by bateau through Lake Champlain, the 70-year-old Benjamin Franklin and John Carroll, later archbishop of Baltimore, failed to persuade the Canadians to join the campaign with the rebelling colonies. When a fresh army arrived from England all hope took wing and the Americans began a retreat that was saved from headlong flight by General John Sullivan of New Hampshire and Arnold, in command at Montreal. The Richelieu River and Lake Champlain were again the scene of the most desperate misfortunes of war. To keep valuable equipment and stores from falling into the hands of Burgoyne, the Americans, many half-dead of smallpox, plunged into icy waters to drag 100 heavy bateaux through the Richilieu rapids, which the spring runoff from Lake Champlain had made treacherous. The camp at Isle aux Noix smelled of the dead and dying. "Another fortnight in this place," Sullivan wrote Washington, "will not leave us men enough to carry off the sick." By the time the army had reached Isle La Motte some three thousand stricken soldiers had been removed to Crown Point.

To the resolute Benedict Arnold, recently promoted to brigadier general, this bleak turn of events was terribly disheartening. He wrote General Gates how deeply it discouraged him "to think that we have lost in 1 month all the immortal Montgomery was a whole campaign in gaining." On July 29 John Trumbull, the painter (son of Governor Jonathan Trumbull of Connecticut) summed up the situation on Lake Champlain in a few stark sentences:

> There are now 3,000 sick and about 3,000 well; this leaves near 5,000 to be accounted for; of these the enemy have cost perhaps 1,000—sickness another 1,000—which leaves near 3,000; in what manner they are disposed of is unknown. Among those who remain there is neither order, subordination or harmony, the officers as well as men of one colony insulting and quarreling with those of another. . . . The soldiers are ragged, dirty and . . . lousy.

On Mount Independence on the Vermont shore (opposite the ruins of Ticonderoga) a general hospital had been set up which, according to a letter from Colonel Samuel Wigglesworth to the New Hampshire Committee of Safety, was, in September, 1776, without medicine—"no emetick nor cathartick; no mercurial nor antimonial Remedy; no opiate or elixir. . . . It would make a heart of stone melt to hear the moans and see the distresses of the dying. . . . Now, Sirs, think how much more unhappy and distressed the conditions of these troops would be should the enemy attack our Lines." Worst of all was the fact that the remaining troops lacked a competent general, since Sullivan, who had managed the retreat as bravely and well as possible, had departed in disgust for Philadelphia, upon the assumption of his command by Horatio Gates.

Hope, if any remained in the northern department, thus rested on the shoulders of Benedict Arnold, who had agreed to build a fleet and sail it against the oncoming British in order that Anthony Wayne might have time to shore up Fort Ticonderoga. Arnold had, of course, a nucleus of ships to start with and carpenters from various New England ports, but when it is considered that the timbers they shaped were growing in the woods in the spring and in action against the British in the fall and that the flotilla consisted of three schooners, one sloop, seven gondolas and one galley carrying, in all, 32 guns and over 500 men, the achievement at the primitive shipyard at Skenesborough seems all the more notable.

At St. Johns, the northernmost point of navigation on the lake, the British also were achieving wonders. Burgoyne's orderly book sketches the rise of one John Schank from his birth in Scotland to the post of chief of the naval yard at St. Johns; and the building of the 300-ton *Inflexible*, the most imposing specimen of his handiwork. Originally laid down at Quebec, the hull of this ship was taken to pieces, carried over the rapids of the Richelieu and in a single day, September 2, 1776, it was completely reassembled under Schank's direction. Twenty-eight days after the relaying of the keel "the *Inflexible* was launched and on the evening of the 1st of October she actually sailed completely manned, victualed and equipped for service."

Far outweighed in ships, guns and men, Benedict Arnold, beating his way north in heavy weather, was not disheartened. On September 3 the American flotilla (now numbering 15 vessels) reached the northern end of the lake and tried, unavailingly, to draw the British out of the Richelieu River. After the enemy began to erect batteries on both shores Arnold withdrew to Isle La Motte, where, on September 18 he wrote General Gates:

> I intend first fair wind to come up as high as Valcour, where is a good harbor, and where we shall have the advantage of attacking the enemy in the open lake, where the row galleys, as their motion is quick, will give us great advantage over the enemy; and if they are too many for us we can retire. . . . We have a wretched motley crew in the fleet; the marines, the refuse of every regiment, and the sailors few of them ever wet with salt water.

On October 4 the British fleet of 53 ships and boats large and small, manned by 670 seamen under the command of Sir Guy Carleton and Captain Thomas Pringle, left St. Johns. On October 11 the squadron passed to the east of Valcour Island without any knowledge that Arnold's ships were lying in wait out of sight on the west side between the island and the New York shore. Passing the southern end of the island and discovering the Americans' position, Captain Pringle brought his ships about and at eleven in the morning the first hot fight in American naval history began. A 19-year-old named Edward Pellew (later Lord Exmouth) saved the 12-gun British schooner *Carleton* from early annihilation by taking command when his officers fell and bringing her back into firing position. Through an unfortunate maneuver of its untrained crew the *Royal Savage*, the American flagship, lost her rigging in a thunderous broadside and had to be beached and put to the torch on Valcour Island.

Arnold could not afford the loss of his finest ship. Although he kept his smashed and leaking flotilla in action all afternoon his own ship, the *Congress*, had twelve holes in her hull by evening. The gondola *Philadelphia* was awash and sank in the darkness. Withdrawing six or seven hundred yards, the considerably damaged British fleet was nevertheless well able to resume battle in the morning. For Arnold, who had used three fourths of his ammunition, this was impossible. Escape seemed equally so, since the only avenue to the south seemed well guarded.

But good fortune veiled the tiny fleet—a mist so dense that Arnold's ships, each with a tiny stern light that could only be seen directly aft, were able to slip past the British lines single file close to the New York shore. When morning came the furious Guy Carleton found no targets for his guns. A whole day elapsed before his scouts discovered the tattered American fleet to the south, a day that enabled Arnold to sail nine miles to Schuyler Island, to plug up the leaks in those of his vessels that were still seaworthy, to sink two gondolas that were not, and to proceed hastily southward toward the protecting guns of Crown Point. But the wind was contrary and, since his exhausted men could row but feebly, the British caught up. Near Split Rock they captured the lagging and leaking gondola *Washington*, drove the galley *Lee* ashore (the crew blew it up), then bore down on Arnold's *Congress*. A fresh hail of shot now enveloped the hull and rigging of this already crippled ship, killing a first lieutenant and three men, yet Arnold would not strike his colors. He continued his desperate running fight until he was so close to capture or annihilation, a mere ten miles from his goal, that he sailed for the Vermont shore. Happily the waters of what was to become Arnold's Bay at Panton were so shallow that the larger British ships could not follow. Thus the *Congress* and four small gondolas were safely grounded and burned after the removal of their equipment.

The last man ashore was Arnold. As flames consumed the splintered evidence of his superb flight, he and his men started off through the woods to safety, arriving at Crown Point on October 14. One sloop, one galley and one gondola, he learned, had arrived safely—all that remained of fifteen vessels (six were burned, three sunk, one blown up, and two captured).

Since the small garrison at Crown Point was no longer defensible, everything of advantage to the British was either destroyed or moved south to Ticonderoga, where the well-entrenched Americans were determined to take a stand. Upon seeing their batteries on the ridges of the New York and Vermont shores the British decided not to attack. A strong eight-day wind from the south had prevented them from taking immediate advantage of their victory over Arnold. The season was late and Carleton returned to Canada for the winter. Much has rightfully been made of the precious year that Arnold gained for the Americans with his battered fleet whose odd complement of ill-trained farmers engaged the energies of the British all through the summer months when otherwise they might have poured south into the Hudson valley, sealed off all New England, and ended the war.

The callousness of the Continental Congress in dawdling over Arnold's promotions, his sterling services at Ridgefield, Fort Stanwix and Saratoga, his court-martial and acquittal, his defection to the British, and the tragic years of anticlimax spent in England are not a part of this chronicle. It is enough to affirm that a military genius passed this way and left his mark upon the land and upon the pages of history.

2

"Gentleman Johnny" Burgoyne was not exactly a gentleman. His intelligence, ability and charm could not conceal an intangible falseness of manner. His biographers mention his questionable conduct at cards, his enthusiasm for drink, his love of glittering society, and his indifference toward his marriage vow. Nevertheless, he was a facile author and parliamentarian and a capable, progressive and inspiring officer. As the result of his early military achievements in Portugal he might have arrived at the summit of his profession even without the wirepulling of his wellborn wife. So clearly had his experience placed him in the limelight that the King chose him to lead the 1777 expedition south from Canada up Lake Champlain against the Americans. According to the British plan, Lord Howe was to move up the Hudson and St. Leger east along the Mohawk to meet him, thus isolating all New England.

After spending the winter of 1776-77 lounging at Bath and quaffing the mineral waters of the ancient Roman springs, Burgoyne arrived in Quebec on May 7 to attend to his 4,000 regulars and 3,000 hired Hessians. Afloat on Lake Champlain in June his polyglot army with its throng of Indians must, as a spectacle, have rivaled that of Abercrombie on Lake George in the French War. A young Britisher, Thomas Anburey, wrote of this armada with its music and banners against a background of mountains so splendid as to suggest a romantic painting:

> When in the widest part of the Lake it was remarkably fine and clear, not a breeze stirring, when the whole army appeared at one view in such perfect regularity as to perform the most complete and splendid regatta ever beheld. In front the Indians went in their birch canoes containing 20 or 30 each; then the advance corps in regular line with the green boats; then followed the *Royal George* and *Inflexible* towing large booms which are to be thrown across 2 points of land, with the other brigs and sloops following; after them the brigades in their order.

(And finally the camp followers, sutlers and women.)

Plodding along through forests on the New York shore were some 1,500 horses drawing the 700 carts that were necessary for the portage from the Champlain to the Hudson valley. The expedition was the most imposing force that had been sent against the Americans, yet all was not as it appeared. Even as the army moved forward Burgoyne immersed himself in the creature comforts of an expensive entourage. There was jealousy between two of his generals, Simon Fraser and Baron von Riedesel. Friedrich Baum and Heinrich Breymann, his Hessian regimental commanders, hated each other. Torn from their hearths, fighting in a distant wilderness for a cause about which they knew little and cared less, the Hessian soldiers were homesick and disgruntled. Burgoyne had not had much experience with Indians, as was proved by his rhetorical lecture to his dusky allies about the evils of the hatchet and scalping knife during a bivouac at Willsboro.

Be it our task from the dictates of our religion, the laws of our warfare, and the principles and interest of our policy, he exhorted them, to regulate your passions when they overbear, to point out when it is nobler to spare than to revenge, to discriminate degrees of guilt, to suspend the uplifted stroke, to chastise and not to destroy. . . . I positively forbid bloodshed when you are not opposed in arms. Aged men, women, children and prisoners must be held sacred from the knife or hatchet, even in time of actual conflict. You shall receive compensation for the prisoners you take; but you shall be called to account for scalps.

Burgoyne's use of the Indians (not to mention German mercenaries) greatly heated the American metal and was denounced roundly in Parliament by Edmund Burke, who asked what the keeper of his Majesty's lions would do if there was a riot on Tower Hill. "Would he not fling open the dens of the wild beasts, and address them thus: 'My gentle lions, my humane bears—my tender-hearted hyenas: go forth! But I exhort you as you are members of civilized society, to take care not to hurt any man, woman or child.' "

That there were weaknesses in the crazy-quilt army that Burgoyne had patched together eventually became all too clear, but at least it had numbers, strength and momentum, which was more than could be said for the Americans. The demands of other campaigns, sickness, jealousy among commanders, and bad blood between Yankee and Yorker had grievously lessened the complement of troops that was supposed to defend Mount Independence, Ticonderoga, and the gateway to the Hudson. General Philip Schuyler, commander in chief in the northern department, had been too much a symbol of the silk-stocking aristocracy of the Hudson to suit the New England farmers. Playing upon this prejudice in Congress, Horatio Gates had succeeded in having Schuyler removed and himself appointed in March, 1777. Two months later Gates was removed and his predecessor reinstated. Schuyler now offered Gates command of Ticonderoga, which he refused indignantly. The appointment finally went to Arthur St. Clair, a distinguished veteran of Louisberg and Quebec, in the French wars, and of the recent Canadian and New Jersey campaigns. Indeed, it had been he who planned the strategy for Washington's victory at Trenton.

But there was little St. Clair could do because less than three weeks after he arrived Burgoyne attacked. He had some 2,500 soldiers (one third of them sick and many others without shoes or adequate clothing) to cover as many vital yards of defense which stretched from the star-shaped fort on Mount Independence, in Vermont, across a floating bridge 400 feet long to the old French lines north of Fort Ticonderoga. (A boom of timbers fastened together and a double iron chain with huge links an inch and a half square, extending across the narrow channel just north of the bridge, were supposed to stop the British fleet.) The long crescent-shaped line needed 10,000 troops to defend it. There had been that many in the previous fall but most of them had been withdrawn during the winter and of those remaining eight out of nine, it is said, did not even have bayonets. "Had every man I had been disposed of in single file on the works and along the lines of defense," asserted St. Clair, "they would have been scarcely within reach of each other's voices; but Congress had been persuaded that the enemy would make no attempt in that quarter."

The weather had for a time vigorously supported the Americans. In late June, at the widest part of the lake, Burgoyne's ships were first hampered by wind, then fogbound, and again caught in so fresh a gale that the crews of five ships had to land on the Islands of the Four Winds (now the Four Brothers). The army paused at Crown Point to reorganize, to set up a hospital, and to await a raiding party they had sent up Otter Creek. (Where once, directly opposite on the Vermont side at Chimney Point, had been a French village and fort now bivouacked Baron von Riedesel's Hessians with their heavy swords and ponderous jackboots.)

On July 2 the British began their advance against Ticonderoga and Mount Independence on both shores, the Hessians slogging through a swamp in Vermont and the regulars occupying a hill on the west shore to the north of the fort that they called Mount Hope and which St. Clair had insufficient troops to defend. Even if there had been enough troops to hold the American position, its most serious weakness was another small mountain called Sugar Hill whose summit commanded the entire American defenses on both sides of the lake. It even looked down upon nearby Ticonderoga to the north, but General Gates had considered it too steep to fortify (arguments by Benedict Arnold and demonstrations by John Trumbull to the contrary). It was the lot of the unfortunate St. Clair to bear the burden of his thickheaded commander's mistake, for the British quickly saw the possibilities of what they called Mount Defiance, drew their guns to its summit, and with this single maneuver put the entire arc of American defenses in jeopardy. On the morning of July 5 St. Clair's troops on Vermont's Mount Independence looked across to the summit of Mount Defiance and saw with astonishment that it was covered with redcoats.

Withdrawal was St. Clair's only way out of a dilemma suddenly so grave that retreat in the daylight was out of the question. It was attempted in the early hours of July 6, although the moon was out and a worthless French adventurer, Roche de Fermoy, St. Clair's commander on Mount Independence, stupidly put the torch to his quarters, further dispelling the cover of night. Although the troops on the New York side managed to escape over the bridge of floats, the cannon which St. Clair placed at the Vermont approach to prevent the British from following were never fired. The British found the gunners drunk beside a cask of Madeira. Somehow St. Clair managed to load the sick and supplies and baggage on five galleys and smaller boats and send them sculling up the lake to Skenesborough with a heavy guard. The rest of the army struck out hurriedly to the southeast over the Vermont hills to Castleton.

The burning sun was no hotter than the scene of retreat and pursuit on the following day. After a brutal trek of thirty miles the bulk of St. Clair's army reached Castleton at nightfall. The rear guard, led by the Green Mountain Boys' towering Seth Warner, bivouacked at Hubbardton. The pursuing redcoats under the veteran Simon Fraser caught up with them early in the morning and a wild, confused battle began. Rallying his troops Warner fought effectively for over an hour until Major General von Riedesel arrived with his detachment of Brunswickers. When Colonel Francis of the Massachusetts regiment was killed and Colonel Hale surrendered his beleaguered regiment, Warner is said to have thrown himself on a log and "poured forth a torrent of curses and execrations." Recovering his composure he ordered his men to scatter through the woods and meet him at Manchester.

St. Clair, hearing gunfire at Castleton, had ordered two of his regiments, encamped only two miles from the battlefield, to Warner's aid, but instead they started for Castleton. Warner had, however, fought a successful rear-guard action. The exhausted British and Germans were in neither mood nor condition for pursuit. Thirty-five of Fraser's officers and men had been killed, 148 wounded (the resistance of the Americans had shocked him), and with some 274 captives to manage in a strange wilderness he and von Riedesel ordered the whole lumbering contingent to Ticonderoga and Skenesborough.

That vital port at the southern end of navigation had fallen to Burgoyne the day after the Americans had abandoned Ticonderoga and Mount Independence. In a half hour the British fleet had sliced through the boom and chain across the lake and was so close behind St. Clair's flotilla that the Americans scarcely had time to set fire to the Skenesborough waterfront before Burgoyne hove into view. Sawmills, forges, sheds, boats, even the dry trees on the hillside were ablaze as the British landed at the northern end of the village and the routed Americans streamed out of it to the south.

Although St. Clair's army managed, on the whole, a successful retreat to Fort Edward, Congress did not allow him a single excuse. There had to be scapegoats and what better ones were available, regardless of the circumstances, than the commanders of an army that had yielded a vital valley to the British—that had run and not fought. "I think we shall never be able to defend a post until we shoot a general," complained John Adams. Even George Washington considered the loss of Ticonderoga and Mount Independence "an event of chagrin and surprise not apprehended nor within the compass of my reasoning." Amidst villainous accusations that St. Clair and Schuyler had sold out to the enemy (who had embarrassed them by firing into their camps silver bullets which their men had scrambled to pick up) they were both court-martialed. Acquittal with honor was inevitable, the facts being what they were, but they could not escape the slander of politicians and blockheads.

There was no relieving the Republic of the gloom that pervaded it in defeat. Nor, on the other hand, were there any limits to the good cheer of the British. The King, upon hearing the news, invaded the Queen's apartments to announce that he had beaten all the Americans. There was an immediate cooling of the warm camaraderie the French had displayed toward America: they did not want to back a loser. New England patriots were aware that there were many more Tories than they had thought. Everywhere in this frightened land, it seemed, the Eagle was taking wing.

3

John Stark was an authentic home-grown general trained not out of European military manuals but out of the hard primer of the northern woods. Born next door to the frontier in Londonderry in 1728, he knew as much about Indian fighting as any Indian, since he had lived as one for a while. Captured by St. Francis Indians during a trapping expedition in 1752, the well-knit, blue-eyed Yankee delighted the old warriors by brandishing a pole as he ran the gantlet at their village, thus warding off the blows of the young braves. He further pleased the sachem, who adopted him, by throwing his hoe into the river, declaring that it was "the business of squaws and not warriors to hoe corn." Years later he said that the savages of the St. Francis had treated him with more kindness than prisoners of war ever received from "civilized" nations. He considered the five weeks he remained with them (before being redeemed in exchange for an Indian pony) as important because in that time he learned their language and modes of warfare.

As a lieutenant and captain in Rogers' Rangers during the French and Indian Wars he served bravely at Lake George, at Ticonderoga in the Abercrombie fiasco, and with General Amherst in his successful quest of the same fort. As a captain of the Rangers he built half the Crown Point Road connecting Lake Champlain with the Connecticut River; as a colonel he led a New Hampshire regiment in the American left wing at Bunker Hill and helped arrange the defenses of New York City. In May, 1776, he arrived in Canada just in time to meet, and retreat with, the ragged army from Quebec. That summer he commanded a brigade which cleared and fortified the wilderness on Mount Independence. Later he led the right wing in the advance guard of Washington's successful assault at Trenton.

In spite of his obvious attainments and the high opinion of him held by officers and men alike, his name was not included among lesser ones appearing on a new list of generals in 1777. Politics was the only reason conceivable unless a general's grammar was not supposed to slip, and Stark was no college man. In vain they tried to dissuade him from leaving the army but declared that an officer who would not stand up for his own rights ought not to stand for the rights of his country; feeling as he did he did not think it proper to hold a commission. He retired to his New Hampshire farm.

(Inconceivable today, such behavior was not considered desertion in a volunteer army to whom the virtues of liberty often seemed intangible. It was one thing to throw tea into Boston Harbor and another to fight in the freezing forests, against not a foreign power but one's own people. The rebellion had split many towns, many families, through the middle. Failing to receive an appointment as commander of a New Hampshire regiment, William Stark, brother of John, had joined the British Army in New York as a colonel of dragoons and was killed in a fall from his horse. The property of the Tory, Levi Allen, was seized and sold at auction to pay the troops in accordance with a law introduced by his own brother Ira, one of the founders of Vermont. Colonel Benjamin Thompson, a schoolteacher who married the young widow of one of the wealthiest landholders of New Hampshire and who, before the Revolution, lived elegantly in Rumford [later Concord], fought at Lexington but because his Tory background prevented his obtaining a commission in the patriot army cast his lot with the British. He became successively a lieutenant colonel of the King's American Dragoons, an assistant to the secretary of state for the colonies in London, a knight of the British Empire, Bavaria's privy councilor of state, commander of the armies, minister of war, and count of the Holy Roman Empire. A scientist and inventor who made many contributions in a variety of fields from the utensils of war to those of the kitchen, Count Rumford, as he chose to call himself, established the American Academy of Arts and Sciences, the Royal Institution in London, and a science professorship at Harvard.)

A professional soldier with nine lives of active service, John Stark was still a colonel while Major General Sullivan, his colleague from New Hampshire, for example, had vaulted through the ranks with little military background other than seizing the ammunition in William and Mary, the crumbling fort in Portsmouth Harbor. Unquestionably Sullivan was able: he had opened a law office in Durham at the age of twenty, represented New Hampshire in the First Continental Congress, and written some of the articles in the Declaration of Independence. Clearly his commission as brigadier grew out of his appointment as chairman of the War Committee. Having attended Washington during the siege of Boston, he was given command of the defeated army in Canada during its retreat, which he managed with skill (Stark was one of his staff), but this was about all he did to become a major general.* Stark was, in any case, at home during the British advance to the threshold of the Hudson valley.

Lord and master of Ticonderoga, Crown Point, Skenesborough, and Fort Ann, John Burgoyne was as filled with confidence as his artillery wagons were with captured cannon, guns, and ammunition. In London the betting odds against America's winning independence changed from even money to five to one. Burgoyne was comfortably settled with his mistress in the great stone house of Colonel Skene, loyalist founder of the town. This resourceful veteran of many campaigns in Europe, the West Indies, and on Lake Champlain in the French War, had received a grant at the lake's southern end for an impressive tract which he had diligently improved. When Ethan Allen's patriots had seized the forts two and a half years previously they had heard the story of a wrinkled corpse of an old woman found in the basement of Skene's house. It developed that the Scotsman had been receiving an annuity which was to continue as long as his mother "remained above ground" and had conceived of a literal interpretation of the phrase which would allow him to receive it long after it was meant to cease. There has been much speculation as to whether the canny Skene induced Burgoyne to advance to the Hudson valley by way of Skenesborough and Wood Creek instead of Lake George with the idea in mind that the General would have to build a road which, after the war, would enhance the value of his holdings. For whatever reason, Burgoyne chose this swampy route with its giant mosquitoes and tangle of timber felled by a thousand American axmen to impede the enemy advance. He had not only to clear away the trees but to build forty bridges in 26 miles and did not arrive at

---

* In the fall of 1776, after receiving his promotion to major general, Sullivan was captured at Brooklyn Heights when leading a charge against a superior force of Hessians. In an exchange of prisoners he was released by the British in time to fight at Trenton (where Stark commanded the advance guard), at Brandywine and at Germantown, and to lead an expedition against the Iroquois in 1779. That his appointment was political in no way affected, in his case, his reputation as an able officer who served well.

Pine Plains (two miles from the American outpost of Fort Edward) until July 28, more than three vital weeks after he had reached Skenesborough.

On the 27th occurred a ghastly episode that did much to rally the Americans—the scalping of Jane McCrea. It mattered not to patriots that she was engaged to an officer in the army of George III; she was one of their own, the lovely daughter of a New Jersey minister, brutally stripped, scalped and shot near Fort Edward by Burgoyne's Indians. When they came into the camp bearing their trophy of bloodstained golden curls, Burgoyne, greatly shocked, wished to execute the murderers but the commander of the Indian troops, La Corne St.-Lue, warned him that if he did all his Indians would desert. So the murderer was pardoned and "Remember Jane McCrea" echoed through the hills and valleys, camps, posts and stations, and what George Washington or the Congress could not do in heating the blood of patriots the slaying of Jane McCrea and the pardon of her murderer did.

With a supply line of some 3,600 miles, long enough to test the ingenuity of any modern army's service of supply officers, Burgoyne needed provisions. Bennington, Vermont, he learned, was one of General Schuyler's collecting points for cattle, corn, flour, perhaps horses, and von Riedesel badly needed mounts for his dragoons. Eight hundred troops, Burgoyne decided, would be enough to take this hamlet. On August 12, from the east bank of the Hudson opposite the heights of Saratoga, he sent Lieutenant Colonel Friedrich Baum on a mission the outcome of which seemed certain. It happened, however, that the Council of Safety of the fledgling Republic of Vermont, on the suggestion of Ira Allen, had decided to confiscate Tory property and sell it at auction for the support of a regiment to protect the frontiers. During the summer troops paid from the proceeds had been at work cutting down the trees that had delayed Burgoyne's progress south of Skenesborough. New Hampshire and many other states had presently adopted the same method of financing defense. John Langdon, speaker of the New Hampshire Assembly (the first in the Union to declare its independence of Great Britain), meanwhile pledged his personal property. "I have $3,000 in hard money," he announced, "I will pledge my plate for $3,000 more. I have 70 hogsheads of Tobago rum which shall be sold for the most it will bring . . . if we succeed in defending our firesides and homes, I may be remunerated. If not, the property will be of no value to me."

The command of the militia went to John Stark, along with the assurance that he was responsible to no one except the Assembly. Since the Assembly did not know how to conduct a military campaign, Stark was responsible to no one except himself. Within a week after he had received his commission some 1,500 volunteers had marched to Charlestown on the Connecticut, where they paused to cast bullets from the only pair of bullet molds in town. From here, during the first week in August, these troops were forwarded to Manchester, where Seth Warner waited with the remainder of the regiment that had fought at Hubbardton. When Stark arrived he found to his consternation that Benjamin Lincoln, one of the generals promoted over his head, was in charge and on Schuyler's orders was about to march the united forces to the Hudson. Producing his orders and commission from the New Hampshire Assembly, Colonel Stark in no uncertain terms told the General that his troops would remain with the Vermonters under Warner to guard the homeland from Burgoyne's left flank. Realizing that the local militia would not follow him, Lincoln diplomatically agreed to leave the troops under Stark and Warner and set out to consult with Schuyler about this decision.

On August 8 Stark marched his militia to Bennington (Warner remained in Manchester with the Vermont regiment, whose numbers had been increased by 200 recently recruited Rangers). It was pure accident that Stark was in Bennington when the Hessians came lumbering through the forest. Actually, until almost the last minute, Burgoyne had planned to attack Manchester instead. On August 13 the troops on the height of land between the Hoosick and Battenkill were as strangely European as those of the vast flotilla that had conquered the lake. One hundred seventy-five unmounted Brunswick dragoons, hoping to find horses in Bennington, were clumping along in their awkward twelve-pound thigh-length jackboots which carried long spurs. Leather breeches, stiff and hot, added to their discomfort, as did the leather gauntlets on their arms, cocked hats with waving plumes and three-and-a-half-pound broadswords and heavy carbines. Two hundred fifty other Germans were clad according to their units: the regular infantry in white breeches and waistcoats, the

Hesse-Hanau artillerymen in buff with blue coats, the chasseurs in green with red trimmings. There were British marksmen in waist-coats of scarlet, some 300 assorted Tories, Canadians and Indians in a variety of dress, musicians, officers' servants, women and camp followers. Lieutenant Colonel Baum could count some 800 effective fighting troops in this motley procession whose ultimate goal was the Connecticut River and whose mission was to advise the inhabitants that this was the advance guard for an assault on Boston.

By the time the British reached Cambridge (New York), 18 miles from Bennington, Stark's scouts had reported a large force, and a courier was sent to summon Warner's regiment from Manchester. Baum, drawing closer, found not a hamlet full of Tories, as he had thought, but a hornet's nest of provincials, and he sent to Burgoyne for help. Despite a flooding downpour that drowned their powder the next day, detachments went forth to harass the enemy from Stark's base about four miles northwest of Bennington.

The morning of the 16th, according to a poetic German named Glich,

> rose beautifully serene . . . not a cloud was left to darken the face of the heavens, whilst the very leaves hung motionless, and the long grass waved not . . . the fields looked green and refreshed, the river was swollen and tumultuous, and the branches were all loaded with dew drops, which glittered like so many diamonds. . . . I beheld immediately beneath me a wide sweep of stately forest, interrupted at remote intervals by green meadows or yellow corn-fields, whilst here and there a cottage, a shed, or some other primitive edifice . . . [reminded] the spectator that man had begun his inroads upon nature, without as yet taking away . . . her simplicity or grandeur.

His deserting Indians having reported that the woods were full of Yankees, Baum had been feverishly throwing up breastworks around the road over which his reinforcements would come. The strategic hill he had chosen might have been impregnable had he not deployed troops to hold what he considered a vital bridge half a mile down the slope. Stark's strategy was to attack from both sides and he sent out groups of his men in shirtsleeves whom Baum mistook for Tory sympathizers seeking safety behind his lines. Stark meanwhile moved up gradually with his main force. When he announced (in one of folklore's great moments), "There are the Redcoats, and they are ours, or this night Molly Stark sleeps a widow," and Colonel Nichols started for Baum's right rear with 200 New Hampshire troops and Colonel Herrick for the left rear with 300 Vermonters, and the shooting, hot and heavy, began from all sides, Baum must have realized with a rush that this was a hellish place for a proud professional to die. As the Hessians under the hill tried desperately to climb to safety, the sharpshooting farmers picked them off. When the Yankees gained the crest of the hill it was war by bayonet, rifle butt, saber and pike. At length Baum received a mortal bullet in his abdomen and by three in the afternoon the routed Germans were retreating from an onslaught that Stark described as "one continued clap of thunder."

But the Battle of Bennington was not over. After a mud-soaked march more in the road from Cambridge than on it (with the Hessians nevertheless pausing every few minutes to re-dress their lines in military precision!) the brave but bullying von Breymann arrived. Stark's forces were not prepared for a new enemy and now in turn it was they who were confused. Fortunately Colonel Warner appeared from Manchester just at this time and urged the tired Stark, who was for retreating temporarily, to fight it out. This they did, one soldier reporting that he fired so often that his musket was too hot to hold.

With his 29,000-acre empire at the head of the lake in the balance, Colonel Skene was struggling mightily in the enemy lines. After his mount was shot from under him he found an artillery horse and rode off for an ammunition cart which exploded as it was brought up. With a flesh wound in his leg and five holes in his clothing von Breymann at sunset had had enough and was retreating with the Americans in pursuit through the dim forest. Stark and Warner abandoned the chase, for they did not want to press too far their luck with their force of citizens-in-arms, who now could not see whom they were fighting. As always fear and bravery went hand in hand. A thirsty and frightened private holding a bullet in his mouth to moisten his throat, who had first run away and then returned and was now leaving again, was commanded by Stark to help move a cannon. The lad replied that he was worn out, whereupon Stark kindly said, "Don't seem to disobey. Take hold and if you can't hold out, slip away in the dark." A corpse in the road was pointed out to Colonel Warner. "Is it Jesse?" he asked. Dismounting, he looked into his dead brother's face and without a word rode away.

It was a greater hour for the Americans than the people of Bennington, untying their rope beds to bind the 700 prisoners, could conceive. The turning point of the Saratoga campaign (which was the turning point of the war), this relatively minor engagement cost Burgoyne heavily in morale, both domestic and foreign; in casualties and captives; in desertions, Indian and loyalist, and in supplies. It was, according to the British secretary of state, "fatal" and the "cause of all subsequent misfortunes," for it "proved the vigor and alacrity of the enemy in that country." To which words of Lord George Germain, Burgoyne gave sad assent: "The Hampshire Grants in particular, a country unpeopled and almost unknown in the last war, now abounds in the most active and rebellious race on the continent and hangs like a gathering storm at my left."

It is symbolic of the awakening spirit and confidence of the colonies that the first American flag to fly in battle flew at Bennington. The fortunes of John Stark were rising as well. Before the battle the indignant members of the Continental Congress had before them a resolution to censure him for insubordination. Now they made him a brigadier.

VII

THE SLAVE OF FREEDOM

General Washington was gravely understating Ethan Allen when he said: "There is an original something in him that commands admiration." The patron (certainly not saint) of Vermont has rather defied classification. Surely it is fair to say that Boone and Crockett were prosaic by comparison; Ethan's personality had so many sides. Among these were, other than the scout, businessman, hunter and soldier, the politician, diplomat and administrator, the pamphleteer, essayist and theologian. He has never been called a poet, yet it seems clear that he was that, perhaps above all else; not a writer of poetry but a speaker and writer of wildly poetic prose. Frequently ungrammatical, even more often profane, it had a certain unharnessed vitality that is as arresting to modern readers as it was to the people whose emotions and logic he swayed with it. If one believes that what a master spirit writes is a far more trustworthy stamp of his individuality than his thumbprint, then Allen's own sayings and writing still reveal more of himself (and of his surroundings) than anything that has ever been written about him.

Reading it all, one is convinced of the courage and determination of an impetuous and loud-talking egotist whose sense of humor saves him from being a buffoon (since he never takes himself quite seriously). At the same time he is a perceptive, ingenious and, strangely enough, sensitive and loyal man with a warm heart and undoubted integrity.

An anecdote revealing his language at its most profane is one of the few known details of his probably not-so-prosaic youth in Litchfield County, Connecticut, where he was born in 1737. With the help of the Philadelphia Revolutionary Thomas Young, his friend and teacher, unquestionably one of the strongest influences in his life, he had received an inoculation of a smallpox serum which, in defiance of a local law, they had concocted. Two justices of the peace, Lee and Stoddard, were threatening him with prosecution. "By————," he told them, "I wish I may be bound down in Hell with old Beelzabub a thousand years in the lowest pit in Hell and that every little incipid Devil should come along by and ask the reason of Allen's lying there; it should be said because he made a promise on earth in cool blood that he would have the satisfaction of Lee and Stoddard and did not fulfill it!"

After a rather fatal speculation in a lead mine and indifferent luck in the iron-smelting business, he tramped north into the New Hampshire Grants to see the country, to buy some land there, to organize his roughneck police force, the Green Mountain Boys, and to become their spokesman in the most volcanic row over land in the history of the Northeast. This quarrel erupted with regularity for over twenty years until Vermont became the fourteenth state in 1791, and its tremblings reverberated in New Hampshire, New York, Connecticut, Massachusetts, Washington, Montreal and London.

The disagreement began with Benning Wentworth of New Hampshire, who considered it his royal prerogative to grant land between the Connecticut River and Lake Champlain. Prior to the Revolution Ethan and his brother Ira had bought 12,000 acres, for a penny each, in Hubbardton and had later purchased a good share of an entire river valley, that of the Onion (Winooski). When in 1764 the King tardily decided that the New Hampshire Grants belonged to New York, that state proceeded to demand of the New Hampshire settlers payment of fees for every acre previously granted. The Allens' answer to this was the formation of the Republic of Vermont, an independent government backed with force to resist the speculators, surveyors, settlers, sheriffs, posses, proclamations and courts of New York. There were as many characters, scenes and incidents in the land wars (which have occupied whole volumes) as in a Russian novel, and the implications for western New England and the democratic idea were just as profound.

The Allens were not fighting for their land alone, but for the New England farmer and his own free spread in the hills. They were fighting, moreover, against the feudal system that had chained many New York tenants to their Dutch and English manor lords. The people in the "back beyond" of the Grants had little in common with the aristocracy of Portsmouth, even less with those who, barred from self-government by suffrage restrictions and proprietors' privileges, wore the badge of serfdom along the lordly Hudson. Ethan declared that the "genius, piety, temper, spirit and manners" of these two peoples were as opposed "as liberty is to slavery. A people so opposite to each other in civil, political and, we may add, religious sentiments, can never subsist long under the same government, for the demonstration whereof we appeal to the current history of mankind."

John Munro, the New York sheriff with whom Ethan had so much trouble, unwillingly reached the same conclusion: that the New Englanders would never become "good and faithful subjects" of New York: ". . . if you was to bestow all your lands upon them without any fee or reward they would never be faithful to this government for they are all possessed of the spirit of contradiction . . . so full of venom and spite against the government and all its authority that tho they are forced yet the sting remains. They talk so smooth and hensom yet the devil lies at the bottom."

Since the Allens owned as much or more land in the Grants as the Hudson River landlords whom they railed against, they were extremely vulnerable to charges of hypocrisy. Yet those who say that they were merely opportunists protecting their vast empire of land and giving lip service to the democratic idea, cannot have read the constitution that they drew up for their new republic. It was the first to deny human slavery. Never, rich or poor, could they have lived in a society in which, as Henry Christman writes in *Tin Horns and Calico*, "a few families intricately intermarried, controlled the destinies of 300,000 people and ruled in almost kingly splendor over nearly two million acres of land. . . . Democracy [in the Hudson Valley] was so little known that a veteran of the Revolution might be refused a seat on the Albany-Troy stage because he was so shabbily dressed. Newspapers found it sufficiently important to report that cigar smoking had lost its charm for the elite, since almost every shop boy and dirty little urchin had taken it up."

It is not within the scope of this chronicle to review in detail or support the boundary claims of New Hampshire, on the one hand, or of New York, on the other, or the vacillating attitudes of the King in Council.* It is enough to say that a small group of settlers led by

* Even the barest outline must suggest that strife and chaos were inevitable even if the Allens had never appeared on the scene:

1731: The western boundary of Connecticut was fixed along a line twenty miles east of the Hudson.

1741: New Hampshire's Benning Wentworth began granting land west of the Connecticut River in accordance with (a) the King's ancient grant to John Mason, which had descended to Wentworth and others, (b) the King's permission that grants be made until they met with *other governments*

Ethan and Ira Allen snatched the prize from these claiming states and spirited it away to found their own free and independent republic.

As a pamphleteer and orator in the heat of the struggle with New York Ethan really came into his own as he described "Women sobbing and lamenting, Children crying and Men pierced to the heart with sorrow and Indignation at the approaching tyranny of New York." He doubted that "the New York scribblers" could "by the art of printing alter wrong into right, or make any person of good sense believe that a great number of hard labouring peasants, going through the fatigues of settlement, and cultivation of a howling wilderness, are a community of riotous, disorderly, licentious, treasonable persons."

With the same effect gained by the muckrakers of a later day against the trusts, Ethan always pictured his people as the humble defendents (which indeed many of them were). "The plaintiffs, appearing in great state and magnificence . . . made brilliant appearance; but

---

(New York on the west, Quebec on the north, and Massachusetts on the south).

1749: Wentworth granted the town of Bennington. New York protested, citing its royal charter of 1664 which gave it jurisdiction of "all land from the west side of Connecticut to the East side of Delaware Bay." New Hampshire claimed that this meant not the west side of the *river* but the west side of the *colony* of Connecticut and thus claimed a northern extension of this line as being its western boundary.

1764: The King in Council decided the eastern boundary of New York "to be" the Connecticut River, thus making questionable all the grants made by Wentworth to settlers who had already moved in and paid their fees.

1767: The Privy Council ordered New York to stop granting lands in the disputed area until "the King's pleasure should be known." This change of heart on the part of the crown was the result of Lord Shelburne's favoring the claims of New England settlers and of the Society for the Preservation of the Gospel in Foreign Parts which, under the grants from New Hampshire, had received an acreage in each town (23,000 acres in all); under the grants from New York: none. Speculators, including the highest officer in the colony of New York continued, however, to buy vast tracts in the Grants and tried to prosecute the New Hampshire claimants. Judge Robert R. Livingston, "who allowed himself to hold the court [became] interested in over 35,000 acres of land involved in the pending suits. His son-in-law, Duane, who prosecuted the cases, held claim to 68,000 acres, and Duane's partner, Kempe, the Attorney General, was interested in a great though unascertained amount."

1773: A northward extension of the New York-Connecticut boundary became the boundary of Massachusetts and New York, thus adding weight to New Hampshire's claim that this line should be extended still farther north to become the boundary between New Hampshire and New York.

the defendents appearing in but ordinary fashion, having been greatly fatigued by hard labor . . . made a very disproportionate figure at court." It was at Albany in 1770 that he made the vague but poetic statement: "The Gods of the hills are not the Gods of the valleys." It seemed to mean that the court's eviction decrees would have no effect whatever on the New Hampshire settlers. (Ethan invited the attorney general to Bennington to find out the true situation). Possibly the phrase may have been in reply to what Ira Allen claimed was a bribe offered by the court to buy off the New Hampshire Grants' leaders.

Thenceforward Ethan maintained the rights of New Hampshire partisans with force; any New York surveyor or sheriff in the Grants was sure to go home in a hail of curses with welts on his back raised by "twigs of the wilderness," but never anything more serious. During all the riotous incidents of the Green Mountain Boys not a man was killed.

In 1771 Governor Tryon of New York offered £25 for the capture of Ethan and his lieutenants; Ethan countered by offering the same amount for James Duane and John Kempe, two of the ringleaders in New York's "jesuitical and cowardly junto of schemers" who had "disturbed the public peace and repose of the honest peasants of Bennington." It was not the Green Mountain Boys, declared Ethan, but the lawyers and speculators who were "the riotous, the tumultuous, disorderly, stimulating faction, or, in fine, the land robbers . . . chiefly . . . a number of gentlemen attorneys (if it not be an abuse to gentlemen of merit to call them so) who manafest a surprising and enterprising thirst or averice after our country . . . our breasts glow with a martial fury to defend our persons and fortunes from the ravages of those that would destroy us." The Green Mountain Boys were merely acting in accordance with "the law of self-preservation, which the law of God and nature enjoins on every intelligent, wise and understanding human being."

Ethan's reply to the legislature of New York (which passed a special act placing a bounty on his head) was one of his more warlike verbal sallies:

> Be it known to that despotic fraternity of law-makers and law-breakers that we will not be fooled or frightened out of our property . . . printed sentences of death will not kill us when we are at a

distance, and if the executioners approach us they will be as likely to fall victims to death as we . . . and provided any of us or our party shall be taken, and we have not notice sufficient to relieve them, or whether we relieve them or not, we are resolved to surround such person, or persons, whether at his or their house or houses or anywhere that we can find him or them, and shoot such person or persons dead . . . if the governmental authority of New York . . . act in opposition to that of Great Britain, and insist upon killing us, to take possession of our vineyards, come on, we are ready for a game of scalping with them; for our martial spirits glow with bitter indignation and consummate fury to blast their infernal projections.

There were no bounds to Ethan's contempt for this "set of artful and wicked men." When in the spring of 1772 Sheriff Munro and a band of Scotchmen succeeded in capturing Remember Baker, one of the stanchest Green Mountain Boys in Arlington, Baker lost his thumb in the ensuing sword play but was happily rescued before the posse had carried him into New York. Ethan called this a "wicked, inhuman, most barberous, infamous, cruel, villainous and theivish act" and particularly castigated the enemy for setting upon Baker "a large, spiteful, willful and very malicious dog, educated and brought up agreeable to their own forms and customs."

By scaring off the Yorkers with threats and displays of force, on the one hand, and heated communiqués to the press (the Hartford *Courant*), as well as logical and persuasive pamphlets, on the other, Ethan managed to repel all intruders until news of Lexington fired his patriotism and moved him to seize Fort Ticonderoga.

Ever since I arrived at a state of manhood, he wrote later . . . I have felt a sincere passion for liberty. The history of nations, doomed to perpetual slavery, in consequence of yielding up to tyrants their natural born liberties, I read with a sort of philosophical horror; so that the first systematical and bloody attempt at Lexington, to enslave America, thoroughly electrified my mind, and fully determined me to take part with my country.

When later in 1775 Ethan tried to enlist the eastern Indians in his vaulting scheme for annexing Canada to the United States, he couched his appeal to them in their own idiom:

I always love Indians and have hunted a great deal with them and I know how to shute and ambush just like Indians. I want your warriors to come and see me and help me fight the Regulars—You know they stand all along close together, Rank and file and my men fight so as Indians do and I want your warriors to join with me and my Warriors. I will give you money blankits tomehawkes Knives and Paint . . . and I will go with you into the woods to scout; and my men and your men will sleep together and eat and drink together . . . but if you our Brother Indians do not fight on either side still we will be Friends and Brothers; and you may come and hunt in our woods, and pass through our country on the Lake and come to our post and have Rum and be good friends.

That he did not succeed with this entreaty was no reflection on its merits. Few in America cared at this time to risk bearding the British lion in his den, for Montreal, whether weakly garrisoned or not, was looked upon as an awesome citadel of English power. But Ethan insisted that America "might rise on eagles wings and mount up to glory, freedom and immortal honour, if she did but know and exert her strength. . . . I will lay my life on it, that with 1500 men and a proper artillery, I will take Montreal." Although his attempt in September with one-fifteenth that many was calamitous, posterity, at least, finds compensation in the lively journal of his captivity.

At the moment of his capture he was fearful that he had been called for by the old gentleman with the scythe. A savage

part of whose head was shaved, being almost naked and painted, with feathers intermixed with the hair of the other side of his head, came running to me with incredible swiftness; he seemed to advance with more than mortal speed . . . his hellish visage was beyond all description; snakes eyes appear innocent in comparison of his; his features extorted; malice, death, murder and the wrath of devils and damned spirits are the emblems of his countenance . . .

Ethan managed to seize a British officer and hold him in such a position that "his danger was my defense." When attacked by a second Indian Ethan whirled the officer around "with incredible velocity" until a Canadian and an Irishman came to his rescue.

It cut me to the heart to see the Canadians in so hard a case, in consequence of their having been true to me; they were wringing their hands, saying their prayers . . . and expected immediate death. I therefore stepped between the executioners and the Canadians, opened my clothes and told Gen. Prescott to thrust his bayonet into my breast for I was the sole cause of the Canadians taking up arms.

Prescott told Ethan he would not execute him now but vowed he would grace a halter at Tyburn. He was cast into the foul hold of a British man-of-war and shackled with 30-pound leg irons in such a way that he could only lie on his back. When one day he chewed off the tenpenny nail that secured his handcuff, one of his keepers exclaimed: "Damn him, can he eat iron?" A padlock replaced the nail and Ethan's only recourse was "to throw out plenty of extravagant language, which answered certain purposes at that time, better than to grace a history."

After a cruel six weeks he was sent to Quebec and then to England in the bottom of a vermin-infested transport, a dreadful crossing of forty days. As he was led from the ship through the streets of Falmouth on the way to formidable Pendennis Castle, the citizens gathered in the streets and on rooftops to gape at the fawn-skin jacket, sagathy breeches and red woolen hat of the strange colossus of the back woods who had captured Ticonderoga.

He was frequently let out of his cell to the well-fortified parade ground within the castle, where people came from distances as great as fifty miles to ask him questions. One man inquired what his occupation had been.

> I answered him that in my younger days I had studied divinity but was a conjurer by passion. He replied that I conjured wrong at the time I was taken; and I was obliged to own that I mistook a figure at that time, but that I had conjured them out of *Ticonderoga*. This was a place of great notoriety in England so that the joke seemed to go in my favour.

Ethan wrote that he often entertained the visitors "with harrangues on the impracticability of Great Britain's conquering the (then) colonies of America." Expatiating on freedom in general he gained

> the resentment of a young beardless gentleman of the company, who gave himself very great airs, and replied that "he knew the Americans very well and was certain that they could not bear the smell of powder." I replied that I accepted it as a challenge, and was

ready to convince him on the spot . . . he answered that he should not put himself on a par with me. I then demanded of him to treat the character of Americans with due respect. He answered that I was an Irishman; but I assured him that I was a *full blooded Yankee*, and, in fine, bantered him so much that he left me in possession of the ground, and the laugh went against him. Two clergymen came to see me and, inasmuch as they behaved with civility, I returned them the same! We discoursed on several parts of moral philosophy and Christianity; and they seemed to be surprized that I should be acquainted with such topics, or that I should understand a syllogism.

While Ethan was talking freedom on one occasion he asked a gentleman for a bowl of punch. The man offered it but did not deign to drink with him on account of his being a state criminal. "However, I took the punch and drank it all down at one draught and handed the gentleman the bowl; this made the spectators as well as myself merry."

It is noteworthy that Herman Melville was sufficiently impressed by Ethan's character and conduct to have written a little-known sketch about his experiences at Falmouth called *Samson among the Philistines* (in *Israel Potter*). He was, says Melville, "a man of Patagonian stature . . . whose defiant head overshadowed theirs, as St. Paul's dome, its inferior steeples." Ethan is also depicted as "swayingly towering over the flashing bayonets and cutlasses like a great whale breaching among a hostile retinue of swordfish. . . . Allen seems to have been a curious combination of Hercules, a Joe Miller, a Bayard, and a Tom Myer, had a person like the Belgian giants; mountain music in him like a Swiss; a heart plump as Coeur de Lion's . . ."

After numerous debates in high conference rooms as to what should be done with the indomitable and somewhat embarrassing Colonel Allen the British sent him aboard a frigate which put in at the Cove of Cork on the way to America. (The ship was part of an invading fleet under Lord Cornwallis, whom Ethan described as a "large and noble looking man who took more ground to stand on than any man I ever saw.") Having heard that a rebel of their own stripe was incarcerated in the harbor, the Irishmen of the town assembled a purse and a hamper of gifts: wines, sugar, coffee, tea, beef, turkeys, fine broadcloth Holland shirts, silk and worsted stockings, shoes, beaver hats (one laced with gold) and two silk suits. Although the captain of the frigate impounded most of the food and wine, Ethan was able to keep the clothing. Supplied now not only "with the necessaries and conveniences of life, but with the grandeurs and superfluities of it" he thanked his benefactors with "joyful heart. Thanks to God, there are still the feelings of humanity in the worthy citizens of Cork towards those of your bone and flesh who, through misfortune from the present broils in Empire, are needy prisoners."

Arriving off Cape Fear, North Carolina, he was transferred to a second ship which skirted the coast northward to Sandy Hook and without landing at New York continued to Halifax, the place of Ethan's execution, according to the captain. For six weeks the prisoners lived like rats aboard a sloop in Halifax Harbor until, as the result of protests sent by Ethan to the Governor, they were removed to the local jail. At last they boarded a ship commanded by a Captain Smith, whose kindness drew tears from Ethan's eyes but whose crew nearly mutinied just before the end of the prisoners' homecoming voyage from Nova Scotia to New York. Off Rhode Island two of Smith's officers tried to persuade Ethan to recruit the prisoners and join them and a number of the crew in killing Smith, seizing the ship, and making off with its cargo of £35,000 sterling.

> Upon which I replied that we had been too well used on board to murder the officers; that I could by no means reconcile it to my conscience. . . . But they strenuously urged that the conspiracy would be found out, and it would cost them their lives, provided they did not execute their design. I then interposed spiritedly . . . that I would faithfully guard capt. Smith's life . . . and that the same honor that guarded capt. Smith's life would also guard theirs, and it was agreed by those present not to reveal the conspiracy. . . . I could not help calling to mind what capt. Smith said to me when I first came on board; "this is a mutable world and one gentleman never knows but that it may be in his power to help another!"

Transferred again in New York Harbor, this time to a transport which was to be his abode until November, Ethan took up the wager of a friendly British officer that his Majesty's troops would capture Fort Washington within three days. They did and Ethan lost the bet. The officer later promised to call when his army came to Bennington. Ethan declared that the Green Mountain Boys would never allow that to happen; he wished he might have seen this man after the defeat at Bennington, but never did.

Still a prisoner of war but now on parole within the limits of New York, Ethan set about rebuilding a constitution

> almost worn out by such a long and barbarous captivity. The enemy gave out that I was crazy and wholy unmanned, but my vitals held sound, (nor was I delerious any more than I have been from youth up; but my extreme circumstances . . . rendered it political to act in some measure the madman); and in consequence of a regular diet and exercise, my blood recruited, and my nerves in a great measure recovered their former tone, strength and usefulness, in the course of six months.

One of the only telling descriptions of Ethan, curiously enough, came from Captain Alexander Graydon, a fellow prisoner also on parole in New York.

> His figure was that of a robust, large framed man, worn down by confinement and hard fare . . . a suit of blue clothes with a gold laced hat . . . enabled him to make a very passable appearance for a rebel colonel. . . . I have seldom met a man, possessing, in my opinion, a stronger mind, or whose mode of expression was more vehement and oratorical . . . Nothwithstanding that Allen might have had something of the insubordinate lawless frontier spirit in his composition . . . he appeared to me to be a man of generosity and honour.

The plight of the prisoners taken by the British on Long Island in 1776 was agonizing to a parolee who was a mere cipher, "exempted from danger and honour." In the churches of New York Ethan saw the prisoners in the agonies of death "biting pieces of chips; others pleading for God's sake, for something to eat, and at the same time, shivering with the cold . . . the filth in these churches in consequences of the flexes, was almost beyond description." In one churchyard

> a large-boned, tall young man from Pennsylvania, who was reduced to a mere skeleton . . . said he was glad to see me before he died, which he expected to have done last night, but was a little revived; he furthermore informed me that he and his brother had been urged to enlist in the British service, but had both resolved to die first; that his brother had died last night . . . and that he expected shortly to follow him; but I made the other prisoners stand a little off, and told him with a low voice to enlist; he then asked, whether it was

right in the sight of God. I assured him that it was, and that duty to himself obliged him to deceive the British by enlisting and deserting the first opportunity; upon which he answered with transport, that he would enlist. I charged him not to mention my name as his advisor, lest it should get air and I should be closely confined, in consequence of it. . . . I was astonished at the resolution of the two brothers . . . it seems that they could not be stimulated to such exertions of heroism from ambition, as they were but obscure soldiers; strong indeed must the internal principle of virtue be which supported them to brave death.

Ethan was removed to western Long Island in January, 1777, and there, during eight months of relative freedom, overstepped the bounds of his parole. As his health improved, so did his voice; on one occasion when he was discussing religion he asserted that if at the time of Noah's flood he had been on Camel's Rump (*sic*) in the Green Mountains, he would not have been afraid to give defiance to all the waters on earth. In August, after the Battle of Bennington, he is said to have climbed the roof of a hotel in what is now Brooklyn and given three lusty cheers. However, these improprieties were probably not the cause of the afflictions to come. Much more likely they were rooted in his insolent reply to the high British officer who had proposed that he join the British Army and promised that if he did he would be paid in hard guineas, not paper rags, and receive large tracts of land in his favorite country at the war's end. Ethan told the officer that he viewed the offer of land to be

similar to that which the devil offered Jesus Christ, "To give him all the kingdoms of the world if he would fall down and worship him;" when at the same time the damned soul had not one foot of land on earth. This closed the conversation, and the gentleman turned from me with an air of dislike, saying that I was a bigot, upon which I returned to my lodgings.

On August 25 a heavy guard seized Ethan and escorted him to a lonely cell above the dungeon in New York's provost jail, a "dark mansion of fiends" whose commissary was a

monster . . . there is not his like in human shape. He exhibits a smiling countenance, seems to wear a phiz of humanity, but has been instrumentally capable of the most consummate acts of wickedness (which were first projected by an abandoned British council, clothed with the authority of a Howe) murdering premeditatedly (in cold blood) near or quite two thousand helpless prisoners, and that in the most clandestine, mean and shameful manner. . . . He is the most mean-spirited, cowardly, deceitful and destructive animal in God's creation below, and legions of infernal devils, with all their tremendous horrors, are impatiently ready to receive Howe and him, with all their detestable accomplices into the most exquisite agonies of the hottest region of hell fire.

Ethan made the eight months he spent here slightly more tolerable by writing letters and petitions in behalf of dying inmates, notably one John Fell, later a member of Congress from New Jersey. This unfortunate was removed to a private apartment as the result of a letter in which Ethan painted his "dying distresses in such lively colors that it wrought conviction on the obduracy of a British general."

Although Ethan was the sort of man who never languishes as long as he breathes, two years and eight months of his imprisonment all but stifled any hope of freedom. During his absence from the north-country his brother Ira, the architect of Vermont (he was the office force, the legal arm; Ethan was the field artillery), had, with the small coterie of settlers from Connecticut known as the Bennington party, drafted a declaration of freedom, assembled meetings of delegates from the various towns to ratify a constitution (1777), and set up an independent republic which enforced its own laws, coined its own money, and held off invaders (New York as well as Britain) with a militia paid out of the proceeds of confiscated Tory properties sold at auction. Ira had helped achieve victory at Bennington, through information gained from his scouts of Burgoyne's movements and astute planning with Stark, Warner and Herrick. The Vermonters had helped cut Burgoyne's supply line and retake some of the lake forts. At Saratoga the legions of Britain had fallen. France, entering into alliance with the United States, had further brightened the morale of the Continentals.

During these thirty-two months, so eventful outside the jail, so purposeless within it, tragedy had struck Ethan's family; word that his only son had died affected the most "tender passions" of his soul.

I fear [he wrote] some quack doctor has murdered him to improve the art of inoculation. If I find it so when I return to the circumstance of Liberty . . . I shall destroy such a wretch from the face of the earth: But on the other hand, if proper measures were taken, and his death has been inevitable—I submit to fate. Tho' I had promised myself great delight in clasping the charming boy in my arms, and in recounting to him my adventures. But mortality has frustrated my fond hopes and with him my name expires.

All this time the principal officers of the army exerted themselves strenuously to have him exchanged for a British prisoner. Hearing that Ethan was being treated without regard for decency, humanity or the rules of war, General Washington wrote Lord Howe that he considered the latter's silence as a confirmation of the truth of the report and warned him that whatever fate Ethan suffered, that exactly awaited the British general, William Prescott, then an American prisoner (the very man who sent Ethan to England in chains).

Finally in May, 1778, Ethan was exchanged for one Colonel Archibald Campbell and as he set foot on "liberty Ground" he wrote that he was in "a transport of joy." On the way to Valley Forge he received the "acclamations of a grateful people" (grateful, perhaps, that the war's most uncommon personality was again in their midst). Washington, too, was pleased. He thought Ethan's "fortitude and firmness to have placed him out of the reach of misfortune . . . his long captivity and sufferings have only served to increase, if possible, his enthusiastic zeal." At Washington's suggestion Congress made Ethan a full colonel for his valor during and before his imprisonment. He enjoyed the company of General Gates on the way to Bennington, where, on May 30, 1778, he appeared "as one rose from the dead. . . . Three cannon were fired that evening, and next morning . . . 14 more were discharged welcoming me to Bennington, my usual place of abode; 13 for the United States and 1 for young Vermont."

The appearance in 1779 of Ethan's narrative of his imprisonment, first as a serial and then as a book (reprinted eight times in two years), greatly revived the spirit of freedom. According to John Pell's biography it "helped enormously the efforts of Revolutionary leaders to enlist men and to rid the land of Tories." The intellectuals, praising it as warmly as the rank and file, thought that if Allen's natural genius had been cultivated with an education he would have cut a wide swath "among the sons of science." Actually, a formal education might have ruined his style. Its forceful, picaresque and poetic qualities might have been lost in the niceties of academic prose. The vigorous account of his captivity exhibits Ethan's style at its best, although it is relatively little known, while his doings and sayings in the Green Mountains before and after his captivity are the very woof and warp of Vermont.

As a returned (if not conquering) hero he was definitely feeling his oats as the Percheron of the new Republic, comfortably back in harness. Just four days after his arrival in Bennington one David Redding was to have been hanged for aiding the enemy. Unaware that he had been illegally tried by six jurors, whereas the law required twelve in a capital case, a great mob had assembled on June 4 and were threatening a lynching if the sentence was not carried out. At the critical moment Ethan shouldered his way through the crowd, mounted a stump and, waving his hat, bellowed: "Attention, the whole!" After explaining why the hanging was to be delayed he counseled the crowd to go home and come back in a week. "You shall see somebody hung at all events, for if Redding is not then hung, I will be hung myself!" The crowd happily dispersed, and returned on the appointed day to see Redding duly and legally hanged.

In one respect, at least, it was as if Ethan had never been away. Throughout the Revolution the land wars had been going on tumultuously, at times somewhat quiescent under the numbing effects of the greater struggle, but again threatening to shake the little republic to its foundations. Ira Allen, the Fays of Bennington, and the wily farmer Thomas Chittenden (who from 1778 until he died in 1797 served almost continuously as governor of the republic and the state) had accomplished a miracle in holding the government together during Ethan's absence. They had been obliged to contend not only with grasping New York and the armies of Britain but with the partisans of a new state in the Connecticut valley who calculated to take roughly half of Vermont and half of New Hampshire under their jurisdiction. Their leader, none other than the tireless divine of Dartmouth, Eleazar Wheelock, visualized Hanover as the center of a lush river principality, a Puritan Commonwealth independent of the seacoast gentry, on the one hand, and the radicals to the west of the Green Mountains, on the other.

Ethan called Wheelock and his minions "a petulant, pettifogging, scribbling sort of Gentry that will keep any government in hot water," but their accomplishments showed political ability of a considerably higher order. In 1778 the College party gathered in its orbit sixteen towns on the New Hampshire side of the river to convince them that they owed no allegiance to the new provincial government at Exeter because they were not allowed enough representation in it. Their next move was to secede from the New Hampshire government and join Vermont, a coup that the Allens were helpless to prevent because the towns on the Vermont side of the Connecticut, led by General Jacob Bayley of Newbury, voted sympathetically to admit them. Thus in 1778 the offspring republic became larger than the parent state, a circumstance that the Allens feared was filled with gloomy foreboding. Hoping as they did that Vermont might free itself of the land claims of New York and presently become the Union's fourteenth state, they worked feverishly to disown the New Hampshire towns; for, as Ethan reported after a trip to Philadelphia in 1778, if Vermont did not "recede from such union immediately, the whole power of the Confederacy of the United States of America will join to annihilate the State of Vermont to vindicate the right of New Hampshire."

All might have been well in February, 1779, when Vermont accordingly rejected the sixteen towns, if the scribbling gentry of Hanover had not retaliated by stealing ten *Vermont* towns *west* of the river. The prospect for the new Connecticut River state never looked better: the College party was supporting New York claims in Vermont west of the Green Mountains—for it hoped to take the rest of the state east to the river, together with all the New Hampshire towns that would secede. There were many more crafty moves and countermoves before it finally was clear that the College party was checkmated. In 1781, as the result of an adroit reversal of strategy on the part of the Allens, who now decided that offense was the best defense, New Hampshire's valley towns and some New York towns in territory to the west that not even they claimed was within the jurisdiction of Vermont, were admitted to that state. This caused such a ruckus in Congress that George Washington intervened to suggest that if Vermont would return the wandering towns Congress would admit it as the fourteenth state. In 1782 Vermont disowned the towns in good faith but Congress, in bad faith, failed to offer it statehood, and so the broils over land continued.

While the College party's hopes for a new river state gradually subsided, New York remained adamant. The Allens were hard pressed to cope with the festering opposition to their government in a county called Cumberland. The home of numerous Yorkers, it was not, strangely enough, contiguous to New York but deep within Vermont to the southeast. At the Westminster courthouse, where Yorkers tried to maintain the authority of their government, two partisans of New Hampshire were killed in 1775 in what Vermonters called the "Westminster Massacre." Upon his return from captivity Ethan used every device short of his sword to compel "the New York malcontents" of Cumberland County to submit to the authority of Vermont. Ambushed on one occasion, and with a bullet hole through his coat, he marched into Guilford and delivered a resounding ultimatum: "I, Ethan Allen, do declare that I will give no quarter to the man, woman or child who shall oppose me, and unless the inhabitants of Guilford peacefully submit to the authority of Vermont, I swear I will lay it as desolate as Sodom and Gomorrah, by God!" A battery of guns could not have spoken with greater effect.

The other incident always recalled in any chronicle of Cumberland County, or of Ethan, had to do with the trial of a number of New York miscreants before the Vermont Superior Court in Westminster. They were charged with armed interference with the military draft law of Vermont. Through the resourcefulness of their lawyer and the acquiescence of the state's attorney, Noah Smith, who had just consulted *Blackstone's Commentaries*, the defendants were about to get off on a technicality when there was a commotion in the back of the courtroom. It was Ethan in full military dress with a huge sword at his side. Waving his hat he announced to Smith: "I would have the young gentleman to know that, with my logic and reasoning from the eternal fitness of things, I can upset his Blackstones, his whetstones, his gravestones and his brimstones."

The judge, slightly aghast, advised Ethan that the court would hear what he had to say as a civilian, but not in uniform. Unbuckling his sword and casting his hat on the table with a flourish, Ethan recited Alexander Pope's illustrious couplet:

> "For forms of government, let fools contest;
> Whate'er is best administered is best."

Then he declared: "Fifty miles I have come through the woods with my brave men, to support the civil with the military arms; to quell any disturbances should they arise; and aid the sheriff and the court in prosecuting these Yorkers—the enemies of our noble state. I see, however, that some of them by the quirks of this artful lawyer, Bradley, are escaping from the punishment they so richly deserve, and I find also that this little Noah Smith is far from understanding his business, since he at one time moves for a prosecution and in the next wishes to withdraw it. Let me warn your Honour to be on your guard lest these delinquents shall slip through your fingers."

From the Westminster jail the sentenced prisoners dispatched a memorial to Governor George Clinton of New York, pleading for relief. Otherwise "our Persons and Property must be at the disposal of Ethan Allin which is more to be dreaded than Death with all its Terrors." That Governor Clinton was not prepared for civil war in a national crisis and would risk nothing, Ethan well knew. He was perfectly safe in lecturing one of the most irritable Yorkers: "You have called on your God, Clinton, till you are tired. Call now on your God Congress, and they will answer you as Clinton has done."

Congress was too busy with a war and too divided in sentiment about the Vermont land controversy to pass judgment on it and so, year after year, the Allens maintained the status quo; the longer they kept it the more authority and weight their own government carried. That they succeeded in scotching the plans of the various claiming states (including Massachusetts, for a time) is convincing enough of their political acumen. That they managed to keep an army of 10,000 British troops from their borders with mere words was an achievement worthy of a Talleyrand or a Disraeli.

The so-called Haldimand Negotiations, named after the Governor of Canada, British General Sir Frederick Haldimand, with whom they were conducted, began in the fall of 1780 under the guise of an exchange of prisoners. Aware that the American Congress had shown little interest in admitting the Vermont republic as a state, Britain's secretary of state and commanding general in America were intrigued with the possibility that, if its leaders were well enough rewarded, Vermont might become a British colony and as such a wedge for invasion to the south. By nourishing British hopes without actually promising anything, and by spinning out the negotiations, the Allens were able to keep the enemy from their borders for two years. In the meantime they applied pressure upon Congress for statehood by virtue of what they were doing for the common cause. Unless Vermont was admitted to the Union, they assured Congress, its people could not be blamed for turning toward Great Britain. Why should Vermont fight for the Union only to be swallowed up by New York after the shooting was over?

Ethan entered into the negotiations gingerly for, as he told Justice Sherwood, the British emissary, he did not wish to engage in any "dam'd Arnold plan to sell his country and his own honor by betraying the trust reposed in him." He realized, however, that to gain the diplomatic advantages of a string of conferences he would have to risk a whispering campaign that he was dealing, or at least conferring with, the enemy. Haldimand's agent, after meeting with Ethan, reported to his commander that he was not able to tell whether things were going well from the British standpoint, or poorly, for "he [Allen] is a most subtle and designing fellow." Ethan was not the least subtle in his memorials to Congress. He made no bones about declaring that since Vermont was an independent republic it had a right to agree to end hostilities with England if it so desired, and that he was "resolutely determined to defend the independence of Vermont as Congress are that of the United States, and rather than fail, will retire with hardy Green Mountain Boys into the desolate caverns of the mountains and wage war with human nature at large."

The most ticklish, indeed untenable, feature of Ethan's role was convincing the British that he spoke for the people of Vermont when actually the government had agreed only to conferences about the exchange of prisoners. Powerful enemies like the Federalist Isaac Tichenor (a later governor) and General Bayley of Newbury, builder of the unfinished Hazen military road through the wilderness of northeastern Vermont for the invasion of Canada, could be counted on to snatch from the Allens any political advantage they could. In 1781 rumors were flying so fast and thick that there was actually a movement in the legislature for Ethan's impeachment. While it failed to pass, he resentfully turned in his commission as brigadier general. His brother Ira, now authorized to take over the negotiations for the exchange of prisoners, continued, however, along exactly the same lines that Ethan had followed, except perhaps with more finesse. Impatient, and wary of the double-talk of the Vermont emissaries, Haldimand at length sent St. Leger up the lake to augment a force that he had sent a year earlier to seize Forts Ann and Edward, but before this huge army could accomplish anything Lord Cornwallis surrendered at Yorktown and nothing remained for St. Leger but to return to Canada.

So Vermont fought this last campaign of the north with conversation. Despite obvious benefits to the Union, Congress still would not reward Vermont with statehood. Thus the Allens resumed conferences with Haldimand, Ethan declaring on one occasion that he would do everything in his power to make the republic a British province. Toward the end of the 1780's, with the adoption of the Constitution of the United States, it at last began to look as though the impossible might be achieved. The final stumbling block was removed when Vermont paid $30,000 to New York to end forever that state's claims to Green Mountain lands, and in 1791 the unwanted stepchild was received into the arms of the Union.

A few latter-day historians have viewed the Allens' conduct in the Haldimand Negotiations with arched eyebrows and a steely glint that suggests a charge of disloyalty. Disloyal to whom? The United States, in which Vermont was so long denied membership but which it had served so well? It is too easy to think of the Continentals in terms of twentieth-century patriotism and to impose upon them attitudes that they never had. The one pervading characteristic that they did have was individualism and among all the individuals in the northcountry the Allens reigned supreme. Admitting that they were bent on keeping their land, is it at all credible to suppose that the liberty-loving Ethan who had been so gallingly misused in British jails had any other than a last-ditch interest in making Vermont a British province? Certainly what he said during the life-and-death Haldimand Negotiations cannot be taken as an index of his real convictions. A sifting of all the substantial evidence still reveals nothing so clearly as that the Allens were playing a clever and successful game, one which can, after all, be viewed only in terms of its results: statehood for Vermont.

As if the affairs of war and state were not enough to occupy mind and heart, Ethan had been busy writing a book that was to cause a greater ferment in eighteenth-century New England than anything he had ever done. Its subject, of all things for a man of action, was religion. Throughout his life there were clues to his interest in the affairs of the universe and the hereafter. Several times he assured his friend, Lieutenant Colonel Graham, probably with a twinkling eye, that he would live again as a large white horse. Again he remarked: "As to the world of spirits, tho I know nothing of the mode and manner of it, I [expect] nevertheless, when I should arrive at such a world, that I should be as well treated as other gentlemen of my merit."

When, after the death of his first wife, he married the elegant young widow, Fanny Buchanan, the unorthodox ceremony revealed his searching mind. He popped in on his bride-to-be in Westminster one morning in February, 1784, to suggest that if they were to be married it might as well be now. Interrupting his friend, Superior Judge Moses Robinson, at breakfast he announced:

"Judge Robinson, this young woman and myself have concluded to marry each other and to have you perform the ceremony."

"When?" asked the judge.

"Now. For myself I have no great opinion of such formality, and from what I can discover she thinks as little of it as I do. But as a decent respect for the opinions of mankind seems to require it, you will proceed." The judge proceeded. When he inquired whether Ethan promised to live with Fanny "agreeable to the laws of God," Ethan stopped him and looked out of the window. "The law of God," he murmured presently, "as written in the great book of nature. Yes, go on."

Thus the General entered his second marriage, although his financial circumstances so far as cash was concerned scarcely permitted it. "I am drove almost to death for money," he complained at the time, for he was trying to build a house at the seat of his vast lands on the Onion (Winooski) River. "I have not a copper of money to save me from the Devil. We are rich poor cursed rascals by God! Alter our measures or we shall be a hiss, a proverb and a bye word and derision on earth."

Ethan was always talking about the devil yet had little real concern that he would meet up with him, either on earth or later, for in his heart he felt that he had acted decently and, that being so, he would be rewarded in the hereafter according to the system of theology outlined in his now completed manuscript, *Reason, the Only Oracle of Man.* Ethan believed in a wise, good and transcendent governor of man, a unified combination of nature and the universe. He did not believe that miracles or divine revelation had ever occurred; he did not expect them in the future or think them necessary. His was a rational religion which refuted the stern, dour determinism of Calvin, the Biblical legends of original sin, the fall of man and the Virgin birth. Priests and clergymen venomously attacked his views as the work of an infidel, for his published opinions (preceding those of Paine and Jefferson) were among the first to attack what were considered immutable doctrines. In *Ethan Allen* John Pell notes certain relationships between Ethan's pioneering tract and Spinoza's description of the universe, in so far as Creation is "an infinite exertion of . . . omnipotent God." An omnipotent and authoritative God he regarded as of course inconsistent with free will and this "is the rock on which Ethan's boat breaks to pieces just when it is approaching the tranquil seas sailed by Spinoza and Emerson." Under no circumstance would Ethan abandon the doctrine of free will. In religion as well as politics he was, says Pell, "the slave of freedom."

There are those who assert that his childhood friend, Thomas Young, indoctrinated Ethan with these ideas and even wrote large parts of the book, but students of semantics, even of phonetics, may find difficulty in subscribing to this theory. The trademarks of Ethan's style are everywhere present; quite obviously he worked on it for years. His brother's widow told Zadoc Thompson, the Vermont historian, that when she called Ethan to dinner while he was staying at her house "he said he was very sorry she had called him so soon, for he had got clear up into the upper regions." Whatever it is as theology, it is certainly not, as James Truslow Adams asserts, a "crude, coarsely written book." On the contrary, Ethan's exciting rhetoric is to be found on nearly every page:

> The globe with its productions, the planets in their motions, and the starry heavens in their magnitudes, surprise our senses and confound our reason . . . [but] we are too apt to confound our ideas of God with his works, and take the latter for the former.

. . . .

Comets, earthquakes, volcanoes, and northern lights (in the night) with many other extraordinary phenomina or appearances intimidate weak minds, and are by them thought to be miraculous; although they undoubtedly have their proper natural causes. . . . But of all the scarecrows which have made human nature tremble, the devil has been chief; his family is said to be very numerous, consisting of "legions," with which he has kept our world in a terrible uproar. . . . All the magicians, necromancers, wizzards, witches, conjurors, gypsies, sybils, hobgoblins, apparitions and the like . . . old Belzebub rules them all. Men will face destructive cannon and mortars, engage each other in the clashing of arms, and meet the horrors of war undaunted, but the devil and his banditti of fiends and emmisaries fright them out of their wits, and have a powerful influence in plunging them into superstition, and also continuing them therein.

. . . .

Protestants very readily discern and expose the weak side of Popery, and Papists are as ready and accute in discovering the errors of heretics. With equal facility do Christians and Mahometans spy out each others' inconsistencies and both have an admirable sagacity to descry the superstition of the heathen nations.

. . . . . .

Moses in his last chapter of Deuteronomy crowns his history with the particular account of his own death and burial. . . . This is the only historian in the circle of my reading, who has ever given the public a particular account of his own death, and how old he was at that decisive period, where he died, who buried him, and where he was buried, and with all of the number of days his friends and acquaintances mourned and wept for him. I must confess I do not expect to be able to advise a public of the term of my life, nor the circumstances of my death and burial, nor of the days of the weeping or laughing of my survivors.

VIII

BEYOND THE BACKBEYOND

Relatively little would be known about pioneer life in the half-twilight under the pines were it not for Jeremy Belknap and Abby Maria Hemenway of New Hampshire and Vermont, respectively. With a diligence bordering on fanaticism they preserved descriptions of what was trivial and what was momentous in the life of the northern frontier. While the fact that a message from John Langdon (the New Hampshire statesman who presided over the first United States Senate) informed General Washington at Mount Vernon that he had been elected president is a matter of consequence, it is, if irrelevant, at least as interesting to learn in Belknap that

> a dog belonging to Mr. Wormwood of Durham, being bitten by a rattlesnake, immediately went in search of a soft loamy spot of earth in which he scratched a hole and buried himself all over except his head. Here he remained, refusing to eat, till the earth had extracted the venom.

In her five-volume chronicle of early Vermont life, Abby Hemenway dutifully reported the marching and countermarching of armies but also informed us that there were no rats in Burlington until they were brought from St. Johns in Gideon King's old horseboat; and that the daughter of Governor Chittenden was for three months the handsomest woman in Charlotte for the very good reason that she was the only one.

Inasmuch as Vermont was not settled for nearly a century and a half after the New Hampshire seacoast (whose local history is rather lost in antiquity), memories of the Green Mountain frontier were still fresh even in the mid-1800's when Miss Hemenway was at work. She could hear of the wilderness from the very old men and women who had settled it, or from their children. Some accounts, no doubt, suffer from embellishment and others may be apocryphal but most of them seem authentic.

In Bridport on Lake Champlain during the Revolution, she reports, a Mrs. Stone saw Indians creeping toward her house and had just time enough to throw some of her valuables out of the back window and stuff others into her bosom. When the Indians entered they found her calmly carding wool in the midst of her wide-eyed children. Suspecting that there were valuables under her dress one young brave started to run his hand below its neckline when Mrs. Stone drew back her arm and hit him smartly in the face with her card. He recoiled quickly while his friends laughed and shouted, "Good squaw! Good squaw!" and shortly departed.

Because of some minor debt Colonel William Barton for years resided in the jail of the town that bears his name. Such treatment toward an officer who had bravely captured a British general during the Revolution seemed ungrateful—or so his friend Lafayette thought when he toured Vermont in 1825, and bailed him out.

In 1774 Amos Story, one of the early settlers of Salisbury, was killed by a falling tree while clearing his land. His wife then performed the work of the farm and during the Revolution gathered her children each night and led them to a cave she had dug out of the east bank of Otter Creek. She was married twice more and lived to be seventy-five.

In the town of Marlboro a hunter named Samuel Whitney emerged from a hand-to-hand fight with a bear with a scar he carried the rest of his life. Once when he was sick with fever his 13-year-old daughter yoked his oxen, drove them into the woods for a load of wood, which she chopped for the fireplace herself.

Disappointed in love, Timothy Knox, a student at Harvard, fled to the wilderness of future Woodstock in 1765 and lived there three years as a lone trapper.

In 1766 John Chipman and fifteen other young men from Salisbury, Connecticut, cut their way through the woods north of what is now Proctor until they reached Otter Creek. Here they made a dugout and paddled it downriver with their oxcart in tow and the oxen lumbering along the bank, until they reached what is now Vergennes.

Struck down with illness nine miles from any neighbor in the town of Windham in 1773, pioneer Edward Aiken sent for his wife in Londonderry, New Hampshire. She mounted a horse and with her youngest child in her arms rode 100 miles to Windham. Under her care Aiken recovered his health.

During the absence of John Strong on a trip to Albany in 1766 the blanket that served as a door to his lakeside cabin in Addison was pushed aside to reveal the large head of a bear. Hurrying her children up into the relative safety of the loft, Mrs. Strong pulled the ladder up after them. The bear, followed by her two cubs, made at once for a pan of milk and kettle of pudding that was to have served as the Strongs' supper. Overturning the milk she stuck her head into the scalding kettle of pudding and swallowed some before recoiling in pain. As she sat howling on her haunches, clawing the pudding from her mouth in front of her bewildered cubs, the children in the loft laughed out loud.

Strong himself had several serious encounters with bears, one of which left him with a crushed thumb for life; but until the end of the Revolution the Indians proved a far greater peril. One June morning when Mrs. Strong was standing at the spring near her house she thought she heard the dipping of a paddle on the lake immediately below, and upon peering through the trees caught a glimpse of a canoeful of redskins bearing aloft a scalp whose golden curls she thought she recognized as those of a little girl from across the lake. Other scalps were fastened to the belts of the Indians, while farther out two more canoes presented a similar ghastly sight. She slipped back into her house in terror and later that day learned that the scalps were indeed those of her New York neighbors. The morning before Burgoyne took Crown Point the Indians burned the Strong dwelling, but the family all escaped. Later they returned to the rich bottom land of Addison—to that ancient thoroughfare of Indians, French, Hessians and Continentals—the Crown Point Road—to build again.

So far as encounters with Indians are concerned the Strongs' hardships were the exception. Other than a raid from Canada on the town of Royalton in 1780 the settlers east of the Green Mountains remained safe on their farms. Those in the northwest along the lake withdrew temporarily to the homes of friends in the south, or to the forts or their old homes in Connecticut and Massachusetts. After the war they resumed their backbreaking labors to make fields in the woods, to burn the trees for potash (one of their few sources of money), to pile the stones left by what Charles Edward Crane calls "the great Labrador plow"; to build their one-room log cabins with roofs of spruce bark; to raise wheat, corn and rye to make bread, peas, beans, and pumpkins. A single cow, perhaps, supplied milk while meat was obtained from the wild animals of the forest as well as some articles of clothing, skins for rugs and for stretching over the crude frames of a bed. With a smoky fireplace often nothing more than a pile of stones on the floor and the entire family bedded down in a single room, winter was a matter of stark survival. Hunting trips for moose meat or venison sometimes ended with the father staggering seven or eight miles through the snow with a hundred pounds of meat on his back.

Isaac Weld, in his *Travels through the States of North America* from 1795 to 1797, wrote of stopping at Vermont farmhouses along lower Lake Champlain for shelter and food. At one dwelling

> we found a venerable old man at the door, reading a news-paper, who civilly offered it to us for our perusal, and began to talk upon the politics of the day; we thanked him for his offer, and gave him to understand, at the same time, that a loaf would be much more acceptable. Bread there was none; we got a new Vermont cheese, however.
>
> The people at the American farmhouses would cheerfully lie three in a bed, rather than suffer a stranger to go away.

Weld speaks of stopping at Chimney Point, the site of a few houses and a tavern. He was surprised to see there a large birch canoe navigated by several Indians.

Leaving the orderly and peaceful Connecticut valley towns of Vermont and New Hampshire in 1789 the dyspeptic minister, Nathan Perkins, was thoroughly shaken by his observations in the raw and much newer settlements west of the mountains. He could not understand why the hungry people in this area seemed to be so much happier than those in the long-settled towns of Connecticut, and so much kinder to their neighbors. Dressed "coarse, mean, nasty and ragged," they were nevertheless cheerful and many of them, he found, were clever.

> When I go from hut to hut, from town to town, the people [with] nothing to eat, to drink or wear—all work, and yet the women quiet, serene, peaceable, contented, loving their husbands, their homes—wanting never to return, nor any dressy clothes, I think how strange! I ask myself are these women of the same species with our fine ladies? Tough are they, brawny of their limbs—their girls unpolished—and will work as well as mules. Woods make people love one another and kind and obliging and good natured. They set much more by one another than in the old settlements.

He got lost riding through the mud up to his horse's belly between Burlington and Shelburne where there was next to no road nor any houses for four miles. It further depressed him to be in the home country of the Deists, of the "awful Infidel," Ethan Allen, where the people hunted and fished on Sunday and at least half of them "would chuse to have no Sabbath—no ministers—no religion—no heaven—no hell—no morality."

Perkins was viewing the last New England frontier—the kind of people in circumstances that Frederick Jackson Turner has called the most important single influence upon American democracy. Like the floodtide wave which reaching highest on the beach must overpower the undertow of lesser ones, the people of the Green Mountains were the last echelon of those seekers after freedom to abandon a succession of older communities and seek their destiny still farther to the north and west. Just as the original settlers of southern New Hampshire found the atmosphere of Massachusetts' Puritan oligarchy too stolid, the settlers of interior and western New Hampshire disliked the proper life of the seacoast; and so in turn did the settlers of western Vermont (coming from western Connecticut) consider the old towns in eastern Connecticut and even the newer settlements along the upper reaches of the placid river too tame and inhibiting. The government of Vermont had from the beginning been controlled by western Connecticut extremists who looked upon the very free constitution of Pennsylvania as a model for their own, but went several steps further to decree, for example, universal manhood suffrage without any property qualifications. Vermont was the first state to guarantee such a freedom.

The fact that a people so homogeneous (they were more than 90 per cent English or of English descent) could develop such different views in a relatively small area can partially be explained by geography. The White and Green Mountain ranges set the people apart. Even today it is possible to distinguish by their accents natives who live east of the Green Mountains from those of the west. There was, moreover, the long interval, owing to the wars, before the area was completely settled. The people who were prospering in the older towns generally stayed there. Those who had nothing moved on, for they had much to gain in the woods. Most of them were prospective farmers but there were also large numbers of artisans who had learned their trades as apprentices in older settlements and moved on to set up shop for themselves in new country where class distinction had not yet taken root. This of course is the story of the whole American frontier.

The social ferment in Vermont and New Hampshire after the Revolution was very much like that following any war. Money depreciated and an army of lawyers tramped up and down the valleys serving writs. Every second person, it seemed, was in jail for debt. Governor Chittenden of Vermont remarked that during the war "we were obliged to follow the example of Joshua of old who commanded the sun to stand still while he fought his battle; we commanded our creditors to stand still while we fought our enemies." Two hundred farmers meeting in Rutland in 1786 to air their grievances served notice on the banditti of attorneys to take care "how you impose upon those who passed thro' the wilderness, and endured fire, famine and the sword so to . . . obtain their rights, and the liberties of mankind." The killing of all lawyers and deputy sheriffs was suggested as a palliative, but a more moderate course of action prevailed.

Conditions were much more serious in Massachusetts than in New Hampshire or Vermont, where the leaders of Shays' Rebellion sought sanctuary. While they received private and official sympathy and understanding, their acts of violence were condemned. The New Hampshire government in particular was hard put to cope with popular resentment against the courts.

In 1782 the judges of Sullivan County, the heart of an incipient rebellion, were afraid to hold court in Keene. Determining that the judges would sit at the appointed time, the Attorney General of New Hampshire, none other than old General John Sullivan, journeyed from Portsmouth to Keene on horseback. Putting on his glittering general's uniform—epaulettes, sword, spurs and all—he rode his splendid gray horse in front of the timid judges, calling out to the crowd: "Make way for the court." Once inside, he laid his sword on the table and declared that the court was now open. It was just as abruptly adjourned for three months, but the brief ceremony had the intended effect, of displaying authority.

In 1786 Sullivan, now president of New Hampshire, again succeeded in warding off anarchy when 200 men marched into Exeter and surrounded the legislature. The House appointed a commission to consider their petition for paper money but the Senate, at Sullivan's bidding, would not consider the grievance of the mob until it dispersed. This time Sullivan called out the militia and after a brief skirmish the mob scattered.

Under such circumstances lawlessness inevitably arose in a population that contained, along with stable homesteaders and tradesmen, many shiftless vagrants and ne'er-do-wells who found the frontier an ideal setting for their mischiefmaking. The autobiography of the criminal Henry Tufts, perhaps the foremost scoundrel in the history of Vermont and New Hampshire, casts interesting sidelights on the low life of the tavern and turnpike at the end of the eighteenth century, and as such is a valuable sociological document. Tufts stole more horses, became involved with more women, and was in and out of more jails than seems credible for one lifetime, yet he writes of his misdeeds with so much detail and concern for names, dates and places that the story is unquestionably authentic. Among the confessions, if they could be called that, of such northcountry miscreants as Seth Wyman and Stephen Burroughs, Tufts's book shines with candor, gusto and humor.

Born at Newmarket, New Hampshire, in 1748, he wrote that his early efforts were confined to the pilfering of apples, pears, cucumbers "and other fruits of the earth." At the age of twenty-one he stole his first horse and became involved with the first of many women. "Being once initiated into the mysteries of this Cyprian goddess a natural warmth of temper enrolled the name of Tufts among the number of her voteries ever afterwards . . . my inclination, always fervid, but now fired with new incentives, impelled me, more strongly than formerly, to sacrifice the shrine of Venus, nor could I resist the impulses of so bewitching a deity."

After his marriage at twenty-two to Lydia Bickford, he temporarily settled down in the village of Lee but presently resumed his philandering and stealing. For robbing a store he was thrown into a jail from which the prosecutor, a man named Picard, promised to release him if he would become a seaman on a three months' trip to the West Indies and turn over his wages to his "liberator." Tufts agreed to this but escaped on the way to the ship and went to Fort Number 4 on the Connecticut, where for a month he worked honestly at driving a sleigh. From there he went to Claremont to clear land for one

Enoch Judd, the father of two unmarried daughters. When asked if he was single, Tufts replied that he was and in due course he married the elder daughter. Presently news reached Judd that his son-in-law had two wives and "such being the state of things, I thought it wise to decamp seasonably, so I left Claremont that very evening." Returning to Lee by a circuitous route Tufts found that his first wife knew all about the second and gave him an "uncouth welcome."

After robbing another store, he received twenty lashes and was thrown into irons in Exeter. He had, however, secreted some small tools and before serving out his sentence drilled a hole through the wall of the jail and was able to squeeze through by removing his clothes. Emaciated from the deprivations of the jail, he returned home to regain his strength. Sallying forth once more he bought for $30 a set of pictures which he called "Shows" and set about exhibiting them, but failing to prosper had to sacrifice them for $10.

As the result of a game with a jackknife he received in his thigh a serious wound which failed to heal and after three months he determined to seek a cure from the northern Indians on the Canadian border. He was cordially received by the chief and kindly cared for by Molly Occut, their "doctress" with her roots, herbs and barks, and recovered so rapidly that he was soon courting Polly Susap, a niece of old Chief Tumkin Hagen. Life with these Algonquins who roamed 80 miles of woods from Lake Memphremagog to Umbago so well suited him that he remained with the tribe to hunt and to learn the art of medicine from Molly Occut. Tufts's account of his three years with the Indians—of every facet of tribal life; birth, marriage and death, law and religion; of their character and temperament, their hospitality and loyalty, and their vindictiveness when wronged— is as authentic as it is little known.

He might have stayed indefinitely if it had not been for the pressure applied by Polly Susap's parents for a marriage ceremony. "I excused the matter by saying I wished to procure, first, a better Indian habit; but Polly's mother thought my dress good enough, and insisted upon a speedy consummation of the nuptials. This pertinacity of theirs put me to numerous shifts . . ." In May, 1775, after treating his Indian friends to five gallons of rum and advising Polly that he must settle his affairs in the colonies, but would return "on wings of love" at the first moment, he departed.

Somewhat chagrined, back in Lee, to face his wife who had been supporting his children all this time, and with nothing to show for his three years with the Indians, Tufts suffered twinges of patriotism and served several separate enlistments in the army. From time to time he prudently employed his light fingers whenever his talents were called for in obtaining, for example, more than his company's share of rations from the commissary. During the intervals between enlistments and afterwards he posed as a doctor, with knowledge gained from Molly Occut. He chanced to attend a meeting of "New Light" revivalists, and taking account of how they preached and prayed, he resolved to become a minister so that he might exercise his excellent memory and talent for mimicry. Investing all the money he had in a black suit, a Scotch-plaid gown and beaver hat, he went to Maine, where he was received as a genuine preacher. At one meeting when the regular minister asked if any of the assembly wished to speak, Tufts arose and preached so eloquently that the local divine announced that he never listened to a louder sermon to his soul. He declared Tufts to be a heaven-born saint. Whereupon a young woman arose and pronounced him to be the "devil incarnate." Upon Tufts's entrance into the meeting, she said, "he first surveyed my face, then my feet, then my whole person in such a carnal way and manner, that I perceived he had the devil in his heart." Spiritedly defended by the local minister, Tufts survived this attack on his character to deliver, the following Sunday, a sermon so powerful as to draw tears from the congregation. Eventually he returned to his family in Lee, at last with some cash for their support.

Chancing to steal a beehive shortly thereafter, he dropped it as the bees caught up and ran like a deer to outdistance them. Now hungry, he broke into a subterranean chamber where he thought he remembered a store of fruit had been hidden. In the darkness he got hold of a box which turned out to be a coffin, and when he heard the bones clattering he was frozen with fear—"my voice clave to my jaws," he wrote. The wanderlust that afflicted him all his life now brought him to many New Hampshire and Vermont towns where he plied interchangeably the trades of medicine, the ministry and thievery. He painted the face, feet and legs of one of the many horses he stole and so changed his appearance that the owner, overtaking him, did not recognize his mount. For a time it looked as though he might prosper as a farmer but a fire and the depreciation of his savings returned him to his old profession, hence to numerous jails, from which he always managed to escape.

He stole and philandered his way to Virginia and back and embarked on a walking tour of Vermont with a small lobster claw which he described to rapt listeners as an enchanted horn enabling him to foresee the future (he explained how he had lost another horn, the counterpart of this one, that made it possible to "foretell past events"). Working in a field in Canterbury he showed a farmer how to blow into pumpkins or gourds to make music. Hearing strange sounds of trumpets or warlike airs in the distance, many of the people of Canterbury were afraid that Judgment Day was at hand. Three different times Tufts sold a large dog he had stolen and each time the faithful animal returned to him so that he "turned him to pretty good account."

To make jailbreaking less difficult he collected an assortment of small knives, augers and saws, spring keys to open any lock, vitriol, aqua fortis and vials of corrosive ingredients to eat iron and hid them in his hair and the soles of his shoes. They were greatly helpful in a prison in Newburyport, as was an ancient weathercock on the roof "fixed on an iron spindle, which as often as the wind blew, emitted a creaking sound that drowned entirely the noise of our saws. We deemed this a fortunate circumstance and never failed to take advantage of it, shaping our course according to the wind." A free man once more, he set up for "horse jockeying" but was badly worsted in a deal for "a gay, spritely looking horse that proved subject to a disorder called the spring-halt, which frequently seized his limbs so powerfully that he would drop down suddenly, as though shot in the head."

Under the name of Gideon Garland he took another wife and went to farming for a while, then to doctoring and pilfering in Norwich, Bennington, Pownal and Wallingford. In 1793 he was almost hanged for stealing silver tablespoons, a theft which he did not commit, and languished five years in an escape-proof prison called the Castle on an island in Boston Harbor. The new Mrs. Tufts remarried, and upon his release in 1798 the incorrigible vagabond returned to his first wife by whom he had nine children—and lived twice as many more years of mischief before he died.

The air of the northcountry proved as invigorating to intellectuals of nonconformist and liberal persuasions as to farmer, tradesman and shiftless malcontent. These citizens of many parts helped the untutored yeomen to put calcium into the bones of government. The fact that many of them were prosperous lawyers only proves the allegation of the farmers that the advocates were reaping what cash there was from their debt-plagued lands.

One of the most honorable of these was Royall Tyler, the rather maverick son of a well-to-do Boston merchant. He was admitted to the bar three years after his graduation from Harvard in 1776 and became engaged to Abigail, daughter of John Adams, who soon returned his ring and married a diplomat named Smith.

In 1787 Tyler became aide to General Benjamin Lincoln, commander of the militia of Massachusetts. Having helped to save the Springfield arsenal from the insurgents of Daniel Shays, he spent the winter pursuing the fugitives into the frosty hinterlands and that, apparently, is how he became interested in Vermont. He was able to trap one group of Shays' men at Sunday meeting (they had stacked their rifles outside and posted but a single sentry) and when their leader concluded a sermon that was more political than religious, Tyler took to the pulpit to announce that they were his prisoners. Reviewing the problems that gave rise to their rebellion he declared that such evils of government were the results of an exhausting war. With such a frank admission he succeeded in making good citizens of them. At this time he formed an acquaintance with a man who held sympathy for the rebels, Ethan Allen. He said that the officials of Massachusetts were "a pack of damned rascals" and that "there was no virtue among them and he did not think it worth while to try to prevent them that had fled into this state for shelter from cutting down our maple trees."

As soon as law and order prevailed Tyler returned to his Boston law office but it was not long before he was heard from in an entirely different quarter. In three weeks during the winter of 1788-89 he wrote a five-act comedy called *The Contrast*, which displayed the character of the straightforward citizens of the backcountry as contrasted to that of city slickers with a good deal of flamboyant language and an occasional gem of plain talk. *The Contrast* was the first comedy written and performed in America. (It has wrongly been called the first

American play: Robert Rogers' tragedy: *Ponteach or The Savages of America,* printed in 1766, seems to merit that distinction.) After producing a second hit called *Mayday in Town or New York in an Uproar,* Tyler seems to have played the social lion, but then disappeared for a number of months. In 1790 he turned up in Vermont and the next year settled in Guilford about the time of the publication of his novel, *The Algerine Captive,* the first of American origin to be published in England. Guilford, where he hung up his shingle, was, according to his grandmother, the outskirts of creation but a good place for lawyers, filled as it was with rogues and runaways.

Tyler's courtship and marriage were rather peculiar. Some twenty years previously when his wife had been a babe in arms he appeared at the home of her parents, the Joseph Palmers of Boston, and announced: "This child will become my wife." And so she did. As she rode over the snowclad hills toward her new home behind a pair of black trotters whom Tyler called Crock and Smut he told her he certainly hoped she would like it in Guilford and that the people would like her.

> If they have a social party [he explained], the whole neighborhood are invited. We have two merchants, the Messrs. Houghtons, two physicians, Dr. Stephens and Dr. Hyde, one lawyer, your humble servant, all men of education, and their wives and families well bred country people. There are several well-to-do mechanics who aim to treat company equally well. In fact, my dear, you will find it a truly primitive state of society, and if you have any adequate idea of the heartlessness of the world in general, you will rejoice in the friendly simplicity of these people, among whom I have spent three or four of the happiest years of my life.

Toward the turn of the century Tyler decided to move his growing family to the promising town of Brattleboro where he had obtained 150 acres surrounding a fine home high on a hill about a mile west of the West Brattleboro meetinghouse. He wrote a friend about the handsome portico of a dwelling that had room to spare for his four children and the hired help. Situated as it was in a little depression on the crest of the hill, with its attendant outbuildings—barns, smoke and ash houses—it bore the appearance of a small neighborhood. In front of the house was a thriving fruit garden with peach, plum, pear and cherry trees; a kitchen garden off to the side supplied his table with asparagus and plenty of red, white and black currants and English gooseberries. A flower garden adorned the third side of the house, a brook ran nearby, and the woods were full of chestnuts and butternuts. In his two orchards grew enough apples to make sixty barrels of cider a year. Wheat and rye grew in the fields and there was enough hay to winter thirty head of cattle. Hogs, poultry, sheep, geese and turkeys added to the comfort of the proprietor, who also conducted a successful law practice.

Writing for *The Farmer's Museum*, or *The New Hampshire and Vermont Journal*, a newspaper printed weekly across the river at Walpole, was Tyler's most satisfying extracurricular activity. Apparently he first met the editor, a young Harvard graduate named Joseph Dennie, at a lively tavern conclave of the lawyers of the upper Connecticut valley. In the mid-1790's the two joined forces and under the names of Messrs. Colon and Spondee promised their readers

> . . . monologues, dialogues, trialogues, tetralogues, and so on from 1 to 20 logues, annagrams, acrostics . . . chronograms, epigrams . . . by the gross or single dozen—sonnets, elegies, epithalamiums, epic poems—a quantity of brown horror and blue fear . . . love letters by the ream—sermons for texts and texts for sermons—old orations scoured, forensics furbished . . . amens and hallelujahs trilled, quavered and slurred.

With a circulation larger than that of any other country paper *The Farmer's Museum* enjoyed astonishing popularity throughout New England, as well as the entire eastern seaboard (President Washington was the most distinguished subscriber). Tyler's tours about Vermont to hold court among the debt-plagued citizenry provided local material which appeared interspersed with witty and satirical reflections on subjects of national interest. Proof that Vermont understatement is at least 150 years old is found in Tyler's anecdote about a visit he had with a ragged settler on a farm that was a mass of boulders.

"Judge," the man said at one point in the conversation, "I am not so poor as you think I am, for I don't *own* this land." A verse Tyler wrote about Governor Chittenden also makes clear that he was much more at home with such material than with the overstuffed rhetoric of his plays and novel. The wise farmer and tavernkeeper who served so long as Vermont's governor had lost an eye in the West Indies when a very young man, which gave him a somewhat formidable appearance but impaired his abilities not the least, as Tyler testified:

> Talk not of your Washingtons,
> Hancocks and Sullivans,
>   And all the wild crew;
> Our Tom set on high
> With his single eye
> Can more espy
> Than they can with two.

In 1801 Tyler was appointed to the Supreme Court of Vermont. Five years later he became its chief justice. In 1811 he was alternately handing down decisions and dispensing wisdom as professor of jurisprudence at the University of Vermont in Burlington. Because of ill-health and politics (he was something of a Federalist) he stepped down as chief justice the following year, but continued to practice as a trial lawyer in spite of a cancer on the left side of his nose which he covered with a patch. Near the end of his life, while defending a client named Richardson, he was malevolently attacked by the opposing counsel as a man who had lost his faculties and who had been removed from the bench for incompetence. Tyler sat immobile throughout this tirade and when his time came he called out to his client.

"Richardson!" he said. "Go home. There is no use of your staying here. I *thought* you had a good case." Turning his back to the judge and jury and facing his client, he reviewed succinctly the arguments of the case and concluded by saying: "I was mistaken in supposing you had any rights that could be maintained because my faculties are failing and I have a patch on my nose. Go home!"

The jury decided for Richardson.

Any account of the pioneers of the White Mountains, the last frontier in New Hampshire, is of no account without mention of the Eleazar Rosebrooks and their granddaughter, Lucy, and her husband, Ethan Allen Crawford. Prior to the Revolution Rosebrook moved his family to what is now Colebrook and managed somehow to survive the mountain cold in a log cabin. He once lugged a bushel of salt from

Haverhill to his home, a distance of 80 miles. During his service in the army his wife lived in nearby Guildhall, Vermont, and after the war Eleazar made a fine farm of his land there. Not satisfied, according to his granddaughter, he moved east to a desolate trough in the White Mountains called "Nash and Sawyer's location" (later known as Fabyan's). In her memoirs Lucy had a good deal to say about life there, particularly about the satisfactions of hardship. She recalled her grandmother's remark that she felt much more comfortable at Sunday meeting in her striped short, loose gown and blue-and-white checked apron than in the silks she could afford later on. And the men had been happy in mooseskins however cold they were to put on in the morning. Then

> the enemy of contentment began to introduce articles of merchandise, which soon created pride, and a sort of rivalship commenced, and as soon as one [woman] came in possession of a newly imported dress, it stimulated others to follow the fashion. . . . In this way has our country been infested with this foolish pride of dress, making gay the outside; while some, it is feared, have neglected the most important part, the soul.

Lucy first became acquainted with her cousin, Ethan Allen Crawford, when she went to nurse his grandfather in a log house at Hart's Location, twelve miles from neighbors in one direction and six in the other. Having crossed the mountains and lake to Plattsburgh, New York, to fight in the War of 1812, Ethan contracted spotted fever and nearly died but managed to straggle home in fourteen days. Upon his recovery he returned to the service and after the war, with two other men and a single yoke of oxen, he built eight miles of a road to St. Johns, Lower Quebec. He had bought land in northern New York but at the request of his dying grandfather he returned to New Hampshire.

In 1818 Ethan and Lucy were married. One new cheese and the milk of the cows was all that remained when their house burned on the day their first child was born. Ethan's youth and energy (he was over six feet tall with a massive physique) did not relieve him from a depression so acute that for some days he "was quite indifferent which way the world went." His usual optimism presently returned, however, and with the coming of the winter of 1819 he had completed a small comfortable house that would have been adequate had it not been for all the travelers who sought shelter there. The lone dwelling was situated at the foot of the long, awesome ravine through which ran the only market road from northwestern New Hampshire and Vermont to the southeast, and since the settlers waited until winter to haul their goods in sleighs, they had no alternative but to put up at Crawford's. Lucy did her best to make them comfortable in makeshift beds on the floor near the hearth.

Stories of Ethan's energy and tremendous strength soon became legendary in the mountains, a reputation gained not from fighting, which he disliked, but from shouldering such objects as large barrels that other men could scarcely raise from the ground. The one occasion that he did fight was disastrous to his adversary. As he told the story:

> . . . there was to be a general muster at Lancaster and as I was lame and not able to walk, Lucy was anxious to visit her parents at Guildhall, and we concluded to go and see them. And on the day appointed I with others went to see the soldiers perform, and while . . . I was sitting . . . there came a man who was celebrated for wrestling and laid hold of me and stumped me to throw him. I eased him off, and then he went to the others in the same way, and received similar treatment, until he upset a whole row of old men sitting on a rail fence or board. He came again and insisted on my taking hold with him. I told him I was not in the habit of that kind of sport and also I was lame and could not, even had I dispositioned to; and he came the third time and caught hold of my vest and rent it several inches in length, and at the same time with his foot gave me such a blow on my lamed ancle that the hurt raised my temper to such a degree that, unconscious of what I did, I put my fist in such an attitude that it laid him prostrate on the ground. He was taken up with rather a disfigured face; for which I was immediately sorry, for I knew he was influenced by liquor; but it was done—and many were glad of it—while I was ashamed to think I had given way to passion, and when I came to where Lucy was, I asked her to forgive my imprudence by mending my vest. I told her it should be the last time I would give way to an angry passion, and I have thus far kept my word.

Ethan was fond of pets and once when a doe with young that he had captured balked at the end of a rope, he picked her up and carried her home. Resolving to lead home a good-sized yearling bear, caught by the forefoot in one of his traps, he struggled mightily for hours before abandoning any hope of a tame bear. He did domesticate two wolves and was particularly proud of his magnificent peacock who

> possessed a sort of pride in showing himself. . . .
> These animals were of no use to us, they were an expense; but I always liked to have such things to show our friends and visitors . . . for they combined, as it were, the nature of the forest and . . . the romantic scenery.

From the company of militia in Whitefield Crawford bought a small piece of artillery which he erected on a mound called Giant's Grave behind his barn. His far neighbors came to recognize the distant booming that echoed from crag to crag as "Crawford's homemade thunder" from Crawford's own Notch.

> After I was sixteen my father improved a little in living. When I was a little over twenty-one I got me a wife—we was both Poor—three knives, three forks, three tea cups, three chairs, a poor bed—hardly could we keep house. But our courage was good—my wife always standing by me, through all my trouble and trials—shoulder to shoulder—heart & hand from the day of our marriage until the day of her Death. No man never had a better wife than I had—always kind to the Poor and to all her relations. She is now in the Grave Yard, and my judgment is, she is well prepared for the next world—and for the good feeling I have had for her for over fifty-six years, I have Erected a monument over her grave weighing 7 tons, and twenty-one feet high—it is a splendid monument—cost me over six hundred dollars.

Once the land had yielded its stumps and boulders to men with as much granite in their own make-up, it was kind to the settlers. During the short growing season nature also must work hard, especially in the hills where so many of the early settlers chose to live. The higher land, they thought, was safer, healthier and more pleasant; certainly it was drier and easier to clear. Covered with hardwood whose stumps decayed more quickly than those of the soft timber in the wet lowlands, the soil was so rich with mold that a settler could expect a yield of fifteen to twenty-five and even forty bushels of wheat per acre the year after he had cleared it. Few hills were too steep for scythe or sickle. The narrow valleys with their spring freshets, their beaver dams and tangled underbrush were often unsuitable for cultivation or for roads which on the hills remained passable with little attention. A farmer could increase the value of 100 acres eight to ten times with the crops he raised in a few years of diligent labor.

What the settlers achieved in high country way beyond and above what historian Toynbee has called the belt of optimum challenge seems extraordinary. Winter wheat, winter and spring rye, barley, oats, Indian corn, hemp, flax, red and white clover, timothy, peas, parsnips, carrots, turnips, cabbage, potatoes, pumpkins; beef, pork, butter, cheese and maple sugar—all this sprang from the dark soil bordering the gray stone walls. And the plank-sided farmhouse sheltered as abundant a crop of children to share the work in the freest and, in some respects, happiest domestic scene this country has ever known.

The years from the end of the Revolution to the War of 1812 are often called the Age of Homespun, for millponds, and water wheels had not yet drawn the people out of the hills. Virtually everything they ate, they grew; almost everything they used, they made; almost everything they wore came from the factory of the hearthside. Every hand was needed every daylight hour of the year if the family was to survive and prosper in an environment it created almost to the last detail. The men drove their oxen or horses with homemade ox yokes or collars from barns they had built into fields they had cleared and planted; fed them with grain they had raised and watered them from wells they had dug through wooden pipes they had bored with home-made augers. The women, according to Hemenway's *Gazetteer,*

> picked their own wool, carded their own rolls, spun their own yarn, drove their own looms, made their own cloth, cut, made and mended their own garments, dipped their own candles, made their own soap, bottomed their own chairs, braided their own baskets, wove their own carpets, quilts and coverlets, picked their own geese, milked their own cows, fed their own calves, and went visiting or to meeting on their own feet.

There were people who from the time they were born until the time they were laid away in their Sunday dresses never saw what was beyond the mountains. Their children worked from the time they could do the simplest chores until they were married and had children, and they taught in turn that to live was to work. An abiding sense of fulfillment came from their labors and from the knowledge that each was dependent upon the other, and because everyone was needed from the youngest tot carrying in the wood to the grandmother knitting in her rocker, contentment and a sense of security pervaded the homestead.

The hiker who climbs the hills and mountains arrayed in battalions throughout the entire length of central Vermont and northern New Hampshire, looking on stone walls wandering aimlessly under the canopy of a great forest, or cellar holes bordered with hollyhocks and apple trees in a pocket of sunshine miles from the nearest village, needs to know that from 1781 to 1810 the population of Vermont grew from 30,000 to 200,000 people and that here, in splendid or not so splendid isolation, many of them were living. In a few decades they would move on with the frontier, but by this time the independence, the spirit and the disciplines of life in the hills would have become part of them.

IX

NOBODY'S WAR

Such was the optimism of Portsmouth's 5,339 people in the year 1800 that they built a great public pier supporting a three-story building which held fourteen shops. This structure standing over the swirling tides lengthened State or Buck Street by 340 feet and served notice upon the new century that this thrifty town with its 626 dwellings was to become a great port. It was the stem which siphoned from the sea the wealth of far countries.

The cluster of buildings that adjoined or faced the bustling pier—among them the New Hampshire Hotel, counting houses, coopers' shops and sail lofts—overlooked that year a trading fleet of some 28 ships, 47 brigs, 10 schooners and 1 barque. An observer of the great parade of June 26, 1788, celebrating New Hampshire's adoption of the Federal Constitution need not have sniffed the coffee, molasses, tar and hemp of the waterfront to know that this was every inch a port. The blacksmiths and nailers with their forges and anvils rolled past, shipwrights and calkers with their tools, ropemakers with hemp around their waists, riggers, mastmakers, shipjoiners, blockmakers, brass founders and coppersmiths, instrument makers with their compasses, carvers, painters, glaziers, plumbers, coopers, stevedores, pilots carrying spyglasses and charts, captains with their quadrants, seamen, and "the ship *Union* completely rigged, armed and manned, under an easy sail with colours flying, elevated on a carriage drawn by nine horses."

The 54-gun *Falkland* rose on Portsmouth stocks as early as 1690, the *Bedford* galley in 1696, the 40-gun *America* in 1749; and for the Continental Navy, the *Raleigh* in 1776, the *Ranger* in 1777, and the 74-gun *America* in 1782. No single individual was involved more deeply in the port and its destiny than the prince of the chosen few, John Langdon, who to his colleagues must have seemed enviably resourceful in enriching himself in the public service while maintaining his stature as a statesman. Certainly his grand dwelling on Pleasant Street—a palace to young Elizabeth Buckmaster, who remembered the pageantry beyond the gate in the years after the Revolution—had not been built on a senator's salary. "And there at the gate of the palace," recalled Elizabeth, "stood daily the chariot and the liveried servants, and the lady [Mrs. Langdon] came forth, stately, powdered, too delicate to press the rough earth with her foot; and when she was seated the two liveried negroes stood behind and thus the pageant passed on."

Langdon had chafed in his role as New Hampshire's representative to the Continental Congress at the beginning of the war, for he wanted to be appointed continental agent for marine affairs in New Hampshire with supervision over privateering. "You say you will re-sign your seat in Congress rather than not have the Agency," William Whipple wrote. "If my advice can have any weight with you, you certainly will not. Such a step would have an avaricious appearance, and on the other hand there cannot be a greater evidence of Patriot-ism than preferring the public good to one's private interest."

Ignoring this advice Langdon accepted, in 1776, the appointment as agent of prizes for the colony of New Hampshire, and thus became director-general in that quarter of the exciting and extremely lucrative business of building and sailing privateers and of dividing the loot between owner, captain and crew. Langdon's biographer, Lawrence Shaw Mayo, quotes a letter from the indignant Whipple describing an entire countryside in a fever of privateering. Indian corn was $6 a bushel because the farmers had gone to sea. No less than five pri-vateers were fitting out at Portsmouth and needed 400 more men to man them. The United States Navy was in danger of annihilation because the officers and men were all resigning to take command of privateers. Navy ships, in Whipple's opinion, would as a consequence soon be officered by "Tinkers, Shoemakers and Horse Jockeys."

Langdon was involved in every department of privateering, from building the raiders in his shipyard to dividing the spoils. He also undertook to build the largest ship in the Continental Navy, the *America*. Work began in 1777. Two years later she had not yet been launched and seemed doomed to rot. Apparently this was not Lang-don's fault; he had all kinds of trouble getting money from Congress and guns from the Naval Committee. In any case, when John Paul Jones arrived in Portsmouth to take command of her in August, 1779, he found to his horror that the *America* was not half finished, nor were the needed materials on hand. Taking over as superintendent of construction, Jones called the long seasons he spent completing the ship "the most lingering and disagreeable service" he was charged with during the period of the Revolution. He seems to have fought bitterly with Langdon as continental agent and he once charged him with having on hand $10,000 of government money which he was spending for his own ships instead of the *America*. Just how Langdon managed this, if indeed he did, and escaped with impunity is not clear. Of course the privateers were accomplishing much toward serving national safety and protection (as well as not-so-enlightened self-interest) since the enemy ships they removed from the sea lanes were craft that the tiny Continental Navy would not have had to worry about.

This largest ship yet built in America was finally launched in 1782 by nearly five hundred men before an audience who looked with kindling eyes upon her splendid lines. Her female figurehead was crowned with laurels. The forefinger of her upraised arm pointed to Heaven, while around her legs circled rings of smoke depicting the terrors of battle.

Other splendid decorations caught the eyes of landlubbers who understood little about the galleries and gunports of a ship. Under her stern windows two carved figures depicting Tyranny and Oppression were shown biting the dust while over their heads waved the triumphant liberty cap. Elsewhere there were large figures of Mars, Neptune, and Wisdom surrounded by dangerous flashes of lightning.

Poor Jones! After all his heroic work he never sailed his good ship. Congress, casting about for a suitable gesture of appreciation for France's comradeship in arms, presented the *America* to the French squadron to replace the 74-gun *Magnifique* which it had lost. Thus sailed away the American Navy's only ship of the line. Actually she had been the second of the ships of the Piscataqua with which Jones had acquaintance. In 1777 Congress had appointed the gallant sailor commander of the locally built *Ranger*, to which he added so many extra spars and so much canvas that, despite sheer "as delicate as the lines of a pretty woman's arm," she was dangerously topheavy. Jones's second lieutenant Elijah Hall of Portsmouth, testified after a voyage to Nantes: "I have sailed with many captains in all kinds of voyages, but I have never seen a ship crowded as Captain Jones drove the *Ranger*. . . . Imagine . . . the situation of the *Ranger's* crew, with a topheavy and crank ship under their feet, and a commander who day and night insisted on every rag she could stagger under without laying clear down." The captain reported to the Naval Committee that it was the honor of his ship to receive from the French fleet the first salute accorded any American naval vessel. The *Ranger* later distinguished herself in company with two other ships in capturing prizes worth about a million dollars.

When a single prize yielded a profit of $328,721, as did one of the many cargoes captured by Portsmouth's *Fox*, the origin of the town's many architectural gems becomes apparent. John Langdon owned three raiders outright and in his strategic position as agent for prizes probably had an interest in as many more. In view of the opprobrium that today accompanies disclosure of a gift to a public official it seems remarkable that an entrepreneur could then be scooping riches off the sea with one long arm and encircling the choicest public offices with the other. Langdon served twice as chief executive of New Hampshire, presided over the first United States Senate, was invited by Jefferson to become secretary of the navy, a post which he refused, as he did the Republican party's offer of the vice-presidency in 1812. He had his enemies but none, apparently, among the principal officers of the country. George Washington, arriving in Portsmouth to pay his repects in 1789, was lavishly feted by all the dignitaries that the new aristocracy could muster, including General Sullivan and Langdon, with whom the President "made an excursion down the harbour; the seamen who rowed the barge in which the President went were dressed in white. . . . The gentlemen composing the band followed at a short distance and performed several select pieces of music on the water."

In 1795 when Jay's Treaty, forbidding large ships to trade with Britain or her dependencies, was ratified, a loud dissent arose from Portsmouth, for it had been doing very well exporting lumber, fish, livestock and agricultural products and importing molasses, rum, sugar, cocoa, coffee and salt. Two effigies in profile of Jay and Livermore, whittled by William Deering, the Water Street carver, were accompanied by drum and fife and 300 indignant citizens to Warner's wharf, the scene of their "execution" and burning. The events leading up to the generally unpopular War of 1812 were not quite so unpopular with the owners, captains and crews of the privateers whose business not only revived but increased manyfold. While the value of the cargoes carried in regular trade by Portsmouth's 22,000 tons of regular shipping plummeted from $795,000 in 1806 to $125,000 in

1808, the billowing sails of schooner-rigged privateers brought new windfalls to the port after war was declared, and rather confused public thinking about national policies. In little more than a month one vessel averaged almost a prize a day. Another captured twenty in thirty days. The 100-odd raiders with the 3,000 seamen who sailed them out of Portsmouth during the Revolution and the War of 1812 had enough action to last them a lifetime and left a rich legacy of adventure, not only to Portsmouth but to Exeter, Durham, Dover and Berwick. These tidewater towns produced thousands of tons of shipping; Exeter alone built twenty-one vessels in nine years, the largest of which was the square-sterned *Hercules*, a 500-ton three-decker 112 feet long.

Early in June, 1813, on her third voyage, the privateer *Thomas* captured the *Liverpool Packet* after a six-hour chase and brought her to Portsmouth. The bête noire of the northern coast, this ship had in two days during the previous December captured no less than ten American craft which she took to Halifax. That she was British was not of particular consequence—what made her a menace was her captain, an American named York who knew the local harbors and sailing lanes as well as the palm of his hand. Rumors persisted that this hybrid raider was at least partly owned by some gentlemen in Boston. The crafty turncoat at the helm had in seven months captured 481 American ships. In an especially daring sortie to the very front door of Portsmouth her crew had even stolen drying fish from the Newcastle flakes, or staging, and left a note explaining that this was the work of the *Liverpool Packet* and that the crew were united in "lending their regards to the people of the town for thus providing for our wants."

So it was a great day for Portsmouth when Captain Shaw of the *Thomas* brought her in. Sold and renamed the *Portsmouth Packet* she set forth in September under command of Captain William Watson of Dover only to fall prey, within forty-eight hours, to the British brig *Phantom*. Conveyed to Halifax, she set sail once again as a British raider. Meanwhile, as William G. Saltonstall relates in *Ports of Piscataqua*, the windjammer *Thomas*, which had originally bagged the *Liverpool Packet*, was herself captured by the British and renamed *Wolverine*. The loss of his namesake did not, however, dishearten Captain Thomas Shaw. Commanding the brigantine

Portsmouth, the harbor's largest privateer and the enemy's most nagging worry (they called her "Devil's Ship Invincible" and the "Ally of the Imp"), he nearly recouped the loss of the *Thomas* in one haul in October, 1814; the British ship *James*, with supplies for the army in Canada—powder, printing presses, glass, rum, gin, tea, pickles, mustard and nuts—valued at $15,000.

They say that a maid named Colbath set the fire because Mrs. Woodward, her employer, took from her some bottles of wine that she had received from a gentleman boarder. "I'll burn her out!" swore the spiteful domestic. Soon thereafter Mrs. Woodward's barn was in flames, then surrounding structures and finally, it seemed, the whole town, as a furious wind bore burning chips from roof to roof. By midnight, December 22, 1813, narrow State Street was a vast arch of orange fire so lighting the sky that its reflection was seen in Providence, 100 miles to the southwest, and as far to the northeast as Windsor, Vermont. The next morning virtually all that stood in fifteen blackened acres were the ruins of 64 stores and shops, 100 barns, and 108 dwellings, among them the home of the rising young lawyer, Daniel Webster.

The fire was a symbol of an even more disastrous loss to Portsmouth that the citizens were not yet aware of. After the War of 1812 economic tides swept shipping to the south and the captains, crews and merchants in the countinghouses of the old town on the Piscataqua had to accept the fact that the greatest entries in its log as a commercial port had already been made.

2

When representatives of the New England states gathered behind closed doors at Hartford, Connecticut, in December, 1814, to vent their grievances about Mr. Madison's war, particularly the embargo, it is curious that only three of the delegates came from New Hampshire and Vermont, and these were not authorized to attend by their legislatures as were the twelve from Massachusetts, the eleven from Connecticut, and the four from Rhode Island. And yet the ban on trade affected no people more adversely than those of Vermont, the geography of which divides into at least as many parts as ancient Gaul.

Lake Champlain flows north and so did the trade of the valley, for the canal south to the Hudson had not yet been built. Many of the people did what citizens of any free government are likely to do when faced with meaningless and oppressive laws—ignore them. Smuggling goods to the Canadians was, however, one thing; entering into what appeared to many to be the treasonable associations of the Hartford Convention was quite another. The people of Vermont were, of course, not all of a mind about the war; their outlook depended upon self-interest and politics—whether they were Federalist or Democrat, anti-French or anti-British. In the present-day environment of strong central government it is hard to conceive of the rampant regionalism of the early nineteenth century, particularly during a senseless war. Comprehension of this is necessary if one is to regard the burlesque of a British army fed with American beef as anything less than the most heinous treason. If Americans were not dying at the hands of British soldiers, the preposterous spectacle of a Canada-bound lumber raft half a mile long loaded with supplies protected by 500 Yankees and a floating bulletproof fort might seem faintly amusing.

Many Vermonters in the contraband belt near the border did not feel that they were trading with the enemy, but with friends and neighbors across the line. The only way most of them could raise any cash to settle their debts and pay taxes was through the sale of potash in Montreal. This was frequently traded for salt, which the settlers needed most desperately, embargo or no embargo. On November 3, 1811, a young father from St. Albans named Brooks, while rowing a skiff load of salt across the border, was chased by the customs officials and driven into shoal water. When the government agents demanded that he surrender, Brooks said that he had only five bushels of salt belonging to five different families who needed it to cure their pork. He would willingly pay the duties if the agents would only let him bring it in. The customs men would not hear of this and demanded that he surrender the boat. Brooks replied that they would have to catch him first and began to row as fast as he could; whereupon the revenue men, maneuvering their boat as close as possible, fired a load of shot at him point-blank. Opening his shirt and baring his breast, which had received twelve bullets, Brooks exclaimed, "See what they have done!" and fell forward dead, covering the salt bags with his blood.

While such violence against unoffending citizens greatly inflamed the people against the government and the War Hawks, bitter feeling arose among the rank-and-file patriots of '76 against opportunists of the Federalist antiwar party who were profiting handsomely from wholesale smuggling. No democrat prayed at the gallows in Burlington for a hardened brigand named Dean who was hanged for killing revenue officers while he was running potash in a boat called the *Black Snake*.

Even less that was just, honorable and glorious can be said for the War of 1812 than for most wars. The New England states would not allow their militias outside their own borders; many southern politicians were fearful that victory might bring Canada into the Union and destroy the zealously guarded balance of power south of Mason and Dixon's line. It has been charged that old generals were sent up to the border, not to advance and conquer, but merely to march their troops back and forth. But America and England were committed to fight. Inevitably Britain would invade the Champlain valley; inescapably America would have to rise to its defense. At dawn, November 20, 1812, a detachment of an army of 5,000 under General Dearborn mistook the New York militia for the enemy and waged a spirited fight until the British appeared. In the ensuing confusion the bulk of the American Army narrowly escaped annihilation and left many dead on the field as they fled south of the border. This closed a year of even more humiliating and disastrous campaigns in the West. Although 1813 was far more satisfactory in that quarter with victories on land and water, such as that of Captain Oliver Perry on Lake Erie, the Champlain valley army of 4,000 under General Wade Hampton twiddled its thumbs all summer, met defeat at the hands of a small enemy force just over the border, and shrank back to the security of winter quarters. Ships of the enemy fleet raided Plattsburg and sailed across the lake to shell Burlington.

The situation was even worse during most of 1814. Sir George Prevost arrived in Canada with one of the strongest armies ever sent to America, some 14,000 troops, many of them veterans of the Napoleonic Wars. In August Prevost reported to England that "two thirds of the army in Canada are at this moment eating beef provided by

American contractors, drawn principally from the states of Vermont and New York." Western New Hampshire joined in this lucrative trade and Massachusetts and Connecticut would have done so on a grand scale if their cattle had not had to travel so far. "Like herds of buffalos they press through the forests making paths for themselves," complained the American commander, powerless to seal a border which leaked all manner of merchandise in dozens of places—horses, furs, even masts and spars for the British Navy! Certainly there were profits to be made—the Federalists might say this much for a mock half-war that seemed to hold little danger, until it was almost too late.

With supreme unconcern for the northeastern frontier the War Department ordered General George Izard (who had replaced Wade Hampton) with two thirds of his 6,000 troops to the Niagara frontier just when he was beginning to make something of the Plattsburg defenses. His protests to the government, about the game of military musical chairs it was playing with its generals and about the disastrous consequences of this folly, went unheeded, and Izard marched away. Soldiers of the third brigade of the third division of the Vermont militia had no sooner crossed the lake to help fill the void than Governor Martin Chittenden ordered them home on the grounds that they had left Vermont's own frontier unprotected. Whereupon Colonel Luther Dixon and seventeen of his officers of the third brigade signed and dispatched a stinging renunciation of the Governor's orders.

> . . . we humbly conceive that when we are ordered into the service of the United States it becomes our duty . . . to march to the defense of any section of the Union. We are not of that class who believe that our duty as citizens or soldiers are circumscribed within the narrow limits of the Town or State in which we reside, but that we are under a paramount obligation to our common country, to the great confederation of States. . . . Viewing the subject in this light, we conceive it our duty to declare unequivocally to your Excellency, that we shall not obey your Excellency's order for returning, but shall continue in the service of our country until we are legally and honorably discharged.

The defiant brigade stayed on and there was not much the outraged Chittenden, at the head of a politically divided legislature, could do about it. This thoroughgoing Federalist felt that the war had been brought on "under circumstances which forcibly induced a great proportion of the people to consider it at least doubtful as to its necessity, expedience or justice" and that peace ought to replace "a protracted, expensive and destructive war." As the military outlook grew gloomier Chittenden relented to the extent of calling for volunteers for the federal army. At Burlington, the main base and headquarters of the army's northern department, an epidemic began to spread through the troops encamped on the battery. Their officers, gazing across the blue lake that had borne so many confident and spirited, sick and ragged armies to victory or annihilation, must have wondered how destiny would deal with them.

There was at least one bright façade to a scene grimy with politics and military mismanagement: Thomas MacDonough, a young naval lieutenant who had arrived in 1812 under much the same circumstances as Benedict Arnold in the Revolution, to do what he might for Lake Champlain's navy, then consisting of two rotting gunboats— "my poor forlorn-looking squadron," as he called it. With the help of fifteen ship carpenters from New York he went to work near Burlington, at Shelburne Harbor, during the winter months of 1813 and by spring sailed out of the bay with three sloops and the refitted gunboats, carrying in all 38 guns. Two of the sloops were lost in action north of the border on the Richelieu River during the summer and their crews of 112 were captured, so MacDonough had only three vessels left by fall.

Seeking a hideaway far out of range of British guns where he might build and plan for the summer of 1814 he sailed seven miles up the winding, placid Otter Creek to Vergennes, the end of navigation. During the winter of 1814 the shore of the basin below the frozen waterfall was a scene of frantic industry. With money from the government, the help of two ingenious New York shipbuilders, Adam and Noah Brown, as well as iron from the mines of Monkton and timber from the hinterlands, the eight forges, blast and air furnaces and rolling mill of Vergennes, MacDonough produced a fleet in eight months. In five and a half days 110 men cut the timber for three ships, the largest of which, the *Saratoga*, was launched forty days after her heavy keelson and planks were growing in the woods. Fittings and armament that could not be made locally were hauled from Troy on wagons; one heavy consignment required eighty teams to draw it from Troy to Vergennes. Late in May MacDonough's 26-gun *Saratoga* sailed into the lake followed by the 16-gun *Ticonderoga* (designed as a steamboat but transformed into a schooner); one sloop and six gunboats. A 20-gun brig, also built at Vergennes, two sloops and five more 75-foot gunboats later joined the fleet. The 900-man British fleet in the Richelieu River consisted of 16 vessels, compared with MacDonough's 17, but the royal flagship *Confiance*, 37 guns, built at Isle aux Noix, outclassed the American *Saratoga*.

During the late summer the Americans were trying desperately to fill the void in their lines occasioned by General Izard's last-minute departure for the west with 4,000 troops at the behest of the transcendentally wise general staff. To match Sir George Prevost's 14,000 troops at Isle aux Noix (twice as many as in the army of John Burgoyne), General Alexander Macomb, replacing Izard, had at the end of August 3,400 men, 1,400 of whom were sick. Of the remainder only 1,500 were well trained. To the General's desperate call for help some 2,000 yeomen on the farms and villages on both sides of the lake seized their muskets and shipped for Plattsburg.

The last great clash of men and ships on the ancient highway of nations took place on Sunday, October 11, 1814. As Sir George Prevost's huge army advanced on Plattsburg, Captain George Downie sailed his fleet south around Cumberland Head to engage the ships of MacDonough anchored in the town's harbor. The first shattering volley from the British flagship silenced most of the *Saratoga's* starboard guns and put a fifth of her crew out of action. MacDonough was nearly killed by a shattered spar. Later the severed head of a gunman hit him with such force that he fell prostrate on the deck. All was chaos in the bright sunshine—smoke and blood and the groans of the dying. MacDonough managed to slip the *Saratoga's* cable, swing her about and bring her port guns to bear upon the *Confiance*; one of her sailors reported that compared to what followed, Trafalgar was a "mere fleabite." Captain Downie was killed. The rigging of the *Confiance* hung in shreds. When she struck her colors her hull was breached in 105 places. The Yankee farmers behind the cannon in their sloops and gunboats realized, incredulously, that the lake was theirs. Their compatriots ashore, fearfully outnumbered, took heart as well and by evening the King's 14,000 troops, shocked at the loss of their fleet, were retreating as madly as the legions of Abercrombie had retreated at Ticonderoga in the French War.

Whether American contractors fed the retreating British Army with beef is not clear; the drums of victory rather muffled the cries of Federalists. From the steamboat *Vermont,* the first in regular service after Fulton's *Clermont,* the hero of Plattsburg stepped onto the Burlington wharf amidst cheers and booming artillery and rode in an elegant coach to the coffee house with an evergreen sprig in his hat. Festooned with flowers and compliments, nearly drowned with toasts, the man whom Theodore Roosevelt called the foremost naval figure down to the Civil War, responded "with that modesty and dignity so conspicuous in his character."

X

WHAT THEY DID THERE

And what were they doing when peace veiled the valleys of the Connecticut, the Merrimack, Ashuelot, Contoocook, Souhegan, Battenkill, Wallomsac, Ottauqueechee, Winooski, Missisquoi, Lamoille, the Otter and the Lemon Fair? Raising cattle, horses and sheep, carding and weaving, tinkering, quarrying stone, cutting trees, digging canals and building boats and ships.

Early in the nineteenth century they began coming down out of the hills to the millponds. Let there be a creek or stream and a dam with a rumbling water wheel and there was a town, for what was a farmer without a gristmill, a housewife without boughten woolens, a lumberman without the up-and-down saw that water from the hills kept in almost perpetual motion? The images and traditions of the Age of Homespun slowly faded as cord roads and turnpikes wandered through the remote valleys and later came the railroads' net of iron. Yankees could and did subsist on self-sufficient farms, but contented and prosperous Yankees were Yankees in trade. Wheat, flour, pork, butter, cheese and beef were products with which hillcountry farmers turned early profits. In 1808 Vermonters drove 12,000 to 15,000 head of cattle to the Boston market.

One does not mention horses as a crop without alluding to the vigorous Morgan, as intimate a feature of the northern landscape as the rock maple. He was named after his owner, Justin Morgan, who brought him to Randolph in 1788. The original horse is the despair of geneticists, since his unique characteristics sprang full-bodied from unknown parentage and he was able to pass them all on. This happens so rarely in the animal kingdom, where new types evolve slowly through countless generations, that it can scarcely be said to happen at all, yet through some remarkable mutation it did happen to Justin Morgan. It was almost as if nature had suddenly decided to have a new type of horse and created him on the spot.

A dark bay whose legs, mane and tail were black, he weighed 950 pounds and was about 15 hands high. A broad forehead and small ears were the noteworthy features of his lean, straight face; his back and neck were short, his shoulder blades and hip bones oblique and long, his loins muscular. He walked fast, trotted with an extremely smooth, short and spirited step, raising his feet only slightly but never stumbling, and on short courses could run like the wind—as owners of long-legged race horses found out. He was gentle and playful but disliked children and hated dogs, whom he chased out of sight every chance he got. His strength and endurance became legendary. By the time horse fanciers began to inquire into his pedigree (there was none) Justin Morgan, the man, was dead and many conflicting stories and theories about the origin of Justin Morgan, the horse, gained credence. Justin Morgan's son claimed the horse was sired by True Briton, an Arabian horse, which may account for some of his characteristics. He founded, in any case, the stable of Morgan, and a mighty one it turned out to be.

In his book on the origin, history and accomplishments of this breed, D. C. Linsley quotes a letter written in 1812 from one Solomon Steele, who before moving to Derby Line had often seen the lively bay in Randolph. Justin Morgan was then a poor man and at the time of the incident described to Steele by a neighbor, Nathan Nye, Morgan had rented his namesake for $15 a year to a man named Evans, who was using the colt to clear fifteen acres of heavy timber.

At the time Evans had this horse, a small tavern, a gristmill and sawmill were in operation on the branch of the White River in Randolph, and in this place the strength of men and horses in that settlement were generally tested. On one occasion I went to these mills where I spent most of the day and during the time many trials were had for small wagers to draw a certain pine log which lay some 10 rods from the sawmill. Some horses were hitched to it that would weigh 1200 pounds, but not one of them could move it a length. About dusk Evans came down from his logging field which was nearby, and I told him the particulars of the drawing match. Evans requested me to show him the log, which I did. He then ran back to the tavern and challenged the company to bet a gallon of rum that he could not draw the log fairly onto the logway at three pulls with his colt.

The challenge was promptly accepted and each having "taken a glass", the whole company went down to the spot. Arrived on the ground, Evans said, "I am ashamed to hitch my horse to a little log like that, but if three of you will get on and ride, if I don't draw it, I will forfeit the rum". Accordingly three of those least able to stand were placed upon the log. I was present with a lantern and cautioned those on the log to look out for their legs, as I had seen the horse draw before and knew something had to come. At the word of command the horse started, log and men, and went more than half of the distance before stopping. At the next pull he landed his load at the spot agreed upon to the astonishment of all present. Not many days after this the beaten party proposed to Evans to run a certain horse against his, 80 rods for another gallon. Evans accepted, went from his work, and matched his horse against four different horses the same evening and beat them with ease.

Justin Morgan more than met the demands of a long, hard life in every kind of service under all conditions in the hands of many owners. After his namesake's death he was purchased by William Rice of Woodstock and used as a farm horse for two years until 1800 or 1801, when he was sold to Robert Evans (the man who had hired him from Justin Morgan). In 1804 Evans was sued for debt and the horse became the property of John Goss of St. Johnsbury, who turned him over to his brother. Under David Goss Justin sired a number of colts and further distinguished himself in heavy work and in a drawing match against much larger horses at General Butler's tavern in St. Johnsbury. Goss sold him to his son, Philip, who sold him to one Langmeade. As one of an overworked six-horse team hauling freight from Windsor to Chelsea, the aging black bay became poor and thin and was turned over to a Mr. Chelsea, who traded him to Joel Goss of Claremont, who in turn sold him to Samuel Stone of Randolph. Here he remained two or three years until 1819, when he was sold to Levi Bean. He died at Chelsea in 1821 at twenty-nine years—not of old age, it is said, but from infection resulting from the kick of another horse while running in an open yard.

By this time the progeny of the horse who better transmitted his characteristics than perhaps any other in history were numerous and distinguished in whatever capacity they served. They were to be seen on long stage runs, such as from Boston to Portland, or hauling cars on New York's Sixth Avenue railroad. The New York *Herald* in 1853 stated that four fifths of all horses employed on that line were Morgans from Vermont and New Hampshire and that they were not only strong for their size but could withstand hard labor that would break down the strongest draft horse. Spirited Morgans helped not only to conquer the West but carried the Union cavalry to battle in the Civil War.

In his *Morgan Horses* Linsley tells the charming story of a mid-nineteenth-century journey by stage through the White Mountains.

The near horse was of a deep chestnut color, about 14 and a half hands high, very closely and compactly made, with a clean, small head and exceedingly small ears set pretty wide apart, very lively and active. The other animal was a gray mare of about the same weight, but at least half a hand higher . . . and she was on the whole a very fair animal, although her muscular development was decidedly inferior to that of her mate. . . .

The mare was impatient and my friend declared that what all horseflesh of her dimensions could do she would. My own fancy had been taken by the . . . chestnut. Accordingly I proposed to back this horse. The driver, after several false starts from the barroom, finally took up the reins and gave them the word. The mare dashed ahead as if she would pull the driver from his seat. The horse struck out with a short nervous step, but did not seem much inclined to pull or move at any but a moderate pace. The mare took us along over the first half mile almost entirely by the bit. My companions laughed at my chestnut horse. A half hour passed and with it some five miles of road. By this time bets were not so freely offered on the mare. She had fallen off on her pace, perspired freely and every few moments gave her head a toss. . . . The day was hot. The horse had worked more freely as he grew warm, but not a muscle moved save those ears. Thus we kept on for about 12 or 14 miles to the end of the first stage, the mare fully satisfied and panting with heat and exertion. Here we were to have a fresh team, but one of them being very lame from a sprain, the driver put in only one, and drove the chestnut through to St. Johnsbury . . . the horse did not appear to mind it in the least, and up the long hill as we entered St. Johnsbury, he pressed on at the same short, nervous trot he had kept almost the entire way.

As we stepped out at the hotel we all took a good look at him. His general appearance was that of a horse about ten years old, but what was our surprise when . . . we learned that he was one of Sherman's [a foal of Justin] sons, 18 years old, and had been running constantly nearly 11 years in the stage team.

Horses, yes, and, until after the Civil War, sheep with golden fleeces covering the hillsides of farmers always ready to experiment. In 1802 Chancellor Robert Livingston imported the first three Merinos, a buck and two ewes, to his manor on the Hudson. David Humphreys,

American minister to Spain, brought in 200 more but these were rather too few to start a revolution at a time when the States were accustomed to receiving wool from England's fine flocks. When the Embargo Act shut off this supply, William Jarvis, Humphreys's successor as American minister at Madrid, arranged to have no less than 4,000 of the finest sheep in Spain shipped to America. He gave two each to President Madison and former President Jefferson and, after selling the preponderance of them at very high prices in New York and Massachusetts, brought 350 to his Connecticut River farm at Wethersfield in 1810.

> They were driven overland to Vermont by a Spanish shepherd, a dark alien-looking man who wore unfamiliar clothes and looked like a picture out of the Old Testament. He looked neither to the right or left as the people of the countryside came to watch, but passed gravely along with eyes only for the fine backs of his flock, which he urged on with unintelligible singing words.

Soon Merinos replaced the nondescript native breeds and by the 1830's the hills of the northcountry were alive with them. At the height of the woolgathering mania in 1840 there were more than 2,250,000 sheep in Vermont and New Hampshire, two thirds of them in the valleys of the Green Mountains and along the shores of Lake Champlain. One farmer refused an offer of $10,000 for his best ram and another is said to have declined a fortune—$50,000—for a flock of 200 Merinos. Today's traveler, finding with astonishment a splendid Greek Revival house with a portico and faded pillars way off in the back beyond, may be sure that it is a house that Merinos built.

Rowland Robinson, born in the heart of the sheep country, wrote romantically of those prosperous days when Vermont (in whose climate this animal and its coat grew even more splendidly than in Spain) was the wool capital of the country.

> Shearing-time was the great festival of the year. The shearers, many of whom were often the flock-owners' well-to-do neighbors, were treated more as guests than as laborers, and the best the house afforded was set before them. The great barns' empty bays and scaffolds resounded with the busy click of incessant shears, the jokes, songs, and laughter of the merry shearers, the bleating of the ewes

and lambs, and the twitter of disturbed swallows, while the sunlight, shot through crack and knot-hole, swung slowly around the dusty interior in sheets and bars of gold that dialed the hours from morning till evening.

The value of wool as a prize cash crop before it was lost to the western prairies after the Civil War, was its nearness to the mills where it was carded and woven. Almost as indelible an image as the white church and the village green is the upland country's valley mill, its moss-covered stones and adz-scarred beams confessing great age. Sometimes it is of brick with many windows and a bell or clock tower, a fortlike memento of the days before the Civil War when wool was king and, for all anybody knew, always would be. Much more rarely in farm country with tentative designs on manufacturing, it was a colossus running on for blocks, as in Manchester, Nashua and Winooski. Rare was the article with a market that could not be made under the maze of shafts turned by the water wheel through clacking belts of leather; but the products that could be grown at the back door of the factory and emerge finished out the front were pre-eminent. Wool was one of these.

Water power was first applied to the carding of wool in 1794 and by 1815 in Vermont alone 139 carding mills and 15,000 hand looms were taking advantage of Jefferson's embargo on British goods. But this output was trifling compared with the miles of cloth that later issued from country mills at Queechee, Cavendish, Springfield and Ludlow (to name but a few of the Green Mountains' one hundred textile towns).

Of all such factories in New England or America none was greater than Amoskeag, with its boundless pavilions of brick on both sides of the Merrimack at Manchester. It was not typical of New Hampshire, even less of Vermont with its farms and small industries, but it happened that at Derryfield, as Manchester was once known, the Merrimack made available a vast source of water power, and Boston capitalists, a reservoir of capital to develop it.

In 1793 an old man named Samuel Blodgett began building a canal around the "hideous waterfall." He was in his eighties when he finished it fourteen years later but well in possession of his faculties, for he declared: "As the country increases in population we must have manufactures, and here, at my canal, will be a manufacturing town that shall be the Manchester of America." By 1810 a company was in business called "Proprietors of the Amoskeag Cotton and Wool Manufactory." Twenty-one years later, when it became the Amoskeag Manufacturing Company, it owned all the water power between Concord and Manchester and all the land at the 60-foot falls. A stone dam replaced the old one of wood and canals led the water behind it to a complex of wheels in an ever-growing community of factories. Within five decades it became so vast and various an enterprise, with its picker houses, miles of spindles, its machine shops and foundries, that the river was dwarfed in a canyon of brick. Textiles were dominant but there were also paper mills, an ax plant, a fire-engine factory, and even a locomotive works which built 252 glittering iron horses in 1859.

The most meaningful account of the people who labored in the dim and dusty corridors of these factories prior to the Civil War and before the arrival of armies of immigrants, was written by Harriet H. Robinson. While she had the downriver factory town of Lowell specifically in mind, what she wrote was quite as revealing of the lives of laborers of Manchester and Nashua, early an industrious cotton center. Stories of ready work and regular pay in these burgeoning communities

> reached the ears of mechanics' and farmers' sons [and] gave new life to lonely and dependent women in distant towns and farmhouses. Into this Yankee El Dorado these needy people began to pour by the various modes of travel known to those slow old days. The stage coach and the canal-boat came every day, always filled with new recruits for the army of useful people. The mechanic and machinist came, each with his home-made chest of tools and his wife and little ones. The widow came with her little flock and her scanty housekeeping goods to open a boarding-house or variety store. . . . Some . . . were daughters of professional men or teachers, whose mothers, left widows, were struggling to maintain the younger children. A few were the daughters of persons in reduced circumstances. . . . There were others who seemed to have mysterious antecedents, and to be hiding from something; and strange and distinguished looking men and women sometimes came to call upon

them. Many farmers' daughters came to earn money to complete
their wedding outfit, or buy the bride's share of housekeeping
articles. . . . Into the barren homes many of them had left [money]
went like a quiet stream, carrying with it beauty and refreshment.
The mortgage was lifted from the homestead; the farmhouse was
painted; the barn rebuilt; modern improvements were introduced
into the mother's kitchen, and books and newspapers began to
ornament the sitting-room table.

Young men and women who had spent their two or three years
of probation . . . often returned to the old places, bought land,
built their modest houses, and became new and prosperous heads of
families. Some of the mill-girls helped maintain widowed mothers,
or drunken, incompetent, or invalid fathers. Many of them educated the younger children in the family and young men were sent
to college with the money furnished by the untiring industry of
their women relatives.

Among the gloomier facets of mill life in winter was darkness
itself, six days of labor from dark until dark and on the seventh,
rest for the six more dark and changeless days ahead. The company
compensated for wages as low as it could pay with a suffocating
paternalism; the roof of the laborer's dwelling belonged to the
company, and the bank into which he put his savings. A miracle
of production had been achieved along the Merrimack, and a tomb
for the human spirit. Not that wages were any higher in the
hinterlands, but there mountains and green fields could be seen
from the windows of the factories which geography and economics
kept as small and personal as the towns they helped support.
Amoskeag was an anomaly in a country of mountains and rolling
hills and the great city it spawned is still a stranger there.

In northern New England the landscape presses in, limiting
the size of communities, making demands of the people and
imposing its individuality upon them. From the earliest days
they have had to make-do; necessity has literally been the mother
of inventions. The list of them is long and varied—the electric
motor, barbed wire, the iron plow, the platform scale, and the
automatic repeating rifle. The small towns of Springfield and
Windsor were nurseries of the machine-tool industry. Unlikely
as it may seem, they turned out more than one twentieth of the
machines that made all the machines in the United States during

the Second World War. Turret lathes, thread grinders, milling machines, multiple spindle automatics, gear shapers, chucking grinders and optical compariters were among the ingenious brain-children which had their forerunner decades before when Asahel Hubbard of Windsor installed his rotary steam pump in the Vermont State Prison. He inaugurated the National Hydraulic Company, which had incalculable effects on water pumping in the United States. What Asahel did with his pump in Windsor and Thomas Davenport with his electric motor in Brandon and Thaddeus Fairbanks and John Howe with their scales in St. Johnsbury and Rutland scores of others were trying to do in drafty machine shops or horse barns. That dashed hopes ended many of their efforts on improbable gadgets does not alter the fact that tinkering was either the heritage of the northcountry Yankee or else an expression of the solitary independence of life in the hills.

Of their triumphs in wood and iron many had greater importance, but none more appeal or was more symbolic of the new frontier in the great West than the Concord coach. The roots of this fabled enterprise reach back into the early nineteenth century when Lewis Downing arrived in the New Hampshire capital and started, alone, to make springless buggies. Within thirty-six months he had a prosperous business in a new shop with ten men working for him. In 1826, a decade after he had started, he hired a coach builder named Stephen Abbot, who soon became his partner in the manufacture of the vehicle for which they became famous.

The Concord coach was an eloquent symbol of a philosophy of production that has died hard in New England—craftsmanship. Downing never took on any more business than he could see to personally. Basswood or poplar could not be seasoned, moistened, heated and bent into body panels overnight. Fashioning a wheel with spokes of sturdy ash, carefully shaped, balanced and weighed, took as long as necessary. Painting and decoration was an art, not a trade. Oil lamps, gleaming from the Downing-Abbot windows, attested a working day of fourteen hours. As many orders as could be comfortably filled—and no more—would be taken. And if any detail of workmanship did not appear perfect to the eyes of Lewis Downing he would smash it, according to tradition, and have it done over. When the finished coach was rolled out into the sun-shine it was "a resplendent and proud thing . . . of beauty and dignity and life . . . as inspiring to the stage-faring man as a ship to a sailor." The white oak body "fairly held itself together by sheer virtue of scientific design and master joinery, for very little iron was used; and this, where needed, was iron only of the best Norway stock."

The nearly oval body of the Concord rested not on springs but on an indestructible cushion of leather running in strips three inches thick from rear to front axles. Thorough braces, as they were called, served the dual functions of transforming the vertical bumps of the road into a fore-and-aft rocking motion of the cradled body and permitting heavy loads without straining the team. When the horses started, the body would roll back, and, rocking forward again, help them overcome the inertia of getting under way. At the same time passengers were protected from the shocks of the wheels. The Concord was no Pullman; it was a heavy-duty vehicle designed for getting there under the worst conditions. Although it was made in three sizes, to carry six, nine or twelve passengers, as many as seventeen were sometimes packed in by adding extra seats on top and behind. Pressed together like kernels of corn, "everybody's back hair comes down," confessed F. J. Vincent in *Ben Holaday, The Stage Coach King,* "and what is nature and what is art in costume and character is revealed."

In 1847 Downing and Abbot dissolved their partnership, each forming a separate factory, presumably for the benefit of their sons, and by 1860 the two firms employed 311 men. When Down-ing retired five years later the rivals became one again under the name Abbot-Downing Company, and as such continued until after the turn of the century. Although the company had always built other vehicles, such as express, circus, and California mud wagons, it was the coach that achieved world renown and so stimu-lated business that by 1890 the shops covered six acres. Stage drivers in Africa discovered that the Concord's sturdy wheels were among the few that would not warp, shrink and fall apart, and in the American West it was found that the coach would float. It could negotiate murderous mountain roads and, as any viewer of "horse operas" is well aware, withstand any amount of gunfire and flaming arrows. Under the seat of the driver, in front of the towering pile of luggage on the roof, the bullion or the deeds to the mine seem destined to travel forever.

The Concord is usually pictured as a scarred and paintless veteran of a hundred holdups but it could be, and often was, very much a lady. An elegant one trimmed with purple goatskin went to Mexico. The coach operated by the Eagle Hotel in Concord itself boasted a lining of red plush, French windows, and an eagle painted on the light-olive body. Potter Palmer of Chicago ordered twelve in canary yellow for his hotel. In choosing their colors—often a dark-green body with vermilion running gear, or a red body with a straw-colored carriage—buyers also specified the paintings they wanted on the doors with such brief instructions as: "ornament up rich and tasty," "neat but not gaudy," "richly ornamented and showy," "put on some nice, neat landscape." Often the paintings were of ladies, political heroes or characters in fiction or mythology.

Among the large fleets under single ownership, that of Ben Holaday, who used 110 coaches in his Overland Mail, was perhaps the most famous, although Wells Fargo's order of thirty in one shipment created a sensation in Concord. It took a year to build them. No two had the same decorations, and when they were shipped in 1868 they departed on a special train of fifteen platform cars and four box cars filled with harnesses and spare parts.

Probably no single coach ever had a more tumultuous career than that called *Deadwood*, which was carried around the Horn by the clipper ship *General Grant*. On its run from Cheyenne to Deadwood it was involved in a deadly attack by Sioux Indians and its strong box was a favorite prize of masked highwaymen. Eventually it came into the ownership of Buffalo Bill Cody, who used it as a feature of his Wild West show. In tours abroad it carried such personages as the Prince of Wales, the kings of Sweden, Denmark, Italy and Greece, the Queen of Belgium, the Emperor of Germany and the President of France. In 1895 Buffalo Bill brought this veteran of Squaw Gap, Red Canyon and Lame Johnny Creek home to quiet Concord and added to *Deadwood's* list of notable passengers its proud maker, Lewis Downing, Jr.

If there was gold in the hills no one had found more than a glimmer of it, but there had never been danger of running out of granite. At Barre, Robert Parker and Thomas Courser, finding more than they could ever cut on Millstone Hill, accepted a contract to supply blocks for the Vermont capitol at Montpelier. Mining marble, a softer, more co-operative stone, had by then (1832) been going on for half a century at Dorset in Rutland County and in northern Lake Champlain at Isle La Motte. There was slate in many colors in as many places and enough iron at Monkton for Commodore MacDonough to cast 177 tons of shot for his fleet at Vergennes, for a short time the iron capital of the Union.

But those who saw the forest for the trees—practically every farmer in New Hampshire and Vermont at one time or another—were cutting timber. They were getting out masts for the Royal Navy "in the infinite thick woods" early in the seventeenth century, and woe unto the farmer who was caught cutting a tall pine, three feet thick at the stump, marked with an arrow by "The Surveyor of the King's Woods." Seventy or eighty pairs of oxen were sometimes needed to skid such a tree out of the woods, even in the snow. "Ride into Swamp," wrote Judge Samuel Sewall about lumbering at Salmon Falls in 1687, "to see a mast drawn of about 26 inches or 28; about 2 and 30 yoke of oxen before and about 4 yoke by the side of the mast, between the fore and hinder wheels. Twas a noble sight."

When the hinterlands of the Piscataqua and Merrimack had yielded to the ax there remained the forests of the Champlain valley and of the Connecticut and its tributaries; yet as early as 1823 few white pines were left standing near the lake. They had been burned for potash or floated north through the Richelieu in rafts so large that sometimes forty or fifty men were needed to row them and protect them from thieves when they arrived in Quebec. It was a tough business, as disastrous to character as to the landscape, for the Quebec waterfront was a den of dissipation and "if a young man has the first year sufficient resolution to withstand the iniquitous temptation, a second season . . . generally gives the finishing stroke."

The $600,000 worth of white pine and oak rowed over the border in 1810 alone (in defiance of the embargo) at times transformed the Richelieu into a vast and incongruous boardwalk floating tents or cabins and cookhouses, not to mention cows. Many of these rafts originated several miles up the Missisquoi River, at the head of navigation, where resourceful woodsmen bridged the dam and rocks to the pool below with an inclined plane to cushion the descent of long sticks for masts, or lashed cribs of three-inch timber. "Here [at Swanton] on the Missisquoi," wrote one zealous observer, "was the sublimity of nature in the ceaseless rush and roar of the swollen current. There the danger, the daring and the skill of man, here also a throng of excited and anxious spectators, their loud hurrah mingling with the roar of the waters when the raftsmen were successful in their task."

From its source in the four crystal lakes high in the New Hampshire north, along the entire tree-lined borders of Vermont and New Hampshire, the wide Connecticut, frothing occasionally over rocky falls but usually blue and calm, became a river of wood throughout the nineteenth century. It came in tumbling logs, in rafts, bearing shingles, laths and clapboards; and life along the well-mannered river has never been as lively since. The rafts queued up for the canal at Bellows Falls, and their crews at that town's saloons, where a half-Indian named Sam Flint, six feet four inches tall, served as keeper of the peace.

The rafts were unpinned in sections, each small enough to enter the locks of the Bellows Falls canal, one of the first to be built in America. Canal fever, infecting the entire eastern seaboard, soon opened the Connecticut for navigation all the way from Wells River, Vermont, at the foot of 15-mile falls, to Hartford 220 miles downstream, and to the sea. Boston and the Merrimack River were joined by the 27-mile Middlesex Canal while Samuel Blodgett's waterway around the falls of Amoskeag and two other ditches upriver at Hooksett and Bow permitted passengers and freight to sail from Concord right through to Tidewater at the Hub.

For roughly forty years, until the railroads came, these canals greatly attracted the commerce of the people of southern New Hampshire and those in the valley of the Connecticut (which drains three tenths of New Hampshire and four tenths of Vermont) toward Boston and southern New England—a pattern that lingers despite the broken barriers of geography of the present day. Hardworking 75-foot freighters, flat-bottomed and narrow, squeezed their 20-ton cargoes through the locks of the Merrimack and Middlesex Canal and passenger packets sailed on regular schedules, providing an economical method of travel for a family and its goods en route to near or distant parts. Time was of little consequence to shipper or trader. The river current eddying past the long steering oar and a breeze in the large square mainsail and tapering topsail were good enough for drifting downstream and locomotion by sculling oars or setting poles was adequate going up.

Flatboats of various sizes also prospered on the Connecticut, although they found difficulty in moving against the contrary current in northern sandbar waters. The boats gave the "landships," or goods wagons, a run for their money for they could carry many tons in a single shipment. There was, moreover, much excitement in their arrivals and departures, like that caused by the comings and goings of the weekly stages or the locomotives of a later day. The weather was no readier subject of conversation than a new anecdote about such a legendary boatman as Bill Cummins, who could "lift a barrel of salt with one hand by putting two fingers in the bung-hole and set it from the bottom timbers on top of the mastboard."

The Merrimack and Connecticut canals could scarcely be said to have altered life in their valleys as dramatically as did the Champlain Canal, the northern branch of the Erie from the Hudson River to the lake. Since Champlain drained north, the people had always looked to Canada for most of their trade. The new canal united, in effect, fresh water with salt and when it opened in 1823 the people of the valley abruptly turned about and faced south toward Troy, Albany and New York. The first vessel to pass through the locks at Whitehall and proceed magically to the Hudson River was the canal boat *Gleaner* from St. Albans. Upon reaching the Hudson a long procession of extravagantly decorated boats escorted "The Barque of the Mountains" to the dock amidst salutes from the artillery and uproarious cheers from a crowd on shore. Escorted to the Troy House "by a procession with music," her owners were feted at a public dinner, and so it went at Albany, Hudson, Poughkeepsie and all the way down to New York.

The arrival of the *Gleaner* symbolized to New Yorkers the nearness of a dimly distant hinterland that now, quite obviously, offered Elysian fields of trade. At the same time the citizens of the

Green Mountains began to reappraise the old enemy empire to the west and south. Upon the opening of the canal, canvas-covered wagons from the backcountry carrying beef, pork, flour, cheese and butter overwhelmed the roads to the ports of Swanton, St. Albans, Vergennes and Burlington, which were hard pressed for boats to float these unexpected tons of merchandise. St. Albans was butchering 200 head of cattle a day, as was Vergennes, which had been dozing since the fleet-building days in the War of 1812. This river port came astonishingly alive, reopening its ironworks and starting a variety of businesses—marble and hemp factories, saw-, grist- and woolen mills, tanneries, and a towpath company to haul canalboats the seven secluded and windless miles from the falls of Otter Creek to the lake.

Within ten years 232 canalboats were at work on the lake and this number doubled in the next decade. In 1843 the opening of the Chambly Canal, bypassing the Richelieu rapids to Montreal and Quebec, brought a great new infusion of tonnage and wealth from the north into and through the Champlain valley. In 1851, $25 million worth of freight moved in both directions across the Canadian border. This amount increased annually until 500,000 tons floated past customs at Rouses Point in 1862. In 1868 ten steamboats, fifteen schooners and 575 sloop-rigged canalboats plied out of local ports, and these did not include foreign-based ships and barges from the St. Lawrence. Such was the traffic out of Whitehall and Troy that boats had to wait their turn at the locks and from one end to the other the lake was flecked with sails.

From the day the southern canal was finished, trade from the Champlain valley flowed mostly south—iron from the Adirondacks, marble from Swanton and Isle La Motte and wool from all eastern Vermont, butter and cheese (about one million pounds of the former and three quarters of a million of the latter in 1846), pork, apples—more food, in fact, than was then passing over the great Erie. In the beginning most of the barges on the canal served to receive northbound Hudson River cargoes at Troy and southbound goods from such lake sloops and schooners as the *Hercules, General Scott, Water Witch* and *Lafayette* at Whitehall. Despite the grumbling of shippers about the transfer and delay of semiperishable cargoes, this system continued for some twenty years until an enterprising Burlington wholesaler named Timothy Follett established the Merchant's Line of sloop-rigged canalboats whose masts could be unstepped and stored at Whitehall (at "Old Billy Cain's Sail Loft"). With their cargoes intact they then proceeded behind mules through the canal to Troy and Albany and from there perhaps to New York in the tow of a steamer. Tooth-and-nail competition ensued, with the Northern Transportation Line and with lake-going steam tugs, but for many years the sloop-rigged canalboats reigned supreme.

The through boats carrying agricultural products and general merchandise had trouble enough competing for hull room with rafts of lumber which for years choked the canal from bank to bank. Round lumber, square lumber, lumber sawed in shingles, staves and hoop poles choked the locks. It came from the backwater areas that the original harvesters of the Champlain forests had passed over in their quest of the virgin timber that they had shipped to Quebec or burned for potash and charcoal. The unwieldy rafts damaged the banks of the canal and when higher tolls were imposed upon them and timber started coming through in special sloop-rigged barges, the vagabonds who traveled for weeks in the rough shanties of their rafts began to disappear. When, in the late 1840's, it at last looked as though the boom in lumber was over, great tows began to come in over the Chambly Canal from the north—from the Canadian hinterlands of the St. Lawrence and even from the Great Lakes.

The effects of a bonanza that made the waterfront below Burlington's sloping terraces for half a century the third largest lumber mart in the world may be seen today. On street after street Victorian mansions, rising like battlements, impart a certain stability and serenity that has prompted John P. Marquand to remark of their elm-arched domain that it is the last in America that looks that way. The houses are monuments of a golden era (for the lumber barons, if not the dockwallopers) when thirty acres of harbor, wharves and even the surface of the breakwater were crowded with 30-foot-high stacks of lumber—and still it came in single tows often scaling three million feet. In 1873 Burlington received, sorted, dressed or manufactured into products and forwarded 169,902,000 feet to Albany and New York by canal or to southern New England by rail.

During the following decade over 400 barges and steamers were engaged in hauling lumber alone.

Life on the hard-working canal was scarcely for the fainthearted, but for the more resolute farmer-turned-boatman prosperity was only as far away as the end of his fists. A struggle for precedence at each lock, where rum and blackstrap molasses were available, often resulted in smashed boats as well as noses, for a heavily laden hull set in motion by straining mules or horses on the towpaths could be a devastating weapon. Barges with names like *Fulton*, *Lady Jane*, *America*, *South Carolina*, *Victress*, *MacDonough* and *Boxer* became as famous or notorious as their adversaries, such white-winged canal-going sloops as the *Napoleon*, *Emperor Alexander*, *North America*, *General Macomb* and *Royal Oak*. The names suggested not an inland waterway but an international thoroughfare, which indeed it was.

Until the railroad came the packet boat was the principal link for passengers from the end of steamboat navigation at Albany and Troy, to Whitehall, where spacious side-wheelers, far too high and large to navigate the canal, waited in the lower basin to speed the traveler through the lake. The passenger business was most competitive and, since the successful canal packet was the packet that reached Whitehall or Troy ahead of time, pugilists often served as deckhands to ensure rapid transit through the locks. The use of horses, in tandem, instead of mules, further hastened the packets on their journey, for they always galloped on the towpath and fresh teams relieved them at a gallop. Except in winter when the canal was frozen, stagecoaches languished on the Troy-Whitehall run since no passenger cared to be jolted over stones and ruts when he might doze peacefully on the deck of a packet as fine as the *Burlington* or *Albany*. Yet the packet cabins were crowded, the berths as narrow, complained Charles Dickens, as bookshelves. For those who could afford staterooms the most peaceful conveyance was, of course, the steamboat.

Under the oak tree behind Isaac Nye's store in Burlington in 1808 Vermonters had built the first lake-going steamer in the world. Laboring through the waves from St. Johns to Whitehall at only five miles an hour this trembling craft nevertheless spelled doom for the commuting sloops *Dolphin, Burlington Packet, Lady Washington* and *Maria* of "Admiral" Gideon King, who had monopolized travel on the lake since 1790. Fattening upon the passenger traffic between New York and Montreal, the Champlain steamboats grew larger and finer by the decade until, toward mid-century, they received one of the few compliments paid anything American by the peripatetic Charles Dickens. In his *American Notes* he declared that the *Burlington* was the most elegantly fitted-up steamboat in the world, one which set new standards of luxury and opulence, dignity and quiet.

For 144 years the Champlain steamboats, some of them three decks high and 268 feet in length, spirited passengers and untold quantities of freight between the lake ports and introduced the wonders of America to tens of thousands of immigrants arriving by way of Quebec and Montreal and bound for New York. The Champlain Transportation Company, founded by Vermonters with headquarters at Burlington and a shipyard in Shelburne Bay, managed to monopolize the steamboat business during most of the era, although fierce outbreaks of competition sometimes turned the lake into a raceway. Whitehall, long the southern terminus of navigation (where passengers took canal packets, stages or cars to Albany and thence the Hudson River boats to New York), became an academy for brawling travel agents and runners.

The steamboat era on the upper reaches of the Connecticut was short and abortive although it was in shallow river water that Samuel Morey became a pioneer in applying the power of steam to paddlewheels. As early as 1790, long before Fulton's triumphant journey in the *Clermont* on the Hudson, Morey was navigating a tiny steam vessel on Lake Morey and on the river at Orford; but like many visionaries he lacked the means, and was born too soon, to convince the world of his prescience. The first steamer to thrash its way into the upper river only to expire, like the spawning salmon, was the *Barnet*, a 75-foot sternwheeler which reached Bellows Falls on December 11, 1826. Judging from the spirited account of its arrival in Hemenway's *Gazetteer* the pressure in the *Barnet's* boiler was no greater than that ashore where dignitaries, aflame with wine, were toasting "The Connecticut River—the grand highway from Canada to the seaboard. Give us steam!"

Captain Blanchard . . . proudly walked the deck of his steamer inspiring increased confidence that greater things were at hand. . . . His advent here was greeted with bonfires, bell ringing, illumination and intoxication. There was loud cheering from the well-lined river bank, and British cannon taken from Burgoyne at Bennington roared out from their brazen throats the joyful news.

But these demonstrations were made before our hero had got into port. He was struggling against the rapids called "The Tunnel.". . . When about halfway up . . . the boat came to a standstill. Notwithstanding the fire was so great that the blaze poured from the smokestack and . . . Captain Blanchard . . . was punching against the bed of the river with a spiked pole, no further progress could be made. . . . Blanchard fell from the boat into the rapids . . . but was fortunately rescued by strong hands which seized him by the collar at the right moment. . . .

Sorrow and disappointment were apparent as swift water now obtained the victory . . . [but] unconquerable will and genius . . . survived this cruel shock. The next trial to ascend proved successful. . . . Now safely moored . . . as the sun went down, the asthmatic breathing and noise of the contending elements in the bosom of the *Barnet* ceased, but the public mind was under a high pressure all that night. . . . Light from the morning sun fell upon broken windows, tables, chairs, crockery, glassware. . . . The survivors . . . aroused by the cannon, bell and hissing steam . . . bravely stepped on the hot, quivering trembling deck of the monster and away they went.

The *Barnet* never again appeared in Bellows Falls; its boiler exploded and scalded the chief engineer to death. This mournful accident failed, however, to discourage the proponents of steam, for in 1829 the stern-wheeler *Vermont* reached Brattleboro and in the following year proprietors of the Connecticut Steamboat Company attended a two-day conclave in Windsor with delegates from 23 New Hampshire and Vermont towns and determined that no less than five steamboats should be built. While capital was obtained and the small vessels duly constructed, the company found as time passed that it was paying out more than it took in. Morale deteriorated as it became clear that the river was too swift, the locks too narrow, the boats too frail. During an excursion from Wells River to Hanover a steampipe burst on the *Adam Duncan*, piloted by Wells River's Captain Nutt.

("This is the day that Captain Nutt
Sailed up the fair Connecticut.")

A passenger was drowned and within a year the small steamer was auctioned for a pittance. Venturing upon one northern cruise the *William Hall*, too large for the canal, navigated the streets of Bellows Falls behind a yoke of eight oxen. The *John Ledyard* ended its career very much as had a famous Dartmouth student of the same name, who drifted in a canoe out of college and into the life of a vagabond. "It is quite true," states his biographer, Helen Augur, "that Ledyard accomplished nothing and died with his dream still burning in his heart." So it was also with the Connecticut Steamboat Company.

Steam solved the travel and transportation needs of the Connecticut valley, not on water but on land via the "iron ligeament" in 1848. In the beginning trains were thought of as feeders for shipping, as in transporting lumber from Burlington through the Green Mountains and down the Connecticut valley to Boston. And yet, for all the goods and passengers trains proved capable of carrying, the fact remained, as it does today, that the Atlantic was east, Lake Champlain was west, and these twain have never really met.

Although it never regained the stature as a port that it had enjoyed in colonial times, Portsmouth continued, after the War of 1812, to depend entirely upon the ocean for its well-being. Fishing remained profitable as did shipbuilding, both private and for the government. Through much of the nineteenth century the Piscataqua's tidal estuaries were busy with small trading vessels called gundelows—not to be confused with the similarly named bargelike gunboats of the Revolution. The gundelow was 60 to 70 feet long, but narrow and shallow of draft. It had a spoon bow, a rounded stern and its large lateen-rigged sail, attached to a stubby, rotating mast, was so hinged that it could be lowered easily and quickly to pass under a bridge. By no means ugly, surprisingly fast and maneuverable with an expert at the tiller, it was known to travel the 25 miles from Exeter to Portsmouth with an ebb tide and a good wind, discharge its cargo of bricks, reload with coal, and reach Exeter on the flood tide by dusk the same day. A more modest version of the gundelow was the passenger-carrying Piscataqua packet, a trim keelboat that also handled freight. In *Ports of Piscataqua* William Saltonstall reports "20 2-horse pungs at the old Durham Inn with beef from Vermont destined to go down to Portsmouth by river, provided the ice didn't interfere."

Other than the vessels engaged in offshore fishing (some 68 with a total complement of 581 men in 1824) there were 33 hauling lumber, fish and agricultural products up and down the coast and 81 sailing to foreign countries in a trade that was gradually diminishing owing to Portsmouth's distance from the large population centers farther south. The irony of it was that the busier harbor of Boston froze in winter while the fast-moving tides always permitted navigation at the superior northern port. Portsmouth could and did continue to build ships to serve luckier ports and of course there was its permanently settled navy yard, which today dominates the city's economy. Established in 1806 on Fernald's Island, it gradually spread out over sixty acres of bayberry and wild strawberries until it became one of the navy's principal armories. The nation's first and third battleships, *America* and *Washington*, were built there. In 1817 work began on the 74-gun *New Hampshire*. When the sloops of war *Saratoga* and *Portsmouth* joined the fleet in 1843 steam was becoming a power to reckon with and the yard turned to the building of side-wheel and propeller ships like the large *Piscataqua*, completed in 1866 (the year the government bought Seavey's Island and added its 105 acres to the naval base).

Unless the era of privateering need be excepted, no period was fairer for the shipbuilders than that of the golden years of the clippers. Portsmouth was only halfhearted about whaling, although it did build perhaps twenty ships for New Bedford, Nantucket, Salem and Boston and four for its own use; but no clippers finer than those from its yards ever sailed. Starting in 1845 the master shipbuilder George Raynes created (for clippers were not just built) at least eight in one decade. Among those who loved these swift ships in Boston, New Orleans, New York and in the far foreign ports where they called, his name and those of such colleagues as Fernald and Pettigrew and Hanscom were bywords, for among their renowned goddesses of sail were the *Typhoon, Witch of the Wave, Sea Serpent,* and *Nightingale*.

In 1851 Fernald and Pettigrew's *Typhoon* sped to England in thirteen and a half days, the shortest sailing passage then on record, and an exciting one according to the testimony of E. F. Sise of Portsmouth.

> One night when blowing very heavy I went on Deck and asked the mate how fast she was going. He said when the Captain went below his orders were if she went 16 knots to shorten sail. He had hove the line over and finding she was going *over* 16 knots, he was taking in sail. However only 15 and ½ knots appears on the log and Captain S. thought it would not be believed.

George Raynes's fleet, slender *Witch of the Wave* contained a library of one hundred books. Her staterooms were paneled in bird's-eye maple, in satin, zebra and rosewood.

The Boston Cadet Band played "The Star-Spangled Banner" at her launching and when the crew hoisted her sails her lady figure-head "in gossamer drapery of white and gold, with one shapely arm extended" and the child in a seashell drawn by carved dolphins on her stern fairly danced over the waves. Figureheads that have survived the clippers that bore them are now recognized as objects of art, infinitely expressive of the spirit of America and priceless in value. The woodworking shop of John H. Bellamy, carver of eagles and probably the most gifted of the maritime sculptors and cabinet-makers, was across the Piscataqua at Kittery Point. He also worked in Portsmouth at 17 Daniel Street.

Across the stern of George Raynes's heralded clipper *Sea Serpent* crawled two immense wooden serpents. A recumbent figure of "the Swedish nightingale," Jenny Lind, a bird on her finger, was affixed to the stern of Samuel Hanscom's *Nightingale* and a second likeness of the popular singer adorned her bowsprit. The frame of this finest of all Piscataqua ships, the fastest afloat in her time, was entirely of live oak. Her rigging was capped with bright brass, her decks were holystoned, mahogany belaying pins decorated her carved and gilded rails, mahogany and satinwood enriched her carved and gilded cabin. At sea, with her skysails, staysails, outer jibs and stun'sails billowing in a hard wind she was as ultimate an expression of beauty as the artisans of a farming country were likely to achieve.

XI

CERTAIN WOODMEN,
WATERMEN, AND HUNTERS

In New Hampshire slavery was not against the law, as in Vermont, but the climate of feeling there was about the same: the people disliked bondage of any kind. It is true that in Portsmouth, prior to the Revolution, there had been slavery, but it was slavery with a difference; the Negroes were household retainers with a certain place in the community and an organization of their own. Cyrus Bruce, Governor Langdon's servant, was in the hierarchy of the colored company and as such wore certain badges of distinction—metal seals, a heavy chain of gold, ruffles, and silver shoe buckles. The king or president, annually elected by some 187 slaves (in 1767) was Colonel William Brewster's Nero, who served also as a judge in handing down sentences for misdemeanors. After the Revolution the Portsmouth slaves were given their freedom, unless they chose to remain as pensioners.

On a voyage to Russia at the turn of the century Captain Charles Coffin employed as his steward a Negro who upon arrival asked permission to see a parade of Russian troops to be reviewed by the Emperor. Apparently the steward was as interesting to the Emperor as his cavalry for Captain Coffin received a message asking if he were willing to dispense with his services. The decision was made by the steward himself. He presently became a butler on the royal staff, and on a voyage to Portsmouth to bring his wife back to Russia he wore clothes of gold lace.

In almost every village square in New Hampshire and Vermont bronze statues, sheathed by the weather in green, commemorate the long columns of men who marched away to the most bitter and tragic of our wars, and never came back. What they did on the battlefields and what the battlefields did to them, and to New England valleys emptied of their youth, is written in every town history and poignantly recalled each Decoration Day. But the influence in high places that other Yankees—the makers of opinion, the planners of strategy—had as a group is less well understood. This much is certain: out of few, if any, states came men who had more to do with the antislavery issue and the tempestuous fortunes of the war itself than certain natives of New Hampshire and Vermont. They were by no means all of a mind about slavery. There were the moderate abolitionists but more violent defenders of the peace, who worked unceasingly to beat out the brush fires started by the radicals on the grounds that total conflagration was to be avoided at all costs. There were the Copperheads, who viewed the problem as none of their business. And there was the militant majority, whose banner was emancipation. That these individuals were effective enough to impress their various views upon the national scene at least affirms the vitality of their rocky homeland.

The more outspoken freemen of the hills had always grumbled about slavery. As early as 1786 the Republic of Vermont adopted a bill prohibiting the sale of Negroes, or their removal from its borders. Montpelier citizens interested in repatriating slaves by transporting them to Liberia formed the first so-called colonization society in America. In the early eighteen-hundreds Vermont senators, congressmen and the state legislature were accustomed to placing before Congress bills and petitions that were invariably shouted down by flushed and angry spokesmen from the South.

Offensive forces in the Green Mountains did not, however, gain much headway until the father of abolition, William Lloyd Garrison, arrived in Bennington in 1828 to edit a newspaper called the *Journal of the Times*. This, as he recalled later, was almost his first effort "in the sacred cause of Universal Emancipation." In it he advocated the gradual liberation of every slave in the Republic. He prayed that he might be "the humble instrument of breaking at least one chain, in restoring one captive to liberty; it will amply repay a life of severe toil." Although the *Journal of the Times* seemed to young Horace Greeley (of the *Northern Spectator* a few miles away in Poultney) "about the ablest and most interesting paper ever issued in Vermont," the furious editor of the *Vermont Patriot* called it and its insidious cause "this fatal snare of disunion, disorganization, humbuggery and fanaticism."

A crusading, hotheaded reformer without diplomacy or a sense of the public temperament, an inveterate swallower of pills and patent medicines, Garrison ushered in his antislavery outbursts with pronouncements for John Quincy Adams—peace, temperance and popular education. Meanwhile he strove to build what any zealot must have if his reforms are to gain acceptance—an organization. Within a few years after he had ended his brief sojourn at Bennington to establish other abolitionist journals, the New England Anti-Slavery Society was a power in the northcountry. In succeeding years the platoon of emancipation became a company, a regiment, a division, a small army.

The hill winds of New Hampshire also bore cries of liberty, but faintly at first. In the vanguard of Granite State abolitionists was Nathaniel Peabody Rogers, husband of a Quakeress reformer, associate of Garrison, and editor of Concord's *Herald of Freedom*. According to James Russell Lowell, he was "a kind of maddened John the Baptist." When chided for preaching abolition on the grounds that Jesus never did, Rogers replied that there would be no slavery if the golden rule were observed. "Admitting—what I deny—that Jesus Christ did not preach abolition of slavery, then I say *he didn't do his duty!*" In the *Herald of Freedom* Rogers tells of a journey with Garrison into the White Mountains. While stopping to water their horses they were shocked at seeing smoke coming out of a carriage of two other antislavery friends. Upon examination they found that one of the men was smoking. They admonished him severely for "anti-slavery does not fail to spend its intervals of public service in mutual and searching corrections of the faults of its friends." It shocked them to think that "he, an abolitionist, on his way to an anti-slavery convention, should desecrate his anti-slavery mouth and that glorious Mountain Notch with a stupefying tobacco weed." The properly chastened friend, announcing that smoking *had been* a bad habit, threw his cigars into the Ammonoosuc.

This was but a mild example of the standards that the reformers expected their crusaders to live up to. Suffering a kind of emotional trauma, Rogers' hearers and the readers of his *Herald of Freedom* fairly breathed the gospel of abolition. Some idea of the environment in which it took root in New Hampshire is to be gained from the journals of Mary Hersey Lincoln, a temperance worker (and later a suffragette) who made a pilgrimage to the White Mountains in the company of other prominent Massachusetts abolitionists in 1844. The location of Nashua was lovely, she thought, "but oh! how marred by eternal factories." At Concord

> Nathaniel L. Rogers, editor of that brave *Herald of Freedom*, though lying sick on the sofa, welcomed us most heartily with his benignant

smile and a pressure of his beautiful hand. . . . Ere long we espied the vehicles drawing near slowly and covered with dust containing the host of Hutchinsons [a popular New Hampshire family of singers]. . . . Mr. Rogers and his family are deeply and enthusiastically attached to them, both on account of their reform spirit and their rare musical talent. The Hutchinsons pitched their tent on the hill nearby, and are to sleep on their buffalos! They have given a fine concert in the Old North Church which was crammed.

A little later during this junket Abbie Kelley, an antislavery companion of Mary's,

told me of the trials and insults of every kind to which she was exposed when she first became a lecturer on anti-slavery. It is marvelous —the devotion and strength she possessed throughout the whole— her body and mind went through a tremendous struggle ere she became free and bold and strong to go through her work. Oh! the nights she has lain in bed sleepless, her head throbbing with her high mission.

A horn blown by Ethan Allen Crawford, echoing among the crags and ravines of the White Mountains, deeply thrilled Mary. "It is glorious!" she wrote. "It is like music from celestial orchestras—a chorus of angels singing. . . . Crawford, who is blowing the first blast, says 'Take some frosty morning and we take the leaves off the trees!' He is a lusty, hearty old fellow, clever and good natured but he tells awfully large stories!"

Parker Pillsbury (the flouring of the family had not yet taken place) was, with Rogers, one of New Hampshire's original spokesmen against slavery—"a tough oak stick of a man not to be silenced, or insulted or underestimated by a mob, because he is more mob than they; he mobs the mob," wrote Ralph Waldo Emerson in 1846. "He is fit to meet the barroom wits and bullies; he is a wit and bully himself and something more; he is a graduate of the plow and cedar swamp and the snowbank and has nothing to learn of labor, or poverty or the rough of farming." Pillsbury grew up in Henniker where his father was a Congregational minister, follower of a calling which the son chose also but one, for him, without serenity. For preaching abolition, and attacking other ministers who would not, he was excommunicated. Garrison admiringly called him a true *revival* abolitionist and Lowell wrote:

> Beyond, a crater in each eye,
> Sways brown, broad-shouldered Pillsbury,
> Who tears up words like trees by the roots,
> A Theseus in stout cowhide boots.

In later years Pillsbury became very much a national figure as editor of the *National Anti-Slavery Standard*. Impatient with Lincoln, he became a foe of President Johnson, whom he considered, in effect, proslavery. As time went on, the house of abolition became divided against itself—the radicals against the conservatives on both state and national levels. But this schism was as nothing compared with that, in New Hampshire, between the abolitionists and the *anti*-antislavery forces. When John Greenleaf Whittier came to Concord to address an antislavery rally he narrowly escaped a violent crowd of egg throwers. R. W. Emerson, for a time Concord's Unitarian minister, reviled the homeland of his wife with the lines:

> The God who made New Hampshire
> Taunted the lofty land with little men—
> Small bat and wren.

Impatient with the enemies of reform, the fiery Garrison in 1844 exclaimed that New Hampshire did not belong to New England "but should be cut from her moorings and float southward, to find a geographical position between Texas and Louisiana. . . . Yet she may not be wholly beyond recovery; she has some of the choicest spirits to be found anywhere in the wide earth."

One of these, in his opinion, was John Parker Hale, a Dover lawyer long notorious as one of the only two abolitionist representatives in Washington (the other was Maine's Hannibal Hamlin). For opposing, in 1845, the annexation of Texas on the grounds that it would enlarge slavery's domain, he was dumped by the old Democratic party, traditionally in control of New Hampshire politics. But independents led by Edward Tuck and John L. Hayes gathered around and, to their astonishment and his, elected him to the Senate. The splinter group he represented became the Free-Soil party, which nominated him for President in 1852. The loss of this election was more painful than it might have been if his fence-sitting adversary, Franklin Pierce, had not also been a native of his own state. But Hale had made his mark as a pediment of the Free-

Soilers, and through their evolution of the Republican party.

As early as 1844 the Vermont scholar and statesman, George Perkins Marsh, in his acceptance of the Whig nomination for the House of Representatives, had paralleled Hale's opposition to the annexation of Texas as a slave state with a strong speech across the mountains. Vermont then embraced the less-conservative Whig party and so Marsh was not confronted with the opposition of the old-line Democrats that his colleague faced in New Hampshire. It remained, curiously enough, for the senator from Illinois, Vermont-born Stephen Douglas, with his Kansas-Nebraska Bill, to annihilate what remained of the Green Mountain State's Whig party in 1856 and to force such splinter groups as Whigs, Democrats, Free-Soilers and Know-Nothings into the bond of Republicanism. Apparently ignoring or repudiating the views of its native Stephen Douglas, the Montpelier Watchman ventured to call the New Hampshire political kettle black for producing President Pierce and several representatives who voted for the Kansas-Nebraska Bill. The Green Mountain State voted solidly against it.

Certainly the climax of antislavery's boulder-strewn path to precarious heights was Abraham Lincoln's arrival in New Hampshire in 1860 to speak and to visit his son Robert at Exeter's Phillips Academy. To New Hampshire's many Democrats it was an event of supreme indifference, but at least one newspaper, commenting upon his speech in Manchester, reported that the "Grand New Party" seemed to be making headway.

> His sense of the ludicrous is very keen. . . . He seems to forget all about himself while talking, and to be entirely engrossed in the welfare of his hearers. . . . He does not try to show off, to amuse those of his own party, but addresses all his arguments in a way to make new converts. For the first half hour his opponents would agree with every word he uttered, and from that point he began to lead them off, little by little, cunningly, until it seemed as if he had got them all into his fold. He displays more shrewdness, more knowledge of the masses of mankind than any public speaker we have heard since Long Jim Wilson left for California.

2

Of his struggle at Exeter Academy to master his terrible shyness about speaking in public Daniel Webster wrote: "Many a piece did I commit to memory and recite and rehearse in my own room over and over again yet, when the day came, when the school collected to hear declamations when my name was called, and I saw all eyes turned to my seat, I could not raise myself from it."

At Dartmouth he appeared rough and awkward to his classmates but by common agreement he was the best speaker in college. The Fourth of July oration he gave as a junior in 1800, described by the *Hanover Gazette*, "would have done honor to gray-headed patriotism . . . and the most celebrated orators of our country."

Webster came from Salisbury, from long generations of New Englanders, a youth with ink-black hair and eyes and, like his father, with a complexion so dark "that burnt gun powder did not change it," according to General John Stark. Since he was not strong enough for heavy chores, he turned to books and early showed a remarkable propensity, if not to analyze, to remember what he had read. This retentive mind served him well in achieving good grades without drudging at Dartmouth. As a teacher in Fryeburg, Maine, where he helped pay for the education of his brother who had helped pay for his, he could rattle off quotations with great feeling and effect. Here he received the nickname "All Eyes" because they completely dominated his tall thin frame.

Under Christopher Gore, later a senator, he studied law in Boston. Admitted to the bar in 1805 he opened an office in Boscawen, where he lived an impatient and lonely life of "writs and summonses." He complained that "an accursed thirst for money vitiates everything." The profession of law was "good if practiced in the spirit of it; it is damnable fraud and iniquity when its true spirit is . . . [supplanted by one] of mischief-making and money-catching." After two years he felt well enough qualified to move to Portsmouth and do battle with his peers. There, learning from such veteran trial lawyers as Jeremiah Mason the strength of plain Anglo-Saxon nouns, he began to abandon the embellishments that had previously marked his writing and speaking.

When he was well on his way to fame his friend, George Ticknor, told him that he had a copy of a eulogy that Webster had given at Dartmouth upon the death of a classmate, called *Oration on Simonds*. "I thought till lately," Webster told Ticknor, "that, as only a few copies of it were printed, they must all have been destroyed long ago; but the other day Bean, who was in college with me, told me he had one. It flashed through my mind that it must have been the last copy in the world, and that if he had it in his pocket it would be worthwhile to kill him to destroy it from the face of the earth. So I recommend you not to bring your copy where I am."

On another occasion when referring painfully to his earlier declamations he remarked: "I had not then learned that all true power in writing is in the idea, not the style, an error into which the *Ars Rhetorica* as it is usually taught may easily lead stronger heads than mine."

If Webster learned much from Mason at Portsmouth, the dean of the local bar quickly came to respect the dark-complexioned newcomer. When the two first clashed in the same courtroom, "He broke upon me like a thunder shower in July," recalled Mason, "sudden, portentous, sweeping all before it." Another perceptive glimpse of Webster at Portsmouth was that of Mrs. Eliza Lee (nee Buckminster, who as a little girl had seen Lady Wentworth and the last days of royal government). She reported that her eldest sister told of "a remarkable person" in the pew with her, and that she was sure he had a "most marked character for good or evil." Mrs. Lee remembered Webster as being "slender and apparently of delicate organization, his large eyes and massive brow seemed very predominant above the other features, which were sharply cut, refined and delicate . . . his complexion was heightened by hair as black as the raven's wing."

His personal qualities seem to have been curiously contradictory. While he liked the sophisticated people of Portsmouth, he married a plain but attractive schoolteacher, Grace Fletcher, from Hopkinton. He was at ease at social functions but preferred reading Shakespeare to close friends before the fire. Town and city were stimulating to him but he loved the woods, fields and streams and everything in them that grew, walked, flew or swam. To his friends he was a warm and entertaining companion but to others he often seemed overbearing. His practice among the important people yielded a lot of money, yet he liked to represent the poor who could not afford his fees. In his economic and political thinking he was conservative, although not reactionary. (He did more in Congress than any other single man to put the currency of the country on a solid footing by fighting for the establishment of a sound United States Bank, while at the same time his personal finances were chaotic.) He wanted changes to evolve slowly in an atmosphere of law and order. Against the excesses of such radicals as Thomas Paine and, later, William Lloyd Garrison, the Constitution to him was a refuge and a shield. An ardent Federalist who bitterly protested the War of 1812, he nevertheless would have nothing to do with the obtrusive policies of New England governors nor the secessionists of the Hartford Convention. The war, he said, "is now the law of the land. . . . Resistance and insurrection form no parts of our creed. . . . By the exercise of our Constitutional right of suffrage, by the peaceable remedy of election, we shall seek to restore wisdom to our councils and peace to our country."

The wave of reaction against the war carried him into the House of Representatives in 1813 when he was thirty-one. As the champion of New England mercantile interests in such issues as tariffs and the embargo, he did everything he could to embarrass the administration. For these services he received loans or gifts from wealthy New Englanders. Accepting money from people whose interests, either immediate or long-term, are involved in the way a congressman votes seemed then to have been considerably less a matter of ethics than now. For a number of years Webster believed in free trade because artificial protection led "the people to too much reliance on government. If left to their own choice of pursuits, they depended on their own skill and their own industry. But if government essentially affects their occupations by its systems of bounties and preferences, it is natural, when in distress, that they should call on government for relief." He later changed his mind because he felt obliged to protect the economic well-being of the area he represented. He could scarcely ignore the importance of its textiles, or the devastating effect upon it of a flood of cheap foreign goods. Thus he came out for tariffs. Few of his biographers can fair-mindedly conclude that he did so just to obtain loans and gifts from rich industrialists. He was too complex a man to be reduced to the denominator of mere self-seeking. Ralph Waldo Emerson, for one, excused his chronic indebtedness on the grounds that "he is known to be generous, and his countrymen make for him the apology of Themistocles, that to keep treasure undiminished is the virtue of a chest and not of a man."

While it is difficult to disentangle Webster's services as a lawyer, on the one hand, and as a public servant, on the other, one gains the impression from a perspective of his entire political career that on the whole he would have voted as he did anyway. But the fact that he was always overextended financially and expected support from his constituents (on the grounds that as long as he was a congressman he could not earn what he might in private life) was not one of the more attractive facets of his character. Certainly a warm heart was one of his stronger qualities. For a family man who basked in the security of his home, who arose with the sun singing hymns, whose interest in everything domestic was inexhaustible, the loss of his Portsmouth home and everything in it in the great fire of 1813, before he moved to Boston, was a severe shock. The death of his daughter Grace in 1817 was a greater catastrophe, from which it seemed he might never recover. (Much later, after the loss of another daughter and a son, he planted on the lawn of his Massachusetts farm at Marshfield two "brother and sister" weeping elms.) As he sat listless through the sessions of the House, government and politics seemed to be total strangers. Thus after finishing his second term he returned to Boston, where he had moved his family during the preceding summer, there to devote himself entirely to private practice. Time and pleasant new surroundings, a prosperous and distinguished practice, eventually restored his spirits. Following his appeal before the Supreme Court in the illustrious Dartmouth College case, he stood at the head of the American bar.

The Dartmouth controversy was no less complex than it had been long-standing. The energies of the college at Hanover had been sapped in a bitter conflict for control among two groups of trustees, one faction representing the private college, with its private charter from King George III, and the other trying to make it into a public institution under the control of New Hampshire. Judging from the comments of those who heard Webster's appeal for the private college, it must have been the most dramatic ever made before the Supreme Court. Justice Joseph Story later testified:

> There was an earnestness of manner, and a depth of research, and a potency of phrase which at once convinced you that his whole soul was in the cause . . . that he had meditated over it in the deep silence of the night and . . . the broad sunshine of the day. . . .

And when he came to his peroration there was . . . in the firey flash-
ings of his eye, the darkness of his contracted brow, the sudden and
flying flushes of his cheeks, the quivering and scarcely manageable
movements of his lips, in the deep guttural tones of his voice, in
the struggle to suppress his emotions, in the almost convulsive
clenchings of his hands without a seeming consciousness of the act,
there was in these things what gave to his oratory an almost super-
human influence. . . . When Mr. Webster ceased to speak [at least
traditionally with the words: "It is, sir, as I have said, a small college,
and yet there are those who love it"] it was some minutes before
anyone seemed inclined to break the silence . . . [of] an agonizing
dream, from which the audience was slowly and almost unconsciously
awakening.

The Court's decision for Mr. Webster and his private college threw
a cordon of inviolability around such chartered institutions. Henceforth no corporations, in Webster's words, would be "subject to the
rise and fall of popular parties and the fluctuations of political
opinions."

The Court's decision was inherently conservative, for it established
a precedent of noninterference by state and federal governments
with the charters of public and private corporations. Of the other
169 occasions in which Webster appeared before the Supreme Court
the so-called Steamboat Case (*Gibbons v. Ogden*) in 1824 was one
of the most important. Whereas his argument in the Dartmouth case
tended to reduce the power of governmental control in one way, his
success in breaking the Fulton-Livingston monopoly on the Hudson
River had, in another, the opposite effect—of making the federal
government supreme in regulating commerce. By throwing open
the waterways, unhampered by the states along their shores, the decision had, moreover, an incalculable effect upon the growth of the
West.

In 1823 Massachusetts sent Webster back to the House of Representatives and from there he went to the Senate. For over a quarter
of a century, as secretary of state in two administrations, as a leader
of the Senate and dominant figure in the Whig party, as an orator,
patriot and defender of the Constitution, he was one of the most
powerful men in America—a Goliath guarding the edifice of Union
and the sacred chamber of the Constitution. The graver the danger—
as when Hayne argued that the states had a right to nullify such acts

of Congress as were repugnant to the individual states—the more inspiring his defense in the hushed Senate chamber. "I have not accustomed myself to hang over the precipice of disunion to see whether . . . I can fathom the depth of the abyss below. . . . While the Union lasts, we have high, exciting, gratifying prospects spread out before us. . . . Beyond that I seek not to penetrate the veil. . . . Liberty *and* Union, now and forever, one and inseparable!"

Champion of the Monroe Doctrine, codifier of criminal law, settler of the boundary between New Hampshire, Maine and Canada, spokesman for enslaved foreign peoples, for the Creek Indians against the aggressions of Georgia, Webster could find—search his mind, his heart and conscience as he might—but one word, but one weapon to hurl against the dark specter of Negro slavery: compromise. He was for freeing the slaves but not at any cost—not at the cost of war or the dismemberment of the great Union. Just as once he had been a freetrader but had come around under pressure for tariffs to protect New England manufacturing, so once he had demanded that the slave traffic of the District of Columbia be abolished. But as the years passed, and he realized the consequences of the Republic's awful dilemma, he backed away from it. And yet to his country place in Marshfield he brought Monica McCarthy, a slave whose freedom he had purchased for $600. He told her she would have to repay this sum in her service as cook but such was his largess that she had $2,000 in the bank when he died.

Because he was so much in the public eye and so much the image of the noble statesman, it was long fashionable among his detractors to take his strengths for granted and magnify his failings. Certainly the death of his precious wife, Grace, in 1828 was a double tragedy, since his second wife, seventeen years his junior, liked the glitter and effervescence of the social world and Webster found himself engaged in a losing battle with food and the vintner. And yet his growing portliness added, if anything, to his majestic appearance. He was the *sine qua non* of every great public occasion. Whenever he appeared to speak a sea of people gathered, sometimes as many as 100,000. His speeches at Bunker Hill and the 200th anniversary of the landing of the Pilgrims, and upon scores of other perhaps less noteworthy occasions, were landmarks in the lives of those who heard him. During the "Log Cabin and Hard Cider" campaign for William

Henry Harrison in 1840 he appeared in Vermont on Stratton Mountain, now a lonely wilderness, before an audience of 15,000 people. Unquestionably he drank more than his share, but reports by his enemies of drunkenness in public are malicious exaggerations. As he grew older he did become fretful and peevish, particularly when besieged with work. He was the first person at his desk in the morning at the State Department and often was observed dictating to two secretaries at once. Unfortunately he did continue to receive retainers from the United States Bank, loans which he was unable to repay, and gifts from friends and business associates in order to afford his residence in Washington, his magnificent farm in Marshfield, and other extravagances. Yet despite the ebb and flow of politics his enemies were unable to discredit him as essentially a man of integrity. "He made money with ease," testified his secretary,

> and spent it without reflection. . . . During his long professional career he earned money enough to make a dozen fortunes, but he spent it liberally, and gave it away to the poor by hundreds and thousands. Begging letters from women and unfortunate men were received by him almost daily, at certain periods; and one instance is remembered where, on six successive days, he sent remittances of $50 and $100 to people with whom he was entirely unacquainted. He was indeed careless, but strictly and religiously honest, in all his money matters. He knew not how to be otherwise.

His most painstaking biographer, Claude M. Fuess, presents the aging Webster through the eyes of some of the most perceptive people of the day. After visiting the Senate in 1835 Harriet Martineau, the English chronicler of America, reported that he was "transcendent." Young Abraham Lincoln greatly respected him. Emerson thought of him as a masterpiece of nature—as "a natural Emperor of men." "Ah! if God had given to this Demosthenes a heart to lead New England," he wrote in his diary in 1845, "what a life and death and glory for him." Edward Everett never knew "a more generous spirit, a safer advisor, a warmer friend." During a trip to England in 1839 (when the renowned orator was presented to the Queen) Thomas Carlyle noted the "amorphous crag-like face; the dull black eyes under their precipice of brows." A man of great dignity, concluded Carlyle, but essentially political. John Kenyon, on the other hand, found him kindly and frank with "thoughtful eyes and a mouth that seemed to respond to all humanities." The Archbishop of York testified: "I met . . . Mr. Webster for only five minutes, but in those five minutes I learned more of American institutions and of the peculiar working of the American constitution than in all that I had ever heard or read."

Despite all that has been written about him, Webster remains indistinct. Why was the presidency always just beyond his reach? Was it because he was physically altogether too prepossessing and mentally too facile, or because he had suffered public and political overexposure? Bad luck undoubtedly had something to do with it, and the fact that he was always a little out of step with the times. He was a Federalist when Federalism was dying and Jacksonianism was on the wing; he was one of the most powerful Whigs, but that party preferred to nominate generals like Harrison, Tyler, Taylor and Scott. He campaigned dutifully for all these; he even worked over Harrison's inaugural address which the General had filled with classical allusions. Webster came home fatigued from this editorial chore saying: "I have killed seventeen Roman proconsuls as dead as smelts, every one of them!" In 1844, much to the surprise of his colleagues, he campaigned for his archrival, Henry Clay.

> Men are nothing, principles are everything. Besides, Mr. Clay is fit to be president. He is qualified for the station. His principles are such as I approve; and his ability nobody can question. Therefore I am bound as an honest man to do everything I can. And when I say that, I am perfectly well aware that Mr. Clay would not do the same thing for me.

The climax of his career was undoubtedly his controversial speech of March 7, 1850, shortly before he left the Senate, again to become secretary of state. Before the speech he despaired: "I know not how to meet the present emergency, or with what weapons to beat down the northern and the southern follies, now raging in equal extremes." The crowd that packed the Senate chamber sat hushed, taut, almost breathless, for three hours and eleven minutes while the great man, splendid in his white stock and dress coat with brass buttons, earnestly summarized the plight of the Union and pleaded for reason, understanding and charity—for a give-and-take solution of the slavery problem. Because Webster appeared to be turning his back upon the abolitionists and currying favor with the South, William Lloyd

Garrison called the speech "indescribably base and wicked" and Whittier wrote:

> Revile him not—the Tempter hath
> A snare for all.
> And pitying tears, not scorn and wrath,
> Befit his fall.

Yet the address profoundly stirred the country at large. It set the stage for compromise measures like the new Fugitive Slave Law and the Kansas-Nebraska Bill—and for a decade longer America remained at peace. Lincoln long expressed the same thoughts of peace and compromise. "If I could save the Union without freeing any slave," he asserted, "I would do it. If I could save it by freeing some and leaving others alone I would also do that."

There are those who say Webster sat on the fence in the hope of capturing the presidential nomination in 1852. Others declare that he knew he was alienating powerful extremists on both sides and that the presidency was irrevocably lost to him. The beginning of the end of almost a very great man came when he found out for certain that it was—when Franklin Pierce, the relatively obscure native of his own state, acceded to the presidency in 1852.

On July 9 of that year the master spirit from the hills of New Hampshire spoke at a great fete in his honor in Boston. The city was decorated and the streets thronged as an open barouche, drawn by six gray horses, brought the sick old man into town. He spoke as strongly as ever for half an hour before a huge audience on the Common, but he was completely spent. Once more he visited the scenes of his memories in New Hampshire, and then returned exhausted to his family and Marshfield neighbors, to his good friends of the wide outdoors—his horses, cattle, deer, his noble oxen. He was still in harness as secretary of state, like his three favorite horses that he had buried upright with their halters on, when the parish bell tolled seventy on Sunday morning, October 24, and the nation awoke hollow and shocked to find that it had lost the most enduring symbol of its national pride.

Of the other natives of the hillcountry who made history during the Union's most perilous hour none loomed larger than "Little

Giant," of Brandon, Vermont, who awoke to the world of politics in nearby Middlebury at the shop of Nahum Parker, a cabinetmaker to whom he was apprenticed. Parker was a conservative Whig and young Stephen Douglas, listening critically to the harangues of old Revolutionary soldiers as he shaped table legs from two-inch planks, decided that he was a Democrat.

Few men in American history have risen faster than Douglas. His career eventually led him to the United States Senate, to which he won re-election over Abraham Lincoln in 1856. Four years later the Springfield railsplitter did him in in the foot race for the presidency. The arch-spokesman of compromise was not among the casualties when the good ship Union foundered, for he died on June 3, 1861.

The birthplace of Franklin Pierce, across the mountains in Hillsboro, was not far from that of Douglas, and neither were his views on slavery. Pierce, however, did not share Douglas' anxiety about slavery as a moral evil. Apparently he was neither against nor for it. It existed; it was an accepted part of the social, economic and political structure of the country; that was enough for him.

Were it not for Salmon P. Chase, Thaddeus Stevens and other "black" Republicans, it might seem that the northcountry was a nursery of compromise. Chase went west when very young but did not like it there and came back home when he was sixteen to go to Dartmouth. Following his graduation he went to Washington to study law, then to Ohio, where he rose to fame as one of the Midwest's most truculent abolitionists. He was senator from Ohio from 1849 to 1855, and governor for another four years. On the third ballot of the Republican convention in 1860 he failed to win the presidential nomination over Lincoln by one and a half votes. Yet the career of this able, if vitriolic and humorless Yankee was not over. He became Lincoln's secretary of the treasury and from 1864 to 1873 he was Chief Justice of the Supreme Court.

And then there was the hard-drinking bachelor from Danville, Vermont, mulish Thaddeus Stevens, a Whig-turned-"black"-Republican. From the University of Vermont and Dartmouth he went to Pennsylvania, where in the practice of law and in the state legislature he won notice as a foe of privilege and oppression—as a tenderhearted champion of free schools and a laborer for him who was "governed, bought, sold, punished, executed by laws to which he never gave his assent, and by rulers whom he never chose."

He was an old man limping around on his club foot, still burning with idealism, when the Republican party was organized, and in 1858 Pennsylvania re-elected him to Congress. During the war he served as chairman of the Committee on Ways, Means and Appropriations of the House. Later he headed the Committee on Reconstruction—a misnomer; it might more aptly have been called the Committee on Retribution.

Thaddeus Stevens was buried as he chose to be—in a Negro cemetery.

3

"Pick as closely as you may," recalled Horace Greeley, "the next plowing turns up a fresh eruption of boulders and pebbles, from the size of a hickory-nut to that of a teakettle." The land was like that in Londonderry, where his Scotch-Irish ancestors had first brought the potato, and it was the same in Amherst, where his parents had moved in 1808. Two years later Horace was born there on a mortgaged farm. It was still mortgaged in 1820, when the sheriff attached everything but the clothes they stood in, so they migrated across the mountains to Westhaven, Vermont, on the border of New York near the southern end of Lake Champlain. Westhaven "might have been," wrote Greeley in his autobiography, "and should be today, a rich grazing township . . . But its pioneers, high and low, were lumbermen; and it has never yet liberated itself from their baleful sway."

Although they never lacked meat, wood, or a little money in Vermont they were always teetering on the brink of poverty, for the land did not yield easily and the elder Greeley may not have been a very good manager. "Flea Knoll," which they farmed for a while, was either too wet or too dry. Greeley mentions a bad run of maple sap, cracked fields with thistles coming up in the corn, and strong drink at haying time. His father never passed a day in thirty years of haying without it, or tobacco. (One of Horace's chores was to fill his mother's pipe before her after-dinner nap.) When one abstemious Irishman with only buttermilk as a beverage was found to have accomplished more with less fatigue than any of the others he was "received with as much wondering incredulity as though it had been certified that he lived wholly on air."

Young Greeley's resolution to become a teetotaler was put strenu-ously to test at sheepshearing time when three older boys held him down and poured liquor down his throat. Later, in Poultney, he helped to organize the pioneer temperance society in town, possibly the first in the country. The cold-water reformers, he recalled, had to withstand a good deal of ridicule. "Alas, that most of our facetious critics have since died, and no autopsy was needed. . . . A glance at each fiery proboscis, that irradiated even the cerements of the grave, was sufficient."

For all the struggle with soil and weather, Greeley looked back fondly to the freshness of the hills and woods, to the cool creeks of Poultney and Castleton and to the winding lake. In summer

we sometimes caught a fine pike or eel . . . in the basin beneath a 50-foot cataract by which the blended creeks tumble into the bay. . . . I sat here alone in the dense darkness of a wooded abyss where the falls drown all sound but its own from 8 to 11 p.m. without being blessed with a bite and then felt my way up through the Egyptian darkness of the forest hillsides of the road and so home pondering the fickleness of fortune, yet eager to try again whenever opportunity should favor.

He thought he probably should have been a farmer, a calling

whose quiet, its segregation from strife, and brawls, and heated rivalries, attract and delight one. I hate earning my bread in any calling which complicates my prosperity in some sort with others' adversity—my success with others' defeat. . . . Blessed is he whose day's exertion ends with the evening twilight, and who can sleep unbrokenly and without anxiety till the dawn awakes him with energies renewed and senses brightened, to fresh activity and that fulness of health and vigor which are vouchsafed to those only who spend most of their waking hours in the free, pure air and renovating sunshine of the open country.

But his inclinations led elsewhere. Even as a child he liked to read newspapers and was a politician, he remembered, when not half old enough to vote. At the age of eleven he tried in vain to get a job as a printer's apprentice in Whitehall. The paper which finally employed him, five years later, was the *Northern Spectator* in East Poultney. The terms of his apprenticeship were that he would receive only his board for six months, and $40 a year after that, and that he must remain until he was twenty. Thus began America's most illustrious career in journalism. He learned to set type, to condense news from the city papers for the *Spectator's* limited columns and, with lame back and blistered hands, to operate the old wooden press. In Poultney he did not fish, hunt, or play ball, but filled his spare time with reading. He recalled that never before or since had he read so much and to so much profit.

He had suffered acutely when his parents moved to Pennsylvania shortly after he began his apprenticeship, but as time passed he become contented and secure in his work. The editor, a Baptist clergyman whose pastorate required that he travel, frequently left the paper, editorial policy and all, completely in his hands. As acting editor Greeley was for paper money but he wanted "it to be *money* —convertable at pleasure into coin—not printed lies, even though they fail to deceive." He thought the admission of Missouri as a slave state was a terrible mistake, but the event that made him a confirmed abolitionist was the appearance of a Negro fugitive in Poultney. He had come across the border from New York, where there was a law that certain born slaves remained in bondage until they were twenty-eight years old. In due time the Negro's master arrived in Poultney "to recover the goods," as Greeley put it.

> I never saw so large a muster of men and boys so suddenly on our village green as his advent inflated; and a result . . . was the speedy disappearance of the chattel, and the return of his master, disconsolate and niggerless to the place from whence he came. Everything on our side was *impromptu* and instinctive; and nobody suggested that envy or hate of "the south" or of New York, or the master, had impelled the rescue. Our people hated injustice and oppression, and acted as if they couldn't help it.

Since he made so many friends in Poultney and so admired the spirit of the people ("I have never since known a community so generally moral, intelligent, industrious and friendly"), it was with painful regret that he climbed on a wagon bound for Comstock's Landing on the Champlain Canal in 1830 and boarded a packet from Whitehall. He was on his way west via Albany and the Erie Canal. In fourteen months he was back east—not in Vermont, but in New York to find employment on a newspaper.

The rest of Greeley is in the national domain. Unquestionably the founding of the New York *Tribune* led straight from the columns of the *Northern Spectator*. Surely there was much of East Poultney in the militant individualist who became leader of the Whigs, founder of the Republican party, and candidate for president. At the end of a tumultuous career Greeley confessed that he might have been much happier as a farmer, but seeing as he was not, he cherished the hope

> that the journal I projected will live and flourish . . . being guided by a larger wisdom, and more unerring sagacity to discern the right, though not by a more unfaltering readiness to embrace and defend it at whatever personal cost; and that the stone which covers my ashes may bear . . . the still intelligible inscription "*Founder of The New York Tribune.*"

Henry Raymond was not born in Vermont but might as well have been; a mortgage on the Raymond farm in Lima, New York, paid for his education at the University of Vermont. He married a girl from Winooski. Burlington was always his intellectual home. His career as founder of the *New York Times* led from there.

Raymond owed part of his heritage to the godfather of Vermont, Ira Allen, who founded the university at Burlington in 1791. ". . . . it is not the Rich that I am Calculating to Assist as the Poor," he had written. "The Rich can send their Sons to what college they Choose But the Poore have it not in their Power yet they may have the most Promising Posterity & if they can obtain good Educations may be in turn Rullers of the Land."

The most immediate influence upon Raymond was James Marsh, professor of moral and intellectual philosophy until 1842 and for seven years (1826-1833) president of the university. Marsh is acknowledged to have started the Transcendentalist movement in America (which always comes as a surprise to those who associate it, roots and all, with Massachusetts) when he introduced to American readers Samuel Taylor Coleridge's *Aids to Reflection*, with a preliminary essay. Within a month Emerson was reading Marsh's book and enthusiastically spreading the gospel. Vermonter John Dewey, a student at the university much later, had this to say about Marsh's views:

It is interesting to note that Marsh makes . . . a distinction between civilization and culture—civilization, he says, in effect is concerned with the adaptation of the arts and services of the individual
to the needs and conditions of existing society—Cultivation is the
development of the powers of individuals with reference to the ends
that make them truly human; it transcends any existing social order
and regime because it elevates them into possession of the spiritual
law of reason, of universal will, and of humanity as such.

As an outgrowth of his philosophy Marsh introduced into the
curriculum modern languages, English, natural sciences, and an
emphasis on speaking and writing. Into this pioneering environment,
at the height of the professor's career, came Henry Raymond, the
farmer's son, in 1836. Under Marsh, who became his good friend,
his interests ranged far beyond the Green Mountain and Adirondack
horizons. Not only did his verse find its way into Greeley's *New
Yorker,* but he served as that paper's Burlington agent.

At the 1839 commencement, held in Charles Bulfinch's Unitarian
church, he spoke for the junior class before an admiring audience
which included Henry Clay in a black frock coat. The illustrious
Whig was stumping the hinterlands for president and upon his arrival
in Burlington by steamboat had been welcomed with loud fanfare.
Only by recourse to his snuffbox, however, had the hard campaigner
been able to keep awake during the commencement ceremonies until
Raymond began his earnest declamation, whereupon Clay, suddenly
alert and interested, turned to the person next to him saying: "That
young man will make his mark. Depend upon it, you will hear from
him hereafter." Such an opinion on such good authority, of course,
stirred in the slender student visions of political glory, but for the
time being he stuck to journalism—literary journalism. Other than
Professor Marsh probably the most powerful influence upon him was
Rufus Wilmot Griswold, a native of Benson, later prominent as
Edgar Allan Poe's literary executor, but at the moment publisher
of a newspaper called the *Vermonter* a few miles south in Vergennes.
Griswold presently went to work for his friend Greeley in New York.
So did Henry Raymond not long after the *Tribune* appeared. For
three years he served as Greeley's most trusted lieutenant. Indeed,
whenever he was ill or went to Vermont on vacation the mercurial

Greeley moaned that it gave him a toothache to look at his (Raymond's) substitute.

The story of Henry Raymond, like that of Greeley after he left Poultney, belongs more to New York and the nation, yet Vermont's influence upon him continued strong. At every opportunity he returned to the hills for relaxation and for the counsel of his friends at the university (which awarded him a master's degree and later elected him a trustee). The fact that he was much more conservative than Greeley may have been the result of formative years spent in the comfortable atmosphere of scholarship and wealth that the growing town of Burlington afforded, whereas Greeley had set out into the world from a hard-scrabble farm and a small village without higher education. Their temperaments differed as widely as their social and economic views. To the knight-errant editor, riding off on his white charger, Raymond served often as an unwilling and scowling second. At the end of three years, after a disagreement about salary, the two parted company. Raymond went to work for the turbulent James Watson Webb, editor of the *Courier and Enquirer*, and it was there that he did much, according to his biographer, Francis Brown, to start the organization which became the Associated Press.

By the time he became managing editor of the new *Harper's* magazine in 1850, Raymond's views were well formed. In an address to the alumni body of the University of Vermont that year he cautioned against the kind of radicalism which, just for the sake of change, seeks to destroy that which has been proved good and, on the other hand, the blind conservatism that resists all change. This was the pith of the policy of a newspaper he had for some time dreamed of establishing and which, in 1851, he did found. It was called the *New York Daily Times*. His partner was George Jones of Poultney, Vermont, the same place, curiously enough, where Greeley had served his apprenticeship. When Raymond was on the staff of the *Tribune*, Jones was in the business department and the two are said to have talked about the newspaper they might own someday. Since not a single resident of New York City invested in the new paper it was, in effect, a New England enterprise. Raymond declared that the *Times* would "seek to allay, rather than excite, agitation—to extend industry, temperance and virtue—to encourage and advance education; to promote economy, concord and justice." This statement bears witness to certain phrases in the Vermont Constitution such as the one which observes that "frequent recurrence to fundamental principles and a firm adherence to justice, moderation, temperance, industry and frugality are absolutely necessary to preserve the blessings of liberty and keep government free."

While George Jones, the business manager, professed to know nothing about editorial matters, after Raymond's untimely death, he did very well in the *Times*'s crusade, for example, against the notorious Tweed Ring. (On one occasion he refused a bribe of $5 million to drop the campaign.) To Charles R. Miller from Hanover, New Hampshire, Jones presently relinquished editorial responsibility. With Carl Van Anda (who learned his trade on the Burlington *Free Press*) as managing editor, Miller guided the editorial policies of the *Times* for more than forty years.

There were other editors from the hillcountry—Charles A. Dana from Hinsdale, New Hampshire, for one—a trustee of Brook Farm, managing editor of the New York *Tribune*, assistant secretary of war (the eyes and ears of Lincoln at the front) and, in 1868, founder of the New York *Sun*.

What, then, is to be said for the land of two seasons—winter and the Fourth of July—beyond the belt of optimum challenge whence came such "woodmen, watermen and hunters" as Webster, Douglas, Pierce, Chase, Stevens, Greeley, Raymond, Jones, Miller and Dana? Does a harsh climate not have its compensations? Could it be said, with propriety, that after a cold night the sap indeed runs better?

XII

WHEN THE PEOPLE
WERE ON FIRE

Unless it is early in October when the sugar maple holds its fiesta of color in the hills, there is little to remind the visitor to Vermont and New Hampshire of the days when the people themselves were on fire. Not to imply that today they are without warmth, as strangers are likely to conclude after seeing all the granite faces at town meeting or the legislature. Though time has rounded off the craggy mountain peaks, deep underneath the granite is molten.

Historians are fond of saying that the northcountry was thoroughly "burnt over" in the nineteenth century, which is another way of saying that the people were effervescing—that their blood was boiling. One consequence of their escape from the clutches of the Puritan towns of southern New England and the rigors of the early wars was a prolonged bath in alcohol. They drank on military training day, at town meeting, in church, and even around the quilting frame. The administrators of justice, lamented Governor Eaton of Vermont in 1855, were often "unable to poise her scales with steadiness." In short

> occasions for drinking were found both in joy and in sorrow; at birth and death; at weddings and at funerals; at meeting and at parting; in sickness and in health; in labor and in recreation; by day and by night; indoors and outdoors; in calm and in tempest; when it snowed and when it rained—and when it did neither.

At the raising of the meetinghouse in St. Johnsbury, according to the Rev. Edward T. Fairbanks,

> all the men and boys were there to put up the timbers and women and girls to give cheer and mix the toddy. The crowning event of the day, as reported to me by an eye-witness, then in his ninety-first year, was the balancing of Zibe Tute on his head at the end of the ridgepole, swallowing the contents of his flask and descending head downwards to the ground.

Watermelon and baker's gingerbread were for sale from peddlers' wagons in the streets of Bennington on parade days, wrote Hiland Hall, and always several barrels of cider were on draught to warm up or cool off the customers. Training day, fixed by Vermont law on the first Tuesday in June, was pungent with burnt gunpowder, gingerbread, root beer, rum and molasses, and potato whiskey. Long before the sun rose the popping of guns far up and down the valleys announced that festivities had already begun. Then on foot, on horseback and by wagonloads Vermonters poured into town where the "music of the toddy-stick" was at least as loud as the roll of drums around the green. By afternoon the streets were a tumult of peddlers hawking their wares above the surging, singing, shouting throng, and by evening the town was utterly dispirited.

The first distillery in the town of Cabot, it is said, was erected in 1809 by a part-time blacksmith who shipped his potato whiskey to Boston and Portland. Within a few seasons the potato growers could scarcely meet the demand of eleven local distilleries supplying an almost inexhaustible market: the British troops across the Canadian border forty miles away. "The good orthodox citizens of this place," observed the town historian in Hemenway's *Gazetteer*, "seemed quite intent on obeying the Divine injunction; 'If thine enemy hunger, feed him; *if he thirst*, give him drink.' . . . It was smuggling, and was rather risky business but the 'Commandment' was plain and imperative and must be followed."

About 1815 Cabot's young apple trees started bearing and from then on no basement was without twelve or fifteen barrels of cider to carry a farmer through the winter. Even if he did not drink it, its value as tender was inflation-proof. Cabot had no monopoly on the liquor business—it was going on even more briskly in other Vermont and New Hampshire towns. It was estimated that in Concord every man, woman and child consumed an average of four and a half gallons a year, which in money represented more than twice the expense of running the town. Judge Jonathan Kittredge, a temperance lecturer who in the past had drunk his share, claimed that in 1828 alone the people of New Hampshire consumed some 732,483 gallons. Then the reaction set in. Temperance clubs, led by steely-eyed clergymen, sprang up in every community and after years of attrition put the monster rum utterly to rout.

If the aftermath of recent wars is any criterion, the good citizens of New Hampshire and Vermont were reacting quite normally during the very wet era that followed the cutting of England's apron strings. The very air was intoxicating and the pioneers' ebullience found expression in many other ways. The so-called Indian Stream Republic affair in northern New Hampshire was a kind of Gilbert and

Sullivan finale to the land wars, which provided excitement as long as there were boundaries to determine. That was just it—the boundary of New Hampshire and Canada had not been entirely fixed during the 1820's and 1830's and the 400-odd settlers on some 200,000 disputed acres in the vicinity of what is now Pittsburg, between the Connecticut lakes on the east and Indian and Hall's Stream to the west, resolved to make the most of it.

In order to deal with such foreign powers as Canada and the United States, they banded together as the United Inhabitants of Indian Stream Territory. They were not, however, united. Some wanted to be citizens of Canada, some, of the United States, and some (doubtless those referred to as persons of "easy morals") did not care one way or the other. They adopted, nevertheless, a constitution, and by 1832 Indian Stream was a full-fledged republic. Foreign relations turned out to be most delicate. For killing wild beasts, the citizens liked to collect bounties from New Hampshire. They did not care to pay the duties imposed upon them for goods exported to the United States. They viewed with positive alarm Canada's proposals for drafting them into its military service. By 1834 some of the people were so irritated by the aggressions of New Hampshire that they appealed to the attorney general of the United States. The freemen of Indian Stream, they said, were willing to be citizens of the United States, but not of New Hampshire. The opinion of the attorney general was a classic of brevity and logic: "If you are within the limits of the United States it is because you are within the limits of the state of New Hampshire." A majority of the frustrated voters of Indian Stream now turned toward the north, but nothing definite came of their petition to Canada for protection.

The ship of state rocked along through shoal waters until, in 1835, it grounded with a crunch. In March of that year a New Hampshire deputy who tried to arrest two inhabitants of Indian Stream was beaten and driven out. In June the New Hampshire legislature decided to send in troops, if necessary, to support the sheriffs in serving their writs. In the fall Justice Alexander Rea of Hereford, Lower Canada, notified the inhabitants of Indian Stream that he would meet with them to discuss means of protecting them from New Hampshire. Early in October a New Hampshire sheriff named Smith served a writ on Indian Streamer John Tyler (who now considered himself a subject of the King) and took him captive for not co-operating. But Tyler was happily rescued by a posse of his pro-Canadian friends. New Hampshire posted a reward of $5 for his arrest. Defiantly Tyler, with others, now captured in the name of the King a pro-New Hampshire deputy named Blanchard who had aided Smith to accomplish his own arrest. A second posse succeeded in re-leasing Blanchard. Shortly thereafter two rash youths named Miles Hurlburt and Ephraim Aldrich, riding boldly into Canada to re-capture Tyler, ran afoul of Justice Alexander Rea, who ordered them off the King's highway. Hurlburt, as he testified later, then pointed his pistol at Rea "and told him to keep his proper distance . . . for if he came any nearer he should take the contents of my pistol." Hurlburt's partner warned Rea that Hurlburt meant what he said. Whereupon Rea and his men tried to seize the bridle of Aldrich's horse. Aldrich brandished his sword and Justice Rea and his men started throwing stones. As a warning Hurlburt fired his pistol into the air.

> About this time, [according to Hurlburt], 30 or 40 more of the party which I left at Parmelee and Joy's store [in Canaan] came into sight. . . . Rea and those with him immediately took to flight, Rea running for the woods and Aldrich after him. When I came up with Aldrich and Rea, Aldrich had Rea down, Aldrich having one hand ahold of the collar of Rea's coat and one hand ahold of the hilt of his sword and Rea having hold with both his hands of the blade of Aldrich's sword with the point of it sticking into the ground and Aldrich was kicking Rea in the side. When I came up Rea was say-ing, "I surrender" and Aldrich replied, "Then let go of the sword and I'll let you alone." Dr. Turrell at the same time came up and remarked to Aldrich, "He says he surrenders. Why don't you let him get up?" Aldrich again replied, "If he will let go the sword, I will," and Dr. Turrell remarked to Rea, "If you will let go the sword, I will guarantee that Aldrich will not hurt you," whereupon Rea let go the sword and Aldrich let him get up and we took him and put him into the wagon and carried him down to the store of Parmelee and Joy in Vermont. While this skirmish was carried on, I heard 4 or 5 guns fired, one of which I fired as before stated. . . . Young was wounded in the groin by a pistol shot. Rea was wounded in the scalp by a sabre. Hurlburt and Wiswald . . . . brought Rea [to

Canaan] about a mile and a half from his home, dressed his wound and sent him back.

This incident was too much for the adjutant general of New Hampshire, who ordered the state militia into Indian Stream. They surrounded the house of one of the most troublesome Canadian partisans, Emor Applebee, and led him to jail, while the wife of one of his pro-New Hampshire neighbors called out: "Well, Mr. Applebee, the old eagle is beginning to scream!"

In January, 1836, the Canadian government advised New Hampshire that it would refrain from further interference pending the setttlement of the boundary. In May the citizens acknowledged, in effect, that Indian Stream was a part of New Hampshire. "Ten years of my life gone for nothing!" sighed Luther Parker, president of the defunct republic as he started southwest across Vermont to make his way by covered wagon, canal packet and steamboat to Wisconsin.

The Vermont border during the late 1830's was no more tranquil than New Hampshire's. In the so-called Canadian Rebellion of 1837, Irishmen of the Green Mountains helped their confrères across the border light the fires of revolt against England, and for several months the people were in great flux. Thereafter, except for epidemics of smuggling, Vermonters along "the line" lived in peace with themselves and their neighbors until 1864, when Bennett Young and his band of Confederates galloped south from Canada to sack the town of St. Albans in the northernmost action of the Civil War. (Although Vermont lost more men, per capita, on the battlefields of the South than any northern state except Kansas, there was, as has been said, nothing like agreement about slavery in the Green Mountains. On the one hand, Vermonters conducted escaped slaves to Canada aboard one of the most efficient branches of the "underground railroad." On the other, Burlington Unitarians dismissed Joshua Young from his pastorate for preaching the funeral service of John Brown when he was buried at North Elba, New York. And John Henry Hopkins, the first Episcopal bishop of Vermont, wrote that the Bible accepted slavery and that there was nothing holy about going to war over it.)

After the Civil War the border between Vermont and Canada again burst into flames in the Fenian uprising against British rule in Canada.

"This is the advance guard of the Irish-American army for the liberation of Ireland from the yoke of the oppressor!" announced General John O'Neill to his Green Mountain wearers of the Green on May 25, 1870. "For your own country you now enter that of the enemy. The eyes of your countrymen are upon you. Forward march!" The well-entrenched redcoats in Lower Quebec, opposite Franklin Center, gave O'Neill a very warm reception and the British flag continued to wave over Canada.

2

It is perhaps in the field of religion that the people of the north-country made some of their most vivid and contradictory experiments. The ground seems to have been plowed in colonial times by George Whitefield, who found New Hampshire a garden for his evangelism. He in fact died there in 1770 after preaching four times in one week to admiring audiences in enemy territory—that of the Church of England minister, Arthur Browne, in Portsmouth.

> My small flock (Blessed be God!) [Browne wrote a friend], have almost escaped the Infection. Three or four only have fallen away, but . . . they were persons of no *extraordinary reputation*. . . . The Enemy's whole artillery Seemed leveled against us . . . pestering & pelting us with Sermons & Lectures, sometimes three & four in a Day.

In colonial New Hampshire the voters in each town determined the "official" churches, and all citizens were taxed for their support whether or not they belonged to them. The path of insurgent religious groups (other than the entrenched Congregationalists) was thus a thorny one. Although none in nonconformist Vermont achieved the fame or notoriety of the Deist Ethan Allen, the irascible Jeremiah O'Callaghan, builder in Burlington of Vermont's first Catholic church, was out of the same mold. A native of York, Ireland, O'Callaghan early became contemptuous of banks and usury, and severely critical of his peers. Shuttled from one diocese to another in Europe and America he was eventually banished to Vermont, far away from the church authorities. Mellowing not the least in the country air, he wrote vigorous critiques against other churches and a book on six-per-centers with chapters entitled: "The Banking

System Is Usury, Fraud and Deception," and "Savings Bank, Satan's Net for Catching Souls."

Then there was Orestes Brownson of Stockbridge (Vermont), the ministerial chameleon, first a Presbyterian, then a Universalist, then an independent, then a Unitarian (friend of Channing, Thoreau and George Ripley of Brook Farm), and finally a Catholic. Author, editor and publisher of some twenty volumes, he is considered by historian Perry Miller to have been in many respects the most powerful of the Transcendentalists.

The age of the revivals, like the temperance movement, was a reaction to the era of the back-yard distillery, which in turn was a recoil from war and Puritanism. Except for the Millerites (who evolved into the Seventh-Day Adventists), the Shakers, the Mormons, the Perfectionists and the Christian Scientists—most of the sects that flourished in the hillcountry during the eighteen-hundreds have vanished without a trace. The last three of the above-named definitely had their roots in Vermont and New Hampshire. Shakerism, imported from New York, prospered in New Hampshire as in few other places. Although the beginnings of Mormonism are associated with New York, both Joseph Smith and Brigham Young were Vermont-born. So was Oliver Cowdery, who claimed to have helped write the *Book of Mormon* from the golden plates that Smith dug up and deciphered in New York. Chosen an apostle as early as 1835 Heber C. Kimball of Sheldon traveled around Vermont gaining converts. He was present at Salt Lake when Brigham Young said, "This is the place," and became chief justice of the "State of Deseret." Other apostles of Vermont birth were Hyrum Smith, Luke Johnson, William Smith and Erastus Snow. The Champlain valley supplied the first of the faithful in New England—a band of 27 men and women from Benson. Indeed, as historian Stewart Holbrook observes, Vermont endowed the prophet with more wives (six) than any other New England state.

The grandfather of Joseph Smith had emigrated to Vermont in middle age and Joseph's father farmed there and in New Hampshire for twenty years—in Tunbridge, Lebanon, Royalton, Sharon (where the prophet was born on December 23, 1805) and Norwich. Joseph Senior, a vigorous six-footer, invested all his savings in a quantity of the legendary ginseng root which flourished in the Green Mountains and which the Chinese considered a cure-all for disease; but the man to whom he entrusted the shipment absconded with the proceeds.

Northern New England at this time was in a fever of fortune hunting. There was boundless interest in buried treasure, as the diggings in Bristol and other pockmarked places still testify. It was a secretive and mystical business conducted in the dead of night with lanterns and in whispers, lest the "spell" be broken and the chest, most certainly but a few feet beneath their shovels, either sink into the earth forever or simply disappear before their eyes. An early historian, writing in Hemenway's *Gazetteer*, felt certain that a band of money diggers led by a preacher named Nathaniel Wood had much to do with the origins of the Mormons. Excommunicated by the Congregational church of Middletown for stirring up a controversy when the parishioners failed to appoint him as their minister, he began to preach to his own family and a circle of neighbors and friends, including the father of Oliver Cowdery. Wood thought God would make Himself known to the people through supernatural agencies. When in 1800 a man named Winchell, armed with a hazel rod, announced that there was buried money in the neighborhood of Middletown, digging for treasure somehow became a part of Wood's strange theology. The hazel rod, it appeared, would indicate who were Jews. There would be a vast convulsion of the earth that would destroy all the "gentiles" (the unbelievers). The pronouncements of Winchell and Wood bear a curious resemblance to certain tenets of the Mormon faith. Certainly its very foundation, the unearthing of the golden plates, was rooted in the Vermont money diggings.

Announcing one night to his spadesmen in Tinmouth that they were about to uncover a chest of money, Winchell warned that there was a divinity guarding it and that the diggers must say nothing during the removal of a huge stone; otherwise the spell would be broken. While the stone was being pried up with bars, one of the workers exclaimed: "Get off my toes!" Whereupon Winchell announced in a loud voice: "The money is gone—flee for your lives!" Which they all did.

Although Nathaniel Wood's flock dispersed some three decades before Mormonism appeared, it is interesting that Winchell (whose treasure hunting some thought to be a camouflage for counterfeiting) presently turned up in Palmyra, New York, where the elder Joseph

Smith and his family went after leaving Vermont. Here the money digging began anew and Joseph Smith, Sr., and later his son engaged in it until about the time the golden Bible was uncovered. So much opprobrium was attached to the Mormons in the early years of polygamy that the leaders were disowned by their native towns, hence much of the early history of the movement has been lost. But now Sharon and Whitingham, the birthplaces of Joseph Smith and Brigham Young, are glad enough to claim them as their own.

The experiment of John Humphrey Noyes in Perfectionism, described by George Bernard Shaw as "one of those chance attempts at Superman which occur from time to time, in spite of the interference of man's blundering institutions," is considered the purest experiment in Communism ever carried on in the United States. Part of its chronicle, like that of the Mormons, belongs to New York, but it had Vermont beginnings and probably would have continued there had Noyes not been forced to leave the state because of his program of "complex," or plural, marriage. Born in Brattleboro in 1811 of well-to-do parents, Noyes attended Dartmouth and studied law for a while, but then decided to go to Andover and Yale to prepare for the ministry. Too independent for the Congregational church, which revoked his license to preach, Noyes strayed further and further from the bounds of orthodoxy and in 1839 founded his daring community at Putney. It was not exclusively religious or social or economic like other contemporary experiments, but all three combined. One student, G. R. Hopwood, describes it as a bold effort, conscious or otherwise, to apply the principles and idealism of Plato to a working human institution.

To finance the Putney experiment Noyes, his wife and mother, his brother and two sisters contributed their inheritances of $38,000. Four years later in 1843, 28 adults and 9 children were sharing the fruits of each other's labors in the store and on the two farms that provided the Community's income. The following year, apparently as a result of the failure of Noyes and his wife to produce more than one living child, they began sharing their wives. It was Plato's conviction that, although licentiousness is an unholy thing, an enlightened soul will dominate the flesh. In order to maintain control of, and quality in, the population of the perfect community, he pictured mating as taking place during festivals under supervision of the leaders. This is nearly what happened at Putney and later at Oneida, New York. Noyes formed a committee of older members to select the parents of the colony's future children. Those excluded from this program were not permitted to have children; without Noyes's permission they were not even allowed to fall in love. For those so privileged, but denied permission to have children, Noyes evolved a strange system called "male continence," which occasionally failed with the result that unauthorized children appeared.

This was too much for the indignant and envious (?) citizens of a state that for all its frontier effervescence was still Puritan in character, and in 1847 the Putney Community broke up. Migrating to Oneida in the wilds of western New York, it continued its experiments unmolested if only for the reason that it had few neighbors. What wrecked Oneida, as it had the Putney Community, was "complex marriage." The orthodox clergy never missed an opportunity to denounce its insidious licentiousness or clamor for the scalp of the man who, under his so-called "selective" program, became the father of nine children by nine different "wives." Yet the experiment in many ways was enlightening. Throughout the history of Putney and Oneida there were overtones of mental healing "beyond the routine of science, which we must take into account in all this dealing with disease." Sociologists have commented upon the distinguished careers of most of the children born under "complex marriage."

At the very least John Humphrey Noyes could claim that he had "made a raid into an unknown country, charted it, and returned without the loss of a man, woman or child."

It is because there is still a Shaker colony in New Hampshire, a handful of old ladies living among the relics of their past on a quiet hill in Canterbury, that their story is told here. For now there have been Shakers at Canterbury longer than at New Lebanon, New York, whence the movement came. Nearly seventeen decades have passed since men and women of the United Society of Believers in Christ's Second Coming first settled at the end of that narrow road to lead lives of humanity and diligence. They were followers of an English blacksmith's daughter, named Ann Lee, who in 1774 came to America to build a church upon the principle that the most spiritual life is the virginal one, the purest life a life of honest labor and self-denial. The doctrine of virginity seems to have arisen from Ann's unhappy married life in England, for it is said that she shrank from her husband's embraces. All of her five children died young. In her misery she groaned and cried at night and was long so sickly that she was under the care of friends.

Like the Perfectionists of John Humphrey Noyes, the Shakers believed in sharing their property. Their adherence to sexual continence, unlike the Perfectionists, is one reason why Shakerism is a dying religion; they could augment their numbers only by converting outsiders to their faith. But for a century and a half there were enough young men and women who wished to withdraw from the world, from disappointments in love perhaps; enough lonely widows and widowers who believed Shaker life to be ideally serene and uplifting, to keep the ranks well filled.

"Do all your work as though you had a thousand years to live, and as though you were going to die tomorrow," Mother Ann Lee had preached. If there were no written evidence that work at Canterbury was done as she had counseled, one could tell from the material objects the Shakers have left: sidewalks of granite, great barns of stone, chairs and tables as spare, unadorned and uncompromisingly erect as the people who made them. At Canterbury and at Enfield, the other New Hampshire colony, there was always an air of repose and of secure well-being that seemed to bid defiance to the gnawing uncertainties and fears of the outside world.

The Shakers achieved such an atmosphere in spite of unremitting labor in kitchen, field and shop. In their dawn-to-dark regimen they built their own dwellings and all the furnishings in them down to the wooden spoons on the table. They curried the leather of their own cattle for shoes and horse collars, wove their clothes from the fine wool of their sheep, and linen goods from home-grown flax. They planted herb gardens for their medicines, cleared, planted and harvested their fields and orchards. At Enfield they dammed a spring-fed mountain stream and at Canterbury they caught the melting snow in eight large artificial ponds to provide water (by way of an aqueduct) for household use and to run mills for carding and spinning wool, sawing pail staves, grinding malt, finishing iron, and even to churn butter and wash clothes in an ingenious water-powered laundry. Outsiders came to know and respect them through their packaged seeds and herbs, candlesticks, stoves, rocking chairs, trestle tables, braided rugs, bonnets, sweaters and linen goods. The Canterbury Shakers prospered through the manufacture and sale of a flat broom and a washing machine; the Enfield colony, through its Eclipse Corn Planter. With its three hundred members, its thrifty livestock, its model houses and factories, the Enfield colony grew so prominent in the mid-1800's that it dominated the whole region of Lake Mascoma, on whose shore it was built. The brethren and sisters contributed one fifth of Enfield's taxes. In two decades they cared for over a hundred of the town's children. So strong was their voice in local affairs that they were instrumental in deciding the route of the railroad from Concord to White River Junction. To gain access to it across the lake from the colony, they built a remarkable half-mile bridge of stone-filled wooden cribbing which lasted ninety years, until the hurricane of 1938. They opened their hearts and purses when fire or famine struck across the country.

Tragedy struck the Enfield colony itself in 1863, when Elder Caleb Dyer, manager of the very profitable Shaker Mills Company (maker of flannels for New York markets), was shot on his way to the office by a drunken father whose children the Shakers had been caring for. As a result of this catastrophe the brethren eventually lost $20,000, but they were by no means destitute. In 1874 they were doing a $30,000 a year business in packaged seeds alone. In 1896 *The Manifesto*, printed by the colony at Canterbury, announced that 2,592 cakes of ice, 22 inches square and 16 inches thick, had been harvested and that 100,000 feet of lumber had been hauled down four miles out of the forests, had been sawed into boards, shingles and laths, and was ready for market.

Industry and unwavering punctuality marked each day in the life of the Canterbury and Enfield Shaker. Two brothers or two sisters, occupying each barren room, awoke at four o'clock in the summer and five in the winter to the ringing of a bell. After dressing they knelt to pray, then made sure that their room, with its low ceilings, pale-blue or yellow walls, its floors of wide pine boards with an occasional rag rug, its wood stove, writing table, its wooden chairs and cot beds were spotless. Coverlets and blankets were removed from the beds and folded over two chairs, placed back to back. Clothes were neatly piled in the homemade chests of drawers that abounded in every Shaker dwelling. Any extra chairs were hung on the even more numerous wooden pegs on the walls. "We hang everything except people, that we leave the world to do," they made a joke of saying. Then they went down to the first-floor dining room, again kneeling to pray (brethren, sisters and children at their separate tables) before eating their breakfast in silence.

Rules governed practically everything they did. In folding their hands, custom dictated that they clasp the right hand over the left; that they kneel with the right leg first and climb stairs with the right foot first. A brother and sister were not allowed to shake hands, to be alone together without a chaperon, even to stop and talk in the halls or to pass each other on the stairs. There was little opportunity for association anyway, since during the day the men were in the fields or shops and the women were busy with the household. If a brother was needed to help with the heavy lifting in the kitchen or in the dairy, where the sisters worked in the summer months, he had many chaperons, as did the sisters when they picked raspberries in the fields.

The sexes did congregate in the evenings for singing and discussion and of course at worship on Sunday, when not even the most casual work was permitted except in an emergency, such as getting the hay in. They sat in rows facing each other and when the time came for marching they would go through all kinds of gyrations, which of course is where the name Shakers came from. They would whirl, leap and thrust their arms out palms upward in time to the music, clap, stamp their feet, groan and tremble. For a long time visitors were permitted to attend Sunday meeting and the marching of two hundred Shakers, the population of the Canterbury colony in the 1800's, was a spectacle. There are scattered reports that in the very early days this shooing-off of evil spirits got out of hand, with the result that it was later very much restrained.

Brethren and sisters met again on Sunday evenings from four to eight for discussion and conversation. Again they sat in rows facing each other, the sisters wearing fresh white hoods and with handkerchiefs on their laps, and the brethren, handkerchiefs across their knees. They could laugh, then, if they wished, and sing their curious songs. The first and fourth stanzas of one of them, called "The Steamboat," went as follows:

> While our steamboat, Self-denial
> Rushes up against the stream,
> Is it not a serious trial
> Of the pow'r of gospel steam?
> When Self-will, and Carnal pleasure,
> And Free Thinker, all afloat,
> Come down snorting with such pressure
> Right against our little boat.
>
> Wretched souls, while hesitating
> Where to fix your final claim,
> Don't you see our boiler heating
> With a more effectual flame!
> When the stream comes on like thunder
> And the wheels begin to play,
> Must you not be torn asunder
> And swept off the downward way?

Their religious beliefs were modest in scope. They considered their founder, Ann Lee, an intermediary between God and themselves—a transmitter of spiritual force. They thought of God as being both masculine and feminine and prayed to "Our Father and Mother which are in Heaven." They considered the Bible as essentially a historical work, and Christ, by birth and otherwise, a human being quite like themselves, except that the will of God was more strongly manifested in Him and in Ann Lee than in any other mortals. From Jesus and the Apostles they adopted the doctrine of celibacy to prove that the spirit could conquer the flesh. They abstained from bearing arms, taking oaths, accepting posts of honor, engaging in politics, or having anything to do with the feverish desires of the outside world. They were, however, most tolerant of other religions, even of John Humphrey Noyes's Perfectionists, with their doctrine of plural marriage. They recognized that the human race could not continue without marriage and childbirth, but that their own state of virginity was the more holy. Historians have found parallels in the doctrines of the Shakers and those later of the Christian Scientists. Ann Lee was known to the Shakers as "Mother," as for a long time was Mrs. Eddy to her followers. The parent church in both sects was known as the Mother Church. Both women claimed that they had the power to heal. The Shakers' church was the Church of Christ; Mary Baker Eddy added the word "Scientist." She also considered God as being both masculine and feminine. The fact that Mrs. Eddy lived but a few miles from Canterbury as a girl probably accounts for these and other similarities.

If life at Canterbury and Enfield had always worked out according to the blueprints, the colonies would have been unique among human institutions. In *The Rise and Progress of the Serpent from the Garden of Eden, to the Present Day* one Mary Dyer (nee Marshall) hurled the blackest charges of drunkenness and immorality at Enfield, where for a time she had lived as a Shaker. She appears to have been a sensuous, jealous and vindictive woman, so few of her charges (or those of others from whom she solicited testimonials against Shaker life) can be taken seriously—particularly since they were all vigorously refuted by her husband, Joseph Dyer, and her children. Whole families, husband, wife and children, were frequently admitted at Enfield and Canterbury, but on an elementary status. Separation of Shaker colonies into groups of about fifty persons called "families," each with their own living quarters, industries and stores, their own elders and deacons, supposedly permitted relationships to be more personable and manageable—more family-like. But since true family life was not allowed, there were bound to be stresses and strains. And of course it was often impossible to keep Cupid from drawing his bow.

In *Fifteen Years in the Senior Order of Shakers* Hervey Elkins tells a poignant story of unrequited love at Canterbury over a century ago. The lovers, whom he gave the assumed names of Urbino and Ellina, suffered long and acutely since the elders forbade them even to speak to each other. Only fifteen rods separated the room where Urbino read and wrote from Ellina's window in the millinery rooms of the third story of a building directly opposite. Resolving to improve a view that was all but obscured by an apple tree, Urbino nonchalantly pruned the trees around the offending one, then succeeded in doctoring the branches that had shielded from his view the dearest sight on earth. Thenceforward the two sat at their windows at every available hour, ostensibly reading books,

and when duty called either away [they] would give the gentle
countersign of their own conception to the other who would respond.
. . . How many times have . . . I seen him, sitting at the window
of his apartment, his head reclining upon his hand and his elbow
resting upon the window stool, watching to see her pass on her way
to the mansion; how many times, under the semblance of the calls
of duty, have they met, though an espionage observed them, to pass
only a look, or a gesture of love.

History records only this glimpse of Urbino and Ellina and does
not tell of their fate.

A fine account of Shaker life during the latter eighteen-hundreds,
and of the outdoors in upland New England, was written by Nicholas
A. Briggs, who spent most of his life at Canterbury. He recalled the
vivid seasons, the joys of sugaring in the early spring when the boys
would wade through deep snow to distribute the buckets, to help the
brethren drill the trees and drive in the spouts. A rare privilege it was
to sit up all night tending the fire which kept the sap boiling in
huge kettles, while hooting owls broke the eerie silence of the woods.
And what a glorious reward, he remembered, were the griddle cakes
and fresh syrup served at the rustic camp, the "stick-chops" made
by pouring syrup on the snow or on a marble slab; or "sap honey,"
the residue of a pail of frozen sap—quite different in taste from that
which was boiled.

Summer was the busiest season and haying perhaps the most de-
manding task of the year, for the livelihood of 200 head of horned
cattle, a dozen horses and 200 sheep depended upon it. It was the
custom to mow one 60-acre field one day and put the hay in the
barn the next. In the morning the boys were lined up in the toolroom,
given pitchforks, which they shouldered like rifles, and marched
double file into the dooryard "then go as you please to the field." As
fast as the boys raked and cocked, the brethren carted the hay away.
It was one man's task to drive the refreshment wagon carrying lemon,
peppermint, checkerberry, raspberry and sweet buttermilk to the
laborers. Then there were vegetable gardens to be tended, oats, barley,
beans, corn and potatoes to be harvested, 400 cords of wood, the
year's supply of fuel, to be cut, grapes and apples to be picked. The
annual crop of a thousand or so bushels of apples had to be sorted
for applesauce or cider and to be cut for drying, a task that required

the combined forces of the brethren, sisters and children two or three nights a week throughout the fall. It would be done in the light of tallow candles on large tables in the laundry, with the brethren paring and quartering with machines on one side of the room and the sisters and children finishing for the kiln on the other. A year's supply of apple pie for the colony and Shaker applesauce for the market was thus assured.

In some ways winter was the dullest season. When they were not studying or attending religious services (three nights a week and Sunday) the older boys were put to work shoveling snow, keeping woodboxes filled and making brooms, while the smaller ones helped the sisters knit stockings. Such a schedule of manual work, study and worship required five changes of clothes a day. Since there were few spare hours, the simplest pleasures on holidays or in other rare moments of freedom were that much more exciting. They roamed the woods or played ball half a day each week in warm weather and on rainy days were allowed to fish. After harvest the teams were harnessed and the children given a whole day's outing to town—Concord, perhaps, where they ate their lunch near the railroad station and watched the trains go by, or on the banks of the Merrimack so they could swim in the afternoon.

Christmas, the most unusual day of the year, was preceded by the devout Shaker Fast Day devoted to the correcting of the errors of the past year, acknowledging and banishing old grudges, and starting the Shaker New Year with clean hands and pure hearts. (Such days were reminiscent of an earlier custom called the "Sweeping Gift." Every so often the elders and a few singers would march through every room in every building crying "Sweep! Sweep!" using their "spiritual brooms . . . to drive out all moral and spiritual uncleanliness that might exist.") On Christmas Day a religious service at nine in the morning was followed by the united gift to the poor. "A bundle of serviceable clothing had been previously prepared for everyone and placed in the waiting room, and now all left the meeting room, everyone took a bundle, and returning, deposited it in one of the large baskets that had been brought in." Union meetings, in which the sexes gathered for conversation in groups of six or eight, were held in the afternoon and Christmas supper was at four o'clock. Gifts to the children of candy, oranges, raisins, and perhaps a diary for the new year were indeed modest in keeping with the Shaker philosophy that it was sinful to have individual possessions.

While Briggs had the warmest remembrances of Canterbury, he could not say that he thought that the life of a Shaker was ideal.

If any boy among the Shakers could be perfectly contented and happy, surely I ought to be that boy, for my lot was cast in pleasant places. I never received an unkind word from my caretakers or teacher, nor do I recall ever a word of reproof. I was favored beyond most, and possibly any other boys, and yet in spite of all favorable circumstances I was not thoroughly contented. Why not? Was it due to a defect in my organism or was it imperfect environment? I think a fair answer will be that I was in an institution rather than a home. It was a boarding school with this essential difference: the boy in the boarding school looks forward to his vacation, when he can spend days or weeks at his home. He knows that a few years at the longest will terminate school, and he will then remain at home or make a home of his own.

Although Briggs's mother lived at the colony and although he was free to visit her,

I knew the sentiment of the people was vehemently opposed to what they termed natural relation, and they continually declaimed against it in their meetings. It was a perpetual testimony of hate for father, mother, brother and sister.

Is it any wonder that embarrassment invariably attended frequent visits to my mother? Once only did I in any way divulge . . . my feelings, but this time I met with her when suffering unusual dejection and sobbingly I poured out my grief. Her sympathy was sweet and she made it very easy for me to say I wanted to return to Providence, and I knew that I had only to say the word and she would take me there. . . . In my ignorance of the true situation, believing that I alone suffered discontent, and, as I have said, feeling a responsibility as the eldest and next to mother the head of the family, I felt it to be selfish and wrong to allow my personal feelings to disrupt the comfort of the others, and I hastened to assure mother that I would try to bear up under it, nor did I ever again burden her with any personal trouble, and, so far as I know, she never knew I had any.

From the schedules of the unending seasons and years, from a life-time association with one sex, Briggs saw no relief. Sometimes when he heard the distant rumbling of trains he wished that he was on one. While he could find no fault with the treatment he personally received, he felt the pressure of the very rigid theocracy that governed the colony. The word of the elders was law and, since they had their favorites, injustice was often done. The only recourse for a brother or sister with a grievance was to appeal to the Ministry, who lived aloof in separate quarters, but since permission to see the Ministry had to be gained through the elders, the aggrieved novitiate really had no recourse at all. For the younger brethren and sisters who had never known the world the fear of falling from what they were taught was a life of grace and salvation was often stronger than their grievance and they suffered on in silence. And yet because many young Shakers had dwelled so long on that which they were deprived of, because they felt that they must try their wings "in order to know the value of a shelter from the evil and sins of the world"—they did leave.

In spite of constant association with a great many people Briggs often felt desperately lonely. As a boy he had one bosom companion his own age with whom he studied, fished and roamed the woods. Then there was the girl whom he gave, in his memoirs, the assumed name of Helen Olney. He had known her since the days he filled the woodbox in the infirmary. When the sisters helped pick strawberries and currants he would sometimes have the opportunity of helping her fill her pail. "A currant bush afforded a nice cozy place for a tryst, a very little bit all to ourselves. No words were ever spoken that might not with propriety have been uttered most publicly, nor did our hands ever touch; but the little exclusiveness of it was most delicious."

Although they both remained at Canterbury for years, nothing came of their friendship because of Briggs's growing responsibilities to the society and because he held tenaciously to his faith in Shaker doctrines. He was first apprenticed to the clothier, then he taught school and was in charge of the vegetable gardens, maple sugaring and the making of 600 to 1,200 gallons of Corbett's Shaker Syrup of Sassaparilla spring and fall. At length he became an assistant elder, a first elder and finally, in 1870 when he was in middle life, a trustee. Although he worked hard and faithfully all these years he occasionally suffered an overwhelming depression—"the inevitable consequence of an unnatural life shut off from the sweetest pleasures that gladden the human heart." He wrote that visitors seeing the smiling faces, hearing the musical voices, and looking upon the neatness and order everywhere in the colony might think that all was fine, but were they to delve into the human heart "to feel its cravings, its almost agonizing longing for pleasures from which the Shaker is, and necessarily must be, debarred, they would understand that which is difficult and almost impossible to describe."

After he had entered into the responsible office of trustee he was going through the dining room where Helen worked one day when she looked up and said, simply, "I shall always love you, Nicholas." It was in a way the supreme moment of his life. He was desperately tempted to take her in his arms and confess his love for her.

> I knew that if I yielded to my impulse, Shakerism with us was at an end. . . . I had never spoken of love to her, nor intimated it in any violation of Shaker propriety. I never meant to go that far. I had not thought of her nor desired her as a wife; that was a sin to be repented in sack cloth and ashes. . . .
>
> If I surrendered to these natural impulses . . . could I meet and dwell with the loved ones who had gone on before, or would I be debarred from their presence as a traitor and the gates of Heaven be closed to me? The weight of the evidence was with Shakerism, and the Shaker within me won.

Certainly one of the most controversial figures in the annals of the northcountry's new religions was Mary Baker Eddy, founder of the Christian Science Church. The controversy has nothing to do with theology or with Mrs. Eddy's phenomenal success in building a church with a zealous membership throughout the world. It is a historical controversy about the kind of person Mrs. Eddy was. There are the sharpest differences in viewpoint among the biographies written by the independent scholars, on the one hand, and those identified with or friendly to the church, on the other.

Ancient prophets had the advantage of living and prophesying before there were any newspapers. Through the ages the events of their lives have been permeated with legend and hearsay. Everything a contemporary figure says, writes and does is exposed to the bifocals of the journalist and historian and to the mechanisms of communication. The more prominent the figure the more prominent the details in their lights and shadows. That there were shadows in Mrs. Eddy's life not even those who deal most compassionately with her deny. That there were lights historians whose own lives could scarcely stand such dissection are inclined to take for granted in their clinical pursuit of the true Mrs. Eddy. Yet what they have written and documented with names, dates and places cannot be overlooked or glossed over in any chapter on the religions of New Hampshire, where Mrs. Eddy was born and where she lived the larger part of her life.

The controversy—at least the literary one—did not gain momentum until after Mrs. Eddy had established her church. It came to a head in the 1880's upon the publication of the *True History of Mental Science,* by Julius A. Dresser, and again two decades later upon the appearance of Mark Twain's *Christian Science* (1907) and Georgine Milmine's *The Life of Mary Baker G. Eddy and the History of Christian Science* (1909). It burst upon the public once more when two other biographies were published: Edwin Franden Dakin's *Mrs. Eddy* (1929), and *Mary Baker Eddy, the Truth and the Tradition,* by Ernest Sutherland Bates and John V. Dittemore (1932). Dittemore, for ten years a director of the Mother Church in Boston, wrote in his foreword:

> My colleagues on the Boston Board, during the early years of my research, were sympathetic and unfailingly helpful. A few years after Mrs. Eddy's decease, however, the newer element sought to dissuade me from my purpose as facts unfolded relating to matters in her history certain to interfere with what had become the unacknowledged but nonetheless actual determination to create a legendary Mrs. Eddy. . . .
>
> For a number of years past I have hoped that I could find time to arrange for having the material that I had collected put in shape for publication. Not, however, until the discovery in 1928 of Mrs. Eddy's wholesale plagiarisms and the later attempt of the Christian Science Church to boycott Charles Scribner's Sons for bringing out the Dakin biography of Mrs. Eddy was my desire energized into action.

When Mark Twain published his book (1907) there was no conclusive evidence of the relationship of Quimby's writings and those of Mrs. Eddy, but he deduced that purely from the standpoint of style a large part of *Science and Health* was not hers. He took the prophetess mercilessly to task for the pretentious ambiguity in her various publications, quoting such of her sentences as: "His spiritual noumenon and phenomenon silenced portraiture."

I realize that noumenon is a daisy [wrote Twain] and I will not deny that I shall use it whenever I am in a company which I think I can embarrass with it; but at the same time I think it is out of place among friends in an autobiography. There, I think a person ought not to have anything up his sleeve. It undermines confidence. But my dissatisfaction with the quoted passage is not on account of noumenon; it is on account of the misuse of the word "silenced." You cannot silence portraiture with a noumenon; if portraiture should make a noise, a way will be found to silence it, but even then it could not be done with a noumenon. Not even with a brick, some authorities think.

It is not a pleasant image that Twain, Milmine, Dakin, Bates and Dittemore present—that of an emotionally disturbed farmer's daughter born in 1821 in Bow, New Hampshire: a girl whose frequent spells, tantrums or seizures of hysteria were so violent that straw or tanbark was laid down on the road outside the house to shield her ears from clattering hoofs. In her youth and young womanhood a soaring imagination and a compulsive need for attention led her to write affected verse, and to dress and speak affectedly. Milmine reports that some of her flowery expressions became local bywords, for example: "When I vociferate so loudly, why do you not respond with greater alacrity?"

She was capable of a great range of moods—gay, affectionate, hopeful, dark, brooding, turbulent. Sometimes she heard voices repeating her name. Her alarmed family could do little with her, particularly during a fit of temper, and let her go her own way. When George Washington Glover, an apprentice at masonry whom she married at twenty-two, died suddenly, she had to return to her father's house in Tilton (Sanbornton Bridge), where the Baker family had moved from Bow and where her son was born. Her old spells of illness and melancholia continued and her family took turns rocking her in a cradle made out of an old sofa, or pushing her in a swing. Another home was presently found for her child, since, according to Mark

Baker: "Mary acts like an old ewe that won't own its lamb." During intervals of health she sewed in a local circle, continued to write fanciful verse, tried twice to teach school, and (according to Milmine) became interested in mesmerism.

Her second marriage to a dentist named Patterson was entirely unsatisfactory (she eventually divorced him, charging desertion), and at forty she was miserably sick, lonely and self-centered. Through Phineas P. Quimby, a native of Lebanon, New Hampshire, then said to be effecting cures through mental healing in Portland, Maine, her life changed dramatically. After a few of his treatments her health improved so markedly that she became one of his most enthusiastic students. In later years her fellow students recalled that she spent her evenings writing down what she had learned in Quimby's office in the afternoon.

> When she left Quimby after his extended tutelage in the early part of 1864 [writes Dakin], she carried with her a copy of his writings called *Questions and Answers*, from which she later taught extensively and which was to be largely incorporated in the pamphlet she copyrighted in 1870 as "The Science of Man, by which the sick are healed, Embracing Questions and Answers in Moral Science . . ." This pamphlet, with numerous changes, was finally to be included in *Science and Health* under the title "Recapitulation."
>
> . . . Mrs. Patterson claimed, in after years, that any similarity between her own ideas and Quimby's was accounted for by the fact that she gave Quimby the benefit of her own theories, which she wrote down for him while he was treating her, and not by the fact that it was she who borrowed from Quimby.

The fact remains, Dakin declares, that the material contained in a Quimby manuscript bearing the date February, 1862, and consequently written before the first meeting between Quimby and Mrs. Patterson, makes such a claim impossible.

Mrs. Patterson's own statements praising Quimby when she was his patient and those she subsequently made are contradictory. Dakin quotes, for example, a letter she wrote to the Portland *Courier* in 1862 saying: "Now, then, his [Quimby's] works are but the result of a superior wisdom, which can demonstrate a science not understood; hence it were a doubtful proceeding not to believe him for the works' sake." Later, in *Science and Health*, she dismissed the man who was called "The Scientist of Transcendentalism" as an ignorant mesmerist:

> The old gentleman to whom we have referred had some very advanced views on healing, but he was not avowedly religious, neither scholarly. I restored some patients of his that he failed to heal, and left in his possession some manuscripts of mine containing corrections of his desultory pennings. . . . He died in 1865 and left no published works. The only manuscript that we ever held of his, longer than to correct it, was one of perhaps a dozen pages, most of which we had composed.

In the light of the Quimby manuscripts that presently turned up, Mrs. Eddy's biographers have found her claims impossible to support and give unqualified credit to Quimby for the basic theories and much basic writing of what (in ten volumes of manuscripts) he called "The Science of Health" and even "Christian Science."

These scholars even question Mrs. Patterson's statement that she discovered the power to heal when she fell on the sidewalk in Swampscott in 1866. She reported the attending physician as saying she had taken the last step she ever would. "Dr. Cushing pronounced my injury uncurable and that I could not survive three days because of it, when on the third day I rose from my bed and to the utter confusion of all I commenced my usual avocations." In consulting the records of Dr. Alvin M. Cushing, her biographers found that he had visited Mrs. Patterson on February 3 (the date she said she cured herself), again two days later, and three times during the following August for the treatment of a cough. In an affidavit signed before a notary public on August 13, 1904, in Springfield, Massachusetts, Dr. Cushing asserted:

> I did not at any time declare, or believe, that there was no hope of Mrs. Patterson's recovery, or that she was in a critical condition, and did not at any time say, or believe that she had but three or any other limited number of days to live; and Mrs. Patterson did not suggest, or say, or pretend, or in any way whatever intimate, that on the third day or any other day, of her said illness, she had miraculously recovered or been healed, or that discovering or perceiving the truth or the power employed by Christ to heal the sick, she had, by it, been restored to health.

The most questioning of her biographers (even if they do not accept all her claims of miraculous cures) give Mrs. Patterson full credit for endowing Quimby's theories on mental healing with overtones of religion and for building her church, although they are often severely critical of the means she employed to justify the end. In an exhaustive portrayal, event by event, year by year, buttressed with interviews with those who knew her, affidavits and documents, Milmine, Dakin, Bates and Dittemore tell of her dreary wanderings in the quest of anyone who would take her in and listen to her. She would first charm, then antagonize her hosts and have to move on. In Stoughton, Massachusetts, after an argument at the home of a family named Wentworth with whom she stayed for many months, she was charged by Horace Wentworth with slashing the matting on the floor of her bedroom, cutting the feather bed to pieces, and building a fire (which happily failed to ignite) of newspapers and coal in the closet.

Although Mrs. Patterson was fifty years old at this time and still in search of her destiny, she did not have long to wait. With a young man named Richard Kennedy, who helped her put the teaching of mind healing on a business basis, she became prosperous. Kennedy was supporting her and paying her half of everything he earned as a healer, while Mrs. Patterson was teaching her system to others in a $300 course of twelve lectures.

> (When God impelled me to set a price on my instruction in Christian-Science Mind-healing [she explained later], I could think of no financial equivalent for an impartation of a knowledge of that divine power which heals; but I was led to name three-hundred dollars as the price for each pupil in one course of lectures at my college—a startling sum for tuition lasting barely three weeks. This amount greatly troubled me. I shrank from asking it, but was finally led, by a strange providence, to accept this fee.)

The partnership ended when Mrs. Patterson accused Kennedy of cheating her at cards (according to Kennedy). Furiously he tore up their contract, paid her $6,000, her share of their earnings, and withdrew to set up his own practice.

In 1875 *Science and Health*, which Mrs. Patterson had apparently been working on for years (but which Dakin, Bates and Dittemore demonstrate was the Quimby manuscripts rearranged and veiled in her bewildering prose), reached an indifferent public by way of a $2,200 subsidy from two of her students. The first edition was viewed by most critics as a kind of stream of unconsciousness, a torrent of confused logic and grammar, yet even the more outspoken of them felt that it had a virtue. Dakin observes that it may have been an accident but that she had either recognized or stumbled upon a working relationship between healing through suggestion, and religion. "Had she sought merely to market a psychological discovery, she probably would have gained only a small audience. What she had on hand was not psychology but religion." The fact that the first edition of *Science and Health* did not sell merely stirred the prophetess to greater efforts—to revisions and revisions of the revisions, including a thorough one by an astute literary consultant, the Rev. James Henry Wiggin. Presently the book became the wellspring of the church and a principal source of Mrs. Patterson's private fortune of some two million dollars.

To say that Mary Baker Glover Patterson Eddy's relationships with many of her associates were stormy, as she rose to power, is to put it moderately—they were as cyclonic as the attacks of hysteria that continued to seize her throughout her long life. Her biographers tell of the series of young students who followed Kennedy into and out of her life: George Barry, who sued her for payment of five years of household services; Daniel Spofford, who as a student and assistant in literary and financial matters was expelled on charges of "immorality" when he paid what proceeds there were from the sale of the first edition of *Science and Health* to the two students who had advanced funds for it, instead of to Mrs. Eddy as royalties.

Mrs. Eddy began to imagine that those in exile were trying to kill her by directing evil thoughts toward her. She came to call this obsession "malicious animal magnetism." Taking up the cudgel against Kennedy and Spofford at every opportunity, even in *Science and Health*, she wrote in the 1881 edition of a certain "Nero of to-day, regaling himself through a mental method with the tortures of individuals, is repeating history, and will fall upon his sword, and it shall pierce him through. Let him remember this when, in the dark recesses of thought, he is robbing, committing adultery, and killing." Dakin says that her students "mounted a sort of guard, each student to stand on guard two hours out of the 24 with instructions to concentrate his mind on Spofford, and prevent him from getting his vibrations through to Mrs. Eddy." Asa Gilbert Eddy, the spinsterish Vermont bachelor she had married in 1877, and a student named Ahrens were even held for trial on charges of attempting to procure Spofford's murder! Appalled at the unchristian discord arising from Mrs. Eddy's lawsuits and countersuits, and at the excesses of malicious animal magnetism, her most trusted students resigned in a body. They declared that they greatly valued her teachings but could no longer stand her temper, her love of money, and her appearance of hypocrisy.

The doctrine, if it could be called that, of Malicious Animal Magnetism almost wrecked Mrs. Eddy's budding church, which was chartered in Massachusetts in 1879. Moving from Lynn to Boston four years later she founded the Massachusetts Metaphysical College, where she continued to conduct her $300 course of lectures and in ten years earned a fortune. Her students became her ambassadors to the public. As they gained adherents through their practices in mental healing, general attendance at Mrs. Eddy's Sunday meetings grew larger. Even some of the Brahmins of Boston were fascinated by the magnetism of this strange, overdressed woman from the backbeyond of New Hampshire with her rouged cheeks, her hair done up in ringlets and her large, luminous gray eyes. Upon occasion she could be positively dynamic. In *Christian Science: Its Encounter with American Culture*, Robert Peel quotes from the journal of the erudite Transcendentalist, Bronson Alcott, who visited Mrs. Eddy and her students in Lynn.

> The evening is passed in discussing metaphysical problems [he wrote]. I find her followers thoughtful and devout, without cant or egotism, students of life rather than of books, and a promising company. The slight touch of mysticism mingling with their faith renders them the more interesting, and Mrs. Glover's influence appears to be of the happiest character.

Of these occasions when she was at her best, one of her students later wrote that she was "calm and undisturbed, without a particle of hysteria" and that she would answer questions in a manner "which, if it did not convince, never failed to satisfy the inquirer of her sincerity." Nor could the inquirer fail to be impressed with her business and administrative acumen, her singleness of purpose, and her unearthly persistence—the persistence of an evangelist.

The most significant years in Mrs. Eddy's life were those after she was sixty-one. Her biographers tell of the burgeoning of a church with 50 members in 1882 to one with 20 incorporated branches and 90 unincorporated societies eight years later; how in 1888 Mrs. Eddy captivated an audience of 3,000 persons in Chicago; how the money began to roll in from new editions of *Science and Health* (each of which her adherents were obliged to buy); how she fled from malicious animal magnetism and the ghost of Phineas P. Quimby to Barton and Barre, Vermont, and at length to Concord, New Hampshire, where in the seclusion of a mansion called Pleasant View she reorganized her empire so that she could rule its farthest outpost with an iron glove; how her Boston congregation paid for and built the so-called Mother Church with a shrine in it called the Mother's Room which held a pure-onyx mantel, a rug made of the down of one hundred eider ducks, and a painting of the humble room of the prophetess in Lynn; how her husband's place (Gilbert Eddy had died in 1882) was taken by another Vermonter, a graduate of her course named E. J. Foster whom she legally adopted; how she suspected Foster-Eddy of falsifying the books and of carrying on with a woman in Boston. (Screaming "Murder!" at him when he returned to Pleasant View, she soon dismissed him from the church. He returned eventually to Waterbury Center, Vermont, where he was reported as being in danger of his life from Mrs. Eddy's followers.) How her seizures of hysteria (for which she is said to have taken morphine) continued; how she was administered to by young Calvin Frye, who now became her household chief of staff; how 3,000 of the Boston disciples made a pilgrimage to Concord and were addressed by Mother Eddy wearing a silk dress trimmed with black lace, a diamond cross at her neck and a D.A.R. insignia in diamonds and rubies; how the *Christian Science Monitor* was started under her aegis; how she rallied, rather magnificently, from enfeebled old age to disprove charges of insanity by her son and nephew in the "Next Friends" suit; how she feared that the faithful and adoring Mrs. Augusta Stetson (builder in New York of a branch church larger than the Mother Church in Boston) might take her place and how she banished her from her pastorate merely on the charge of being too worshipful of Mother Eddy.

(Beloved Student [Mrs. Eddy wrote Archibald McLellan, chairman of the Board of Directors]: Learn at once if the Mother Church can be prosecuted for suspending a student or even expelling them, who is giving us so much trouble as Mrs. Stetson does, and if it can be done safely drop Mrs. Stetson's connection with the Mother Church. Let no one know that I have written you on this subject. Lovingly yours, Mary Baker Eddy.)

And finally they tell how she died on Saturday night, December 3, 1910, at the age of eighty-nine, still tightly clutching the reins of the vast caravan of Christian Science.

The severest judgment of Mrs. Eddy was that of Mark Twain, who considered her "grasping, sordid, penurious, famishing for everything she sees—money, power, glory—vain, untruthful, jealous, despotic, arrogant, insolent, pitiless where thinkers and hypnotists are concerned, illiterate, shallow, incapable of reasoning outside of commercial lines, immeasurably selfish." Twain recognized that in the eyes of her followers Mrs. Eddy was "patient, gentle, loving, compassionate, noble-hearted, unselfish, sinless, widely cultured, splendidly equipped mentally, a profound thinker, an able writer, a divine personage, an inspired messenger whose acts are dictated from the throne, and whose every utterance is the Voice of God." She is viewed in this light by a whole group of biographers with utterly different interpretations of the events described by most of them on the preceding pages.

"One dedicated, like Mary Baker, from her birth to the religious life," writes Lyman Powell in *Mary Baker Eddy: A Life Size Portrait*, "would early learn to pray; and when her mother read to her from the Bible that Daniel prayed three times a day, for spiritual good count she prayed seven times a day, chalking down on the shed wall each prayer in succession, for a while as a settled habit."

In *The Life of Mary Baker Eddy* Sibyl Wilbur writes thus of her delicate childhood: "Mary, who could not endure to hear the calves bawl or the pigs squeal in their own farmyard without an effort to comfort them, was depressed or excited by the turbulence of school life. She was therefore soon taken out of that experience and went on with her books at home." This biography asserts that Mark Baker "dowered her with beauty, educated her with care, gathered her safely into the church, clothed her delicately and without parsimony. As finely and nobly bred was she as any bride who ever left her father's home in all New England."

Regarding her child's being cared for by others: "But it seemed she was too tender and devoted, too weak physically to exercise a mother's care, and when she had overtaxed herself her parents would send little George home with Mahala Sanborn, or it may be they merely permitted the spinster nurse to take him, indulging her fondness." In her own account of her separation from her child, Mrs. Eddy wrote that

> a few months before my father's second marriage to Mrs. Elizabeth Patterson Duncan, sister of Lt. Governor George W. Patterson, of New York—my little son, about 4 years of age, was sent away from me, and put under the care of our family nurse, who had married, and resided in the northern part of New Hampshire. . . . The night before my child was taken from me, I knelt by his side throughout the dark hours, hoping for a vision of relief from this trial. . . . My dominant thought in marrying again was to get back my child but after our marriage his stepfather was not willing he should have a home with me. A plot was consummated for keeping us apart. The family to whose care he was committed very soon removed to what was then regarded as the Far West.

Concerning her alleged debt to the theories and writings of Phineas P. Quimby, Wilbur says:

> The Quimby claim is a purely intellectual one . . . which provokes unjust and invidious suspicion as to the origin of the fundamental principles of Christian Science. . . .
>
> It has been shown that Mrs. Patterson in 1862 wrote certain manuscripts for Quimby and gave them to him. She repeated this generous, if unprofitable, act in the early part of 1864, when she spent two or three months in an uninterrupted effort to fathom and elucidate "Quimbyism." It seems almost incredible that a woman of her intellectual and spiritual development should have devoted so long a period to the struggle of formulating a philosophy out of the chaotic but dogmatic utterances of this self-taught mesmerist. . . .
> He received from Mrs. Patterson manuscripts to which she unselfishly and unguardedly signed his name. These manuscripts in

Mrs. Eddy's handwriting, interlined with Quimby's emendations, may still be in existence.

In an article in the Boston *Post,* March 7, 1883, Mrs. Eddy declared that any letters or newspaper articles she may have written praising Quimby when she was his patient were written under his mesmeric influence.

> Did I write those articles purporting to be mine? I might have written them 20 or 30 years ago, for I was under the mesmeric treatment of Dr. Quimby from 1862 until his death in 1865. He was illiterate and I knew nothing then of the Science of Mind-healing, and I was as ignorant of Mesmerism as Eve before she was taught by the serpent. Mind Science was unknown to me; and my head was so turned by animal magnetism and will-power, under his treatment, that I might have written something as hopelessly incorrect as the articles now published in the Dresser pamphlet. I was not healed until after the death of Mr. Quimby; and then healing came as the result of my discovery in 1866, of the science of Mind-healing, since named Christian Science.

Dr. Alvin Cushing, who, says Wilbur, "drove a dashing pair of trotters and was much in evidence on the speedway when not in the consulting room," did not cure her when she fell on the ice.

> She was not responsible for the calling of the physician and only took his medicine when she was roused into semi-consciousness to have it administered, of which she had no recollection. After the doctor's departure . . . she refused to take the medicine he had left, and as she expressed it, lifted her heart to God.

Richard Kennedy, her student and aide in Lynn, did not leave because she accused him of cheating at cards.

> When Mary Baker began to rid herself completely of the relics of the influence which Quimby exerted over her mind she ordered all her students to desist from stroking the head while treating her patients mentally. . . . Now it was that Richard Kennedy absolutely rebelled and left her.

She did not leave Lynn for Boston because some of her best students rebelled and resigned in a body. Powell asserts that she "was outgrowing Lynn. Then—as now—Lynn had people of importance. But small town curiosity cabined her spirit and cramped her individuality. Backdoor gossip always annoyed this woman of the stars." Wilbur writes that "in leaving Lynn with these humble people Mary Baker took a radical step. She had tried for months to persuade those who were more akin to her in social and intellectual heritage to accept the truth she had to impart."

The Rev. James H. Wiggin, Mrs. Eddy's literary consultant, did not revise *Science and Health*. He was just a proofreader. Wilbur says that Mrs. Eddy "believed that her book might be entrusted to his hands without fear that he would overstep his privilege and tamper with its subject matter or context. Such proved to be the character of his workmanship."

As for Foster-Eddy, her adopted son, Wilbur writes that "away from her personal influence, he was not as attentive to business as the requirements of his office demanded, and he engaged in certain fopperies which brought him scathing criticism from other students, not entirely unwarranted. It became necessary for Mrs. Eddy to remove him."

What the biographers friendly to Mrs. Eddy have to say about the enforced resignation of Mrs. Augusta Stetson from the church she built in New York City seems intangible. She was asked to resign because of her "blatant independence"; because a newspaper article reported authorities in Mrs. Stetson's church as announcing "a church edifice, rivaling in beauty of architecture any other religious structure in America." Mrs. Eddy's letter to the trustees asking them to remove Mrs. Stetson has been quoted. Prior to that she had written Mrs. Stetson: "Awake and arise from this temptation produced by animal magnetism upon yourself, allowing your students to deify you and me. Treat yourself for it and get your students to help you rise out of it. It will be your destruction if you do not do this."

Even an exhaustive study of Mary Baker Eddy's life leaves the student with the feeling that she has somehow eluded him. This may be because the independent biographies have tended to be exposés, while those that have the sanction of the church paint her in lavender. But in view of the powerful church that arose from her labors none can deny Mrs. Eddy a commanding place in the annals of the world's religions and in the history of her native New Hampshire. Even Mark Twain did not begrudge her this.

> When we do not know a person—and also when we do [his daughter quoted him as saying]—we have to judge his size by the size and nature of his achievements, as compared with the achievements of others in his special line of business—there is no other way. Measured by this standard, it is thirteen hundred years since the world has produced anyone who could reach up to Mrs. Eddy's waistbelt.

Stefan Zweig perhaps comes nearest, at least for the layman, in assessing her contribution when he writes that she gave great momentum to contemporary psychology. "Despite all her exaggeration, despite her defects of character and despite the hopeless confusion of much of her thought, Mary Baker Eddy was unquestionably a woman of genius. She discovered or rediscovered some of the fundamental laws of the mind and turned them into account in her practice."

XIII

EXODUS

When the West was young a hundred years ago New Hampshire and Vermont were already old. Like the shadow of a summer cloud the frontier had drifted clear to the Pacific. With it went tens of thousands of New Englanders. By 1860 Vermont had lost to the four points of the compass a larger proportion of its population than any other eastern state, some 145,000 people—almost half as many as were then living in Vermont itself. Because of the mill cities on the Merrimack which attracted many workers, New Hampshire's loss of population was not severe, but its farms were suffering.

Acknowledging the drain of young men from the hills into the vacuum of the prairies, an orator at a railroad convention declared that he was not afraid—that, if the northcountry could not sell wheat, it could grow corn and potatoes. If it could not sell beef and mutton on the market at midwestern prices, it could export rock and ice. "And when we cease to export everything else, we will not have ceased to export men—men whom the land shall honor."

The exodus out of the hills had begun after the War of 1812— and the summer of 1816 when there was frost every month of the growing season had augmented it. After a heat wave on June 5 the temperature fell to freezing and killed the vegetation, the new leaves of the forests, and the yellow cucumber bug, which failed to appear again for ten years. Birds were numbed, newly sheared sheep died. Then it snowed. There were frosts July 8 and August 20. From September 26 through 29 temperatures at sunup in Hanover ranged from 20 to 25 degrees. Drought accompanied the cold. Other than snow no moisture fell upon northern Vermont from May to September. The people lived on oatmeal, for oats survived in places, and upon fish, for the rivers and lakes abounded in trout, salmon and pike.

There were other reasons that the people went west: hardships caused by the embargo of the War of 1812, an epidemic of "spotted fever" in 1813, the exhausting of New England forests, the depletion of the shallow mountain soil, the lure of cheap rich lands beyond the sunset toward which they might journey by way of the newly opened Champlain and Erie canals; the coming of the steamboat and the railroad to the Midwest, the gold rush, the collapse of the sheep-growing boom, the excitement of the slavery controversy, and the Free-Soil movement. Perhaps the greatest of all motives was plain wanderlust in a people born to migrate, to build, and to migrate again. Middlebury, Michigan, was named for Middlebury, New York, which was named for Middlebury, Vermont; Woodstock, Minnesota, stemmed by way of Woodstock, Illinois, from Woodstock, Vermont. Northern New Englanders settled and overflowed New York into Pennsylvania, Ohio, Indiana, Michigan, Illinois and Wisconsin. Name your town in these states: there was likely a Yankee schoolmarm, a Yankee editor, preacher, storekeeper, banker, patent medicine salesman, a Yankee horse thief. In *Migration from Vermont* Lewis Stilwell quotes Herman O. Miles of Waverly, Iowa, immodestly summing up his life's labors:

> I . . . made the first assessment of property that was ever made in Butler and Bremer Counties. I taught the first school that was ever taught in Bremer County. I built the first house that was built from sawed lumber in the County. I was elected the first constable and first clerk of the District in County Court, one of the first School Directors, one of the first law graduates, started and published the first newspaper, called together the citizens and organized the Republican Party, and have the honor of filling the only County office . . . that has never been held by a democrat. I have acted as Justice of the Peace, Mayor, Constable, Road Supervisor, . . . School Director, Secretary of the School Board, Postmaster . . . Sheriff, Auctioneer, farmer and lawyer. I had charge of building the first schoolhouse in town. I built the piers and abutments for the second bridge. I have done more to break up and close whiskey shops and gambling dens in Waverly than any other man, for which my life was sought and threatened, my office gutted, books, records and everything burnt up and thrown into the river.

To multiply Herman by 145,000 is to understand that Yankee energy, idealism, resourcefulness, and thrifty, close-fisted one-track-mindedness were making large areas of the West into the kind of New England that New England was when it was new. Since Yankees were likely the ones to hold the purse strings and vote the laws, their effect upon their new environment was out of proportion even to their large numbers.

New Hampshire and Vermont newspapers tried to dam the westward flood with editorials like "Stick to the Farm, Young Man" but it was no use, particularly when advertisements in the same papers boasted cheap accommodations from Lake Champlain to Lake Erie. In winter Vermont or western New Hampshire emigrants could, and many did, cross the icebound lake to New York in sleighs. From there in due course many of them continued west by covered wagon. In summer there were steamboats every day from Burlington to Whitehall, stages and canalboats to Albany, the terminus of the great Erie. Even at Vergennes, seven miles up the Otter, emigrants could board canal packets every summer Tuesday and Saturday during the 1830's and 40's and float all the way to Buffalo without ever setting foot on dry land. For a time the fare without board was 1½ cents a mile, and many a restless youth with no more in his pocket than passage money started out with little idea of just where he was going or what he would do when he got there. "One such career," writes Stilwell, "began with a basket of lemons, passed to a wagonload of clothespins, then advanced to a line of tinware and ultimated in a dry goods' store together with speculation in town lots in Evansville, Indiana."

The emigrants often started out in colonies or emigration societies. In 1836 the settlers who founded Vermontville, Michigan, gathered at East Poultney and Castleton under the aegis of Sylvester Cochrane, a Congregational minister, to adopt a constitution. They pledged themselves to observe the Sabbath out west just as they had in Vermont, to maintain the same literary privileges, and to ban ardent spirits. Any member of the colony who contributed $12.50 to the common fund was entitled upon arrival to a farm lot of 160 acres and a village lot of 10 acres. In this manner (if not as formally) Vermonters founded Bennington, Michigan; Vergennes, Illinois; Montpelier, Indiana, and uncounted other communities with new names. Beloit, Wisconsin, owes its place in the sun to a group of very resourceful pioneers of the New England Immigrating Company of Colebrook, New Hampshire. One of the earliest settlers in Beloit was Lucius G. Fisher from Danby, Vermont, who arrived in a canoe when wigwams were standing on the prairie near Turtle Creek. He became sheriff, land expert, commissioner of territorial roads, bank president, railroad builder, and subscriber to Beloit College. The three Strong brothers, born in Brownington, Vermont, were all useful citizens of Beloit. Henry P. was physician, mayor, postmaster, and later president of the Wisconsin Medical Society; James W., a teacher, became superintendent of schools and agent of the Milwaukee and Mississippi Railway. William B., assistant in the railroad office at the age of fifteen, became president of the Atchison, Topeka and Santa Fe. Under his eleven-year administration the railroad stretched from 2,200 to 6,960 miles, which explains the remark of one of his directors: "Strong is all right, but he won't let us make any money."

Charles Hosmer Morse of St. Johnsbury, organizer of Beloit's sprawling Fairbanks Morse Company, later became its president and chairman of the board. Stowe's Ira Dutton went with his mother to Janesville, a few miles north of Beloit, when he was only twelve. A wandering career led him to Catholicism, to a Trappist monastery as a missionary, and to the leper colony of Father Damien at Molokai Territory, Hawaii, where he served selflessly until he was eighty-five.

"It seems almost reasonable to assert," remarks Stilwell, "that the northern and southern limits of migration from Vermont were respectively the north and south poles." Both he and Stewart Holbrook (in *The Yankee Exodus*) have tracked many of these stalwarts across the land. Although sampling the more conspicuous of them seems like name-dropping on a grand scale, how else is one to demonstrate the vigor of this breed? They were whaling in the North Atlantic, building subways under Times Square, and they were in the Rockies selling daguerreotypes to miners for $16 each. An Illinois farmer from New Hampshire named Joseph Glidden was patenting what he called "barbed wire." In Moline Charles H. Deere of Rutland was making iron plows for turning up the hard prairie sod and laying the groundwork for an empire in farm machinery. In Ohio Alphonso Taft from Townshend, Vermont, was founding a family of statesmen.

Soon after his arrival in Chicago (first named for Major General Henry Dearborn, a native of Hampton, New Hampshire) Long John Wentworth of Sandwich, New Hampshire, was running a fledgling newspaper, the *Democrat*, and interesting himself in a charter for the young city. Gurdon Hubbard of Windsor, Vermont, was already (1836) slaughtering pigs there and smoking pork in a vast warehouse he had built. Silas Cobb of Montpelier was selling leather buckets to fire brigades and dreaming of his forthcoming fortune in horse-car transportation. Looking after the whole commonwealth was

General Lewis Cass of Exeter, New Hampshire, governor of Michigan for eighteen years and senator for eleven more; secretary of war in Andrew Jackson's Cabinet and secretary of state for Buchanan. Detroit's land-rich senator and political boss, Zachariah Chandler, formerly of Bedford, New Hampshire, became secretary of the interior for U. S. Grant. John D. Pierce of Chesterfield, New Hampshire, became Michigan's superintendent of public construction and reserved a million acres of good rich land for the future of education.

The prairies never swallowed up the Yankees in them; wherever they settled it was the environment, it seems, that yielded. Certainly the far West did to the cofounder of Wells Fargo and the American Express Company, Henry Wells of Thetford, Vermont, as did Minnesota to John Pillsbury and his kin and the other New Hampshire and Vermont Yankees who made this new state practically their own. From Corinth, Vermont, came Ebenezer Knight, manager of the Atlantic and Pacific Mail Company; from Holland, Vermont, went the notorious prince of Leadville and of Colorado folklore, Horace (Silver Dollar) Tabor. Stilwell quotes a letter from a young Green Mountain emigrant in Tahiti, as saying that he had met Vermonters from Putney, Peru, Ludlow, Windsor, Hartford, Woodstock, Bradford, Peacham, Lyndon, Middlebury, Vergennes and other towns he couldn't recall.

The exodus from the hillcountry was south as well as west: college graduates went to the cities even of the deep South to teach, preach or practice law; unmarried girls went to the great river factories of central and southern New England. (In 1846 twelve hundred Vermont girls were working in Lowell, Massachusetts, a town which owed its origin to Nathan Appleton, a native of New Ipswich, New Hampshire, who had set in motion the first power loom in the United States.) But the hillcountry women were not all making cloth. Emma Willard from Middlebury, Vermont, pioneered in Troy with her seminary for young ladies; Sarah Josepha Hale from Newport, New Hampshire, for half a century editor of America's foremost magazine for women, *Godey's Lady's Book*, was in the vanguard of the feminist movement. Mary Gove Nichols, also from New Hampshire, attracted a faithful following in both England and America with her theories about water cures, vegetarianism and social experiments.

The glitter of the circus drew Benjamin Franklin Keith, a farmer from Hillsboro Bridge, New Hampshire, into the employ of P. T. Barnum. Presently he opened his own museum and theater in Boston and through his traveling shows spread the name of Keith on every covered bridge and billboard in the country. Long before the Civil War Henry Augustus Willard of Westminster, Vermont, who as a young man had worked in Chase's Hotel in Brattleboro and on the Hudson River steamboats, became proprietor of Washington's best hotel. John F. Winslow from Bennington, builder of the Union Navy's *Monitor*, was busy with Bessemer steel, Elisha Graves Otis, from Halifax, Vermont, was ascending in the elevator business, and A. B. Chandler, from West Randolph, Vermont, was creating the Postal Telegraph system. Several Dartmouth graduates were founding the American petroleum industry. Dr. Francis Brewer, curious about some oil he had skimmed from a Pennsylvania creek, took a sample back to New Hampshire to have it analyzed by his surgery professor, Dr. Dixi Crosby, and by Oliver P. Hubbard, professor of chemistry. Their friend, George Bissell, a New York lawyer from Hanover, became interested in their findings and in 1854 organized the Pennsylvania Rock Oil Company. With Colonel Edwin L. Drake of Castleton, Vermont, he was responsible for the drilling of the first well in Titusville, Pennsylvania, five years later.

Jim Fisk of Brattleboro was advancing by way of a peddler's cart to the presidencies of the Fall River Steamboat Line and the Erie Railroad in the select company of robber barons Daniel Drew and Jay Gould. From the plans of Richard Morris Hunt of Brattleboro rose the Lenox Library in New York and the William K. Vanderbilt house, to mention but two buildings with northcountry designers. William Rutherford Mead, also of Brattleboro, was a founder of McKim, Mead and White, architects. William Ladd, migrating merely from New Hampshire to Maine, defined the principles of international government in *An Essay on a Congress of Nations*, which he wrote in 1840. George P. Rowell, founder of *Printers' Ink*, the first newspaper directory, and also of the country's first advertising agency, came from Concord, Vermont. Wilbur F. Storey, James R. Spaulding, Charles G. Greene, Stilson Hutchins and George W. Kendall from Salisbury, Montpelier, Boscawen, Whitefield and Amherst, founded respectively the Chicago *Times*, the New York *World*, the Boston *Post*, the Washington *Post*, and the New Orleans *Picayune*. New Hampshire's Henry Houghton of Sutton and E. P. Dutton of Keene became book publishers.

In public life, in the field of education, in the military and naval service the list of celebrated emigrants from New Hampshire and Vermont gets out of hand, for they became governors and chief justices of other states by the dozens, congressmen and senators, Cabinet officers, ministers and ambassadors, college presidents, generals and admirals by the score. It has always seemed odd that a native of the only New England state without a seacoast rose to the command of the United States Navy, but that was true of George Dewey from Montpelier, the only officer ever to hold an approximation of the six-star rank of admiral of the navy.

So many outposts in the railroad empire were captured by north-country Yankees that their success seems almost to have been the result of a conspiracy. It was not that by any means. Generally it was the consequence of a dogged advance over a lifetime from brakeman or tracklayer or engineer to the oak-paneled directors' room. The conquests of the sons of upland New England included presidencies of the Arkansas Central, the Atchison, Topeka and Santa Fe, the Baltimore and Ohio, the Burlington, Cedar Rapids and Northern, the Chicago, Burlington and Quincy, the Erie, the Georgia Central, the Galveston, Harrisburg and San Antonio, the Grand Trunk, the Long Island, the New Orleans, Texas and Pacific, the New York Central, the New York, New Haven and Hartford, the Northern Pacific, and the Union Pacific.

If the railroad had not wound across his father's land in North Hartland, Vermont, where Daniel Willard was born in 1861, he might have been a farmer. He shoveled out cow barns to pay his tuition at Massachusetts State Agricultural College but was always picturing himself at the throttle of one of the Vermont Central's brassbound wood-burners that trailed white smoke through the Connecticut River meadows. He knew their schedules by heart, and when the *General Taylor* or the *Sheridan*, in his memory two of the most impressive engines ever built, whistled by leaving a bouquet of hot steam and cylinder oil in the wake of its cavalcade of shiny cars, he knew that he could never be a farmer.

At eighteen he went to work on a Vermont Central section gang headed by Owen Pierce, a friend of his father, and then switched to the Connecticut and Passumpsic, a 64-mile stretch of track between Wells River and Newport (the northern route between Boston and Montreal). During his first winter (1879-80) with the C & P he fired, not its wood-burning locomotives, but the boiler of a pile driver used in building a trestle over an inlet of Lake Memphremagog. For working a day on the ice, wading home two miles through the snow to a boardinghouse for supper, then returning, sometimes through 30 below zero cold to keep steam in his donkey engine lest it freeze, he received $2.50.

Before long he was firing the *Dartmouth*, which hauled the night passenger express. Then he became engineer of a freight locomotive, a promotion of considerable distinction at his age. Now he was entitled to wear an engineer's "frock"—overalls with shoulder straps and a jacket. He remembered the pride he and his fellow engineers took in keeping themselves and their engines tidy, for there was not much soot in a wood-burner.

"I remember clearly that it was the well-established habit of all the enginemen to carry their bootbrush and box of blacking in their seat-box, and they usually were quite particular about polishing their shoes before they left the engine." Engineers of fast passenger trains commanded as much respect as bank presidents and dressed accordingly—white shirts, fancy vests and gold watch chains. Willard remembered it was not the practice, however, for those without beards to shave every day. Twice a week was often enough.

Six decades later he still enjoyed recalling the names of the Connecticut and Passumpsic engines—the *Caledonia, Green Mountain Boy, Orleans, Dartmouth, Enterprise, Magog*. He particularly admired the *W. K. Blodgett* and her performance on the hill over the line near Lennoxville. The president of the Baltimore and Ohio—the dean of American Railroads, as Willard was known to his colleagues—had made a long haul from the days he had laid track on the cinder beds along the winding Connecticut.

XIV

FACES OF THE LAND

Someone has remarked that if Vermont were flattened out it would be as large as Texas. Its forested peaks, bowed like veterans of old wars, parade in broken ranks 157 miles all the way from Massachusetts to Canada. Although none of the Green Mountain or Taconic ranges aspire to Mount Washington's 6,288 feet, or quite to the commanding mile reached by its five other rugged companions in New Hampshire's Presidential Range, Vermont is much the more mountainous of the two states. It is the most mountainous state in the Union.

As the mammoth ice sheet ground southward a million years ago, enveloping even the highest peaks in its brutal grip, it somehow carried away less soil from Vermont than from New Hampshire; and when finally it melted back into the arctic it dropped less stone on the Green Mountain State. Because of this and of the way the mountains were formed, Vermonters found a livelihood in nearly every remote valley. Vermont is less industrial because geography so widely scatters its people. New Hampshire is less agrarian because the White Mountains are high and jagged and because their blanket of boulders and stones is so heavy that the land in many places has never been reclaimed.

Early in the nineteenth century Granite State people began to congregate in the mill cities of flat lands to the southeast. Yet there are areas in both states in which a native, upon removal of a blindfold, would be at a loss to tell whether he was in Vermont or New Hampshire. On both sides of the Connecticut River one sees the same wrinkled hills and steepled villages. There are those who swear that Vermont is greener, which it may be because of soil and topography, and that they can tell the difference the moment they cross the border. But to the stranger it is very much all one countryside. The people of the rural areas, at least, seem to be very much the same, which indeed they should be since they all came from the same Yankee stock. They have the same outlook—the outlook of mountain people.

Whole volumes have been written about the Taconic, Green and White Mountains and there are even single peaks like southwestern New Hampshire's Monadnock with a literature all their own. From Lake Champlain, only a few feet above sea level, Vermont's ancient Mansfield and Camel's Hump, just shy of a mile in height, look less grand but, because of their rounded contours, more stately than Rockies twice their height. There is this about such comfortable mountain scenery; you can lie down in it. It starts at your feet and with becoming variety stretches away as far as you can see. Nature here is never overpowering; there are no fortissimos except perhaps Mount Washington.

Lying in the heart of New Hampshire's Presidential Range, this highest mountain in the northeast is anything but understatement. Held in fear by Indian and white settler it is respected in modern times by meteorologists who have recorded the raging weather at its summit. It dominates White Mountain history in proportion to its size. It has never been described more poetically than by Captain John Smith, who saw it from the sea in the great distance and called it the "Twinkling Mountain of Angososico." Of the death of the great chief of the Pennacooks, Passaconaway, who in 1660 urged his people to make peace with the white man or be annihilated, it was said that he was carried to Mount Washington in a sleigh drawn by wolves and that he rose toward heaven in a chariot of fire. Through the names on the land the vanished redmen are with us today.

An Irishman named Darby Field, who managed to reach the summit in 1642, filled his pockets with quartz crystals that he thought were diamonds. Strangely enough, the pass through the cliffs of the Presidential Range was not known until 1771 when a moose hunter named Timothy Nash saw it from a treetop. Upon learning of this discovery Governor John Wentworth offered Nash a large tract of land if, by leading a horse through the notch, he could prove that it was passable. With the help of an indomitable mount, which was lowered over precipices by rope and tackle and prodded across swift streams, Nash managed to do it. After the Revolution a primitive road and then a well-traveled turnpike, financed by a lottery, ran from Littleton to Portsmouth through the Notch.

The tragedy of Samuel Willey, one of the first (with Ethan Allen Crawford) to make the awesome ravine his home, is always told in any account of Mount Washington and its environs. Things went well for Willey upon his arrival, for many paying guests sought shelter with him. In June, 1826, when a landslide roared down the gorge opposite his home, he wondered if he ought to move out. The mild early summer allayed his fears, but in August an incessant rain began and the Saco River rose twenty feet. No one ever knew just what happened at the Willey House on the night of August 28 when the frightful landslide crashed down the gorge behind it. In a strange twist of fate the house was completely spared, but not a soul was left in it, although food was in the pantry and a Bible lay open on the table. Later, when the bodies were found not far from the house, it appeared that the Willeys had rushed out into the night only to be buried by a cataract of stone, while their house, directly in its path, was protected by a large ridge behind it which, serving as a wedge, diverted the landslide.

The alchemy that a master storyteller employs in endowing an episode like this with a sense of reality and meaning more powerful than the truth itself is shown in Nathaniel Hawthorne's *The Ambitious Guest*. In his wanderings through the mountain country Hawthorne delved deeply into fact and folklore. It is possible that his tale about the Old Man of the Mountain, called *The Great Stone Face*, will endure longer than that natural curiosity, the head itself, which has beguiled so many generations of travelers. (Its features have twice been shored up to prevent erosion, most recently by Governor Sherman Adams). In Hawthorne's story a prediction is made that a man will appear whose features are identical to the godly ones of the Great Stone Face. Each time a famous person travels through Franconia Notch, Ernest, the central character, thinks that the newcomer may be the one. There is the rich Mr. Gathergold, a soldier called General Blood and Guts, and a statesman, Old Stony Phiz.

> His tongue, indeed, was a magic instrument: sometimes it rumbled like the thunder; sometimes it warbled like the sweetest music. It was the blast of war,—the song of peace; and it seemed to have a heart in it.

When Old Stony Phiz arrives in a cavalcade of troops, banners and music, Ernest is sure that the great man is the living embodiment of the Old Man of the Mountain.

> The brow, with its massive depth and loftiness, and all the other features, indeed, were boldly and strongly hewn. . . . But the sublimity and stateliness, the grand expression of a divine sympathy . . . might here be sought in vain. Something had been originally left

out, or had departed. And therefore the marvelously gifted statesman had always a weary gloom in the deep caverns of his eyes, as of
a child that has outgrown its playthings or a man of mighty faculties
and little aims, whose life, with all its high performances, was vague
and empty, because no high purpose had endowed it with reality.

As the trials of the passing years leave their marks upon Ernest,
however, it is he who becomes the image of the Great Stone Face.
Hawthorne's tale is two things at once—an evocation of northcountry
atmosphere and an allegory about the character of Daniel Webster
of far greater poignancy than Stephen Vincent Benét's story *The
Devil and Daniel Webster.*

Much less well known, but just as deserving of a prominent place
in the literary history of the hillcountry, is *Canterbury Pilgrims,*
Hawthorne's story about two young lovers leaving the New Hampshire Shaker colony at Canterbury to find their way in an untried
world at the same time that a discouraged countryman with his
forlorn wife and their children are escaping from it to seek refuge
with the Shakers. In *Sketches from Memory* Hawthorne seems almost
ready to frame another tale of the White Mountains as he remembers
his visit to Ethan Allen Crawford's house in the Notch in 1832. He
recalls a green-spectacled minerologist "bearing a heavy hammer
with which he did great damage to the precipices," a young man with
an opera glass set in gold who "seemed to be making a quotation
from some of Byron's rhapsodies on mountain scenery," a pretty girl
with the complexion of an alpine flower; two Vermont traders, one
from Burlington and another returning from a trip to Portland,
two pairs of newlyweds, two Georgian gentlemen "who had chilled
their southern blood that morning on the top of Mount Washington," and a squire from the Green Mountains who described the
perils of travel through this country fifty years before. Ethan Allen
Crawford's features were such "as might be molded on his own
blacksmith's anvil, but yet indicative of mother wit and rough
humor."

Thirty-two years later, in 1864, Hawthorne returned to the White
Mountains for the last time. His friend, former President Franklin
Pierce, had hoped that the upland air would restore his health, as
it had before, but he was very feeble when he reached the Pemige-
wasset House in Plymouth, and he died there on May 19.

Rare is the early journal or diary of the White Mountains that does not refer to the cheerful giant who served as both pioneer host and guide up Mount Washington over a trail he and his father had hewn in 1819. Harriet Martineau, the English chronicler of America, speaks of "alternations of throngs of guests with entire loneliness," of bustling Julys, solitary Septembers and jolly winter gatherings, with good liquors and loud songs for the entertainment of guests who came in sleighs. In 1824 Captain Alden Partridge, an early superintendent of West Point and founder (in 1819) of Norwich Military Academy on the Connecticut, descended upon the Notch with fifty-two cadets, and it was up to Ethan and Lucy Crawford to feed them and provide quarters. Overflowing the house, many of them slept in the barn and "a number of them stacked themselves up in a pile by the side of the fence in the bright moonshine." The next year Crawford went to Portland and bought a tent and a sheet-iron stove which he carried up the mountain on his back so that his ever-growing clientele might have shelter at the summit.

In 1852 stone for the Summit House was blasted from the top of the mountain and anchored with stays and bolts. Lumber was carried up by horses and when the roof was in place four stout cables were passed over it and secured to the ledge. Another hotel, the Tip Top House, was constructed the following year. It was such an attraction that Sylvester Marsh, a local engineer, decided to build a cog railroad up the mountain. There was no precedent anywhere in the world for such an undertaking. Brilliant in conception, it was so costly that the first Mount Washington Railroad Company failed. As a young man Marsh had been one of the founders of Chicago and inventor of a number of devices in the fledgling meat-packing industry. He was not to be discouraged by the skepticism of his neighbors and the gentleman in the legislature who proposed an amendment to the charter of his company permitting him to build a railroad to the moon. Climbing three miles over the west side of the mountain into the realm of lichens, liverworts, scrub spruce and dwarf birch, the road was at last finished in 1869. Every stick of the trestle and every piece of iron for the engines and rails had been drawn through the woods by oxen (the nearest railroad station was 25 miles away). The hard-working locomotives, belching steam and black smoke, have since pushed tens of thousands of passengers to the world above the clouds and the road remains a testimonial to the resourcefulness of one Yankee a century ago.

Although the capstone of New England has succumbed even to automobiles, man and machine there must forever remain at the mercy of that vile-tempered despot of the summit, the weather. For every moment of clear calm, with its lavender tableaux of the extreme distance, there are hours or days when the visibility is only a few feet. The chronicle of Mount Washington is filled with encounters with the most desperate weather in the Western Hemisphere—weather that has terrified even hardened climbers of the great peaks of the world who had not considered the Twinkling Mountain of Angososico very high or very steep. On October 25, 1855, Dr. B. L. Ball, a Boston physician, a veteran climber of the Alps as well as the difficult cone of Marapee on the island of Java, undertook to climb Mount Washington. He became lost in a snowstorm and passed the whole night on the mountain with only an umbrella and some scrub branches for a shelter. The next day, with waning strength and with limbs congealed with cold and stinging sleet, he struggled forward, but was not able to find his way back to the Glen House. By evening he discovered to his utter despair that he was back in the same place he had started from in the morning, and he had to pass a second night on the mountain trying to fight sleep and a compulsive shaking that drained his little remaining energy. The third morning he was nearer dead than alive. Although his hands and feet were freezing, he again struggled into the wind through deepening snow. About noon he saw directly ahead of him some men coming around the bluff. They could scarcely believe he was Dr. Ball, for it was not possible that he still lived. No one had ever survived two such nights on the mountain.

Dr. Ball's feet and hands were indeed frozen and it was twelve weeks before he was able to walk even a short distance. Although he never fully recovered, at least he lived to tell a story of moments on Mount Washington that seemed like hours, hours that seemed like years. Like Jack London's story *To Build a Fire*, it is a classic of the cold; unlike London's story, it is true.

Although attempts were made to establish a weather observatory on the extreme summit of Mount Washington as early as 1854, it was not until seventeen years later that government meteorologists constructed there a building strong enough and tight enough for habitation through the winter. It was occupied continuously from 1871 to 1887 and what previously had been conjecture about the extremes of wind and temperature there became fact. In February, 1886, during the worst storm in the history of the observatory, the mercury sank to 51 below zero and the anemometer was carried away after registering a wind velocity of 184 miles an hour. It was so cold in the observatory that, even though the stove glowed bright red, water froze within three feet of it and the icy wind, penetrating the insulated walls, actually raised the rug from the floor. The storm shutters blew in. It was all the two observers could do to anchor them back by using a board nailed to the floor as a brace. For fear that part or all of the building would be carried away into Tuckerman's Ravine the men wrapped themselves in heavy blankets tied with ropes and weighted with bars of iron. Fortunately, the cables over the roof held fast, although the engine shed blew away.

The weather station was abandoned in the summer of 1892 and observations in winter were not resumed until forty years later when more accurate meteorological equipment, together with a wireless and gasoline-driven dynamos, was installed. Robert S. Monahan, leader of the expedition, wrote in his log that on the clear evening of October 23, 1932, the lights of St. Johnsbury, Portland, Bath, Biddeford and Lakeport were very clear and the following day Mount Thetford in Canada, the Bonnefield lighthouse off the Maine coast, the Isles of Shoals off Portsmouth, Mount Monadnock to the south, Mansfield and Camel's Hump in Vermont, and even Whiteface and Marcy in the Adirondacks 120 miles to the west across Lake Champlain could be identified. On other occasions, when they could see clear to the plains of Canada and the forests of Maine, the thin blue line of the Atlantic at the edge of the eastern horizon, the sweeping circumference of mountains and lakes and the winding silver threads of rivers, they could only stand in silent wonder at the many faces of the land.

Chocorua, of the Sandwich Range to the south of the Presidential peaks, might be little known in a land of mountains were it not for the associations it has had with famous men. Longfellow wrote a poem called "Jeckoyva" about an Algonquin chief, Chocorua, who perished among its crags. Visiting the White Mountains in 1828, Thomas Cole, a young painter of the Hudson River school, was fascinated by both the jagged peak and a second version of its legend: that Chocorua had died at the hands of a white man who thought the chief had betrayed him. The well-known painting that resulted shows the dying Chocorua on a lofty rock with the white man standing below, his gun smoking. Now that there was visual "proof" of the legend of Chocorua it gained in fame through the embroidery of retelling, as did the stature of the mountain itself.

Although Monadnock, perhaps the most literary mountain in America, sounds as if it were named for an Indian, it is a term of physical geography, meaning a hill or mountain that has resisted the wearing down of the land around it by water and ice. Monadnock commands respect because it is alone and unchallenged by the surrounding hills of southern New Hampshire. Emerson wrote a poem about it. Thoreau, viewing it from the southeast, wrote of its

> masculine front. . . . As we beheld it, we knew that it was the height of land between the two rivers, on this side, the valley of the Merrimack, on that of the Connecticut, fluctuating with their blue seas of air,—these rival vales already teeming with Yankee men along their respective streams, born to what destiny who shall tell?

From Naulahka, his beloved Vermont home in West Dummerston, Rudyard Kipling counted Monadnock as a friendly witness to the writing of the *Jungle Books* and *Captains Courageous*. Under the heading: "In Sight of Monadnock" (in *Letters of Travel*) he refers to the lone mountain as a wise old giant

> "busy with his sky affairs," who makes us sane and sober and free of little things if we trust him. . . . Monadnock came to mean everything that was helpful, healing and full of quiet and when I saw him half across New Hampshire, he did not fail. In that utter stillness a hemlock bough, overweighted with snow, came down a foot or two with a tired little sigh; the snow slid off and the little branch flew nodding back to its fellows.

Mark Twain, too, was moved to tell of Monadnock as he rocked on the veranda of a cottage in Dublin, New Hampshire, in 1905.

> From the base of the long slant of the mountain the valley spreads away to the circling frame of the hills, and beyond the frame the

billowy sweep of remote great ranges rises to view and flows, fold upon fold, wave upon wave, soft and blue and unworldly, to the horizon 50 miles away. In these October days Monadnock and the valley and its framing hills make an inspiring picture to look at, for they are sumptuously splashed and mottled and betorched from sky-line to sky-line with the richest dyes the autumn can furnish; and when they lie flaming in the full drench of the mid-afternoon sun, the sight affects the spectator physically, it stirs his blood like military music.

With her quiet workshop for artists at Peterborough, the widow of Edward MacDowell has made the literary traditions of Monadnock secure. Here, through her legacy of inspired hard work, creative people may find the repose that was so precious to Kipling on the afternoon side of the mountain in Vermont.

> What I required, or at least wished for [wrote Edwin Arlington Robinson], was a place in the country, not too far from the civilized conveniences of life, that would afford comfortable lodging, good food, a large and well-windowed sleeping room with a good bed in it, an easy walk to breakfast at about seven-thirty, a longer walk to a secluded and substantial building in the woods, a large open fireplace and plenty of fuel, a free view from the door of the best kind of New England scenery, a complete assurance of a long day before me without social annoyances or interruptions of any kind, a simple luncheon brought to my door by a punctual but reticent carrier, a good dinner at night with a few congenial people, and evening without enforced solitude or enforced society, and a blessed assurance that no one would ask me to show him or her what I was writing.

On 600 rolling acres of pine and clover in the shadow of Monadnock Marian MacDowell built twenty-five isolated studios where Thornton Wilder, Aaron Copland, Roy Harris and many other notables in the literary, art and music worlds have found the peace and repose necessary to doing their best work.

Early in the nineteenth century it had already become clear that New England was also flowering in the hills. The umbrellas of artists like Durand, Homer, Bierstadt, Cole, Kensett and Church dotted the banks of the Saco River; poets of the landscape like Lowell, Longfellow, Whittier and Holmes were finding much to see in this wild romantic country, and a good deal to say about it. And the public at large, particularly upon the arrival of the railroads in the White Mountains, was discovering that there was a rocking chair and a piazza half a mile up to suit almost any purse. For well over a century the great white summer hotel with its varnished hardwood floors, its string quartets set in groves of potted palms, its golf links and serene prospects of distant ranges, has flourished in the White Mountains; only now does the seemingly inexhaustible supply of old ladies in their green rockers show signs of giving out.

The large hotel era was at its height in the days before the automobile, during the last quarter of the nineteenth century, when those who could afford it arrived by train for the entire summer, and those who could not, stuffed themselves with four-course dinners for a week, or as long as their cash held out, and returned forlornly to the steaming cities. In front of Bethlehem's Saratoga-like phalanx of hotels ran a boardwalk two miles long. To replenish gossip gone threadbare, the rocking-chair brigades had only to look up from their novels to the cavalcade of parasols and pearl stickpins in front of them. Henry Ward Beecher, escaping the hay fever of the lowlands, was preaching fashionably under a tent at Twin Mountain every Sunday. Among height-of-the-season throngs such luminaries as William Dean Howells might be identified, or P. T. Barnum, who presented a unique circus at the Profile House with his employees disguised as animals. The lucky coachman who delivered Cornelius Vanderbilt and his party safely at Plymouth received a tip of $100.

In a tour of the White Mountains on his way from Portland to Canada, Anthony Trollope was astonished that a range he had thought was somehow connected with the Alleghenies and the Rockies and "inhabited either by Mormons, Indians, or simply by black bears" was dotted with hotels almost as thickly as the Swiss Alps. The scenery, he thought, was superior here when autumn laid on the hills its carpets of rose and bronze. That the hotels were shuttered down during this spectacle was incomprehensible to one who did not understand the lemminglike migration of Americans to the hills or seashore during the summer and the mass exodus to the cities the 1st of September.

Some of the sprawling hostelries viewed by Trollope are still in business. A few have for generations been family owned; others have gone through as many fortunes as they have regimes. The site of

The Balsams at Dixville Notch, according to Roderick Peattie, was once owned by Daniel Webster, who lost it apparently by failing to pay the interest on his note. It was acquired eventually by an inventor named Henry Hale who one season showed to George Pullman a revolving chair he had designed in a local barn. Pullman, delighted, offered a contract on the spot and Hale's chair was soon revolving in nearly every parlor car. Because he was free of hay fever in the mountains Hale spent his new fortune in Dixville Notch on an immense structure with 800 rooms and was so successful in establishing it as a fashionable watering place that at the outbreak of the First World War he was richer than ever. At the behest of his German son-in-law, however, he invested in German bonds, and was wiped out financially and socially.

At this desperate point in the fortunes of The Balsams, Frank Doudera, a young New York policeman, rescued from a burning house a baby named after the wife of Harry K. Thaw, then in the public eye as the murderer of Stanford White, the architect. So much publicity attended the rescue of Evelyn Nesbit Thaw's namesake (the baby's last name was Walker) that Doudera received a handsome reward. Having always dreamed of being not a policeman but an interior decorator, Doudera took a year's leave of absence to try his hand at it. The result was the successful Doudera Decorating Company. His quest for further fields to conquer led him, of all places, to The Balsams, where he built a polo field and golf course. So tasteful was the Doudera Decorating Company in the refurbishing of the 800 rooms that The Balsams and Dixville Notch again joined the company of such select establishments as Sugar Hill, the Mountain View House, Peckett's and Bretton Woods (site, in 1944, of the International Monetary Fund conference). While it is doubtful that any of the other hotels could boast a more eventful existence, their rise and, it is feared, their forthcoming demise in the vagabond era of the motel is very much a part of a country whose economy has for a century partially relied upon recreation.

The Green Mountains, with views just as satisfying, historical and literary traditions quite as significant, also proved to be a natural habitat of the Goliaths of the large hotel era. In Stowe, at the foot of Mount Mansfield was built in 1864 a hotel four and a half stories high with the inevitable piazza running across the front almost its entire length of 300 feet. Subsequently two wings 45 by 90 feet were added in the rear. Among the accouterments were a landscaped park, bowling alley, a pond for fishing and boating, and a cavernous stable for the horses that drew Concord coaches from the railroad depot at Waterbury. At the opening Hall's Band from Boston played for the fashionable assemblage.

Mansfield's reputation was not made by the new hotel, however. A carriage road already wound steeply up to the Summit House just below the 4,389-foot crest with its lordly outlook over Lake Champlain to the Adirondacks to the west, the valley of the St. Lawrence to the north, and to the east beyond innumerable green peaks the bold high crags of the White Mountains. At the Summit House the morning ritual called for the ringing of a bell and a man shouting "Sunrise!" as the guests trooped sleepily out to the balcony. Ascending the mountain in indifferent weather from the Underhill side, Ralph Waldo Emerson found Lake Champlain

> a perpetual illusion, as it would appear a piece of yellow sky, until careful examination of the islands in it and the Adirondack summits beyond brought it to earth for a moment; but if we looked away for an instant, and then returned, it was the sky again. When we reached the summit we looked down upon the "Lake of the Clouds" and the party which reached the height a few minutes before us had a tame cloud which floated by a little below them.

Smuggler's Notch, a counterpart in Vermont of New Hampshire's Tuckerman's Ravine, led those who preferred to look up rather than down through a cool, deep and heavily forested gorge from Stowe to Jeffersonville.

Samuel de Champlain saw Mansfield and Camel's Hump from the lake on his voyage of discovery in July, 1609, and wrote that the Green Mountains were covered with snow. He was usually a careful observer but, unless snowlike mist or clouds shrouded their summits, his imagination must have misled him that day. The Indians called Mansfield Moze-O-Be-Wadso: Mountain with Head Like a Moose. White men have likened it to the head of a man in repose, with the forehead, nose and chin clearly defined from the west. One of the first mountain towns to fall victim to the still-continuing migration from the hill farms was Mansfield, which in 1838 had 279 people. When the western part of the town joined Underhill the people

east of the mountain had no alternative but to annex themselves to
Stowe. With splendid independence, an original settler named Ivory
Luce refused to accept the dismemberment and continued to appear
in the legislature as representative of the defunct Mansfield until he
was thrown out. Then, according to tradition, he picked up a butcher
knife and went hunting for those he considered responsible for this
disaster.

Stowe's large-hotel era was brief, for in 1889 the Mount Mansfield
House burned to the ground and the town fell back upon its farms,
its woodlots, its stores and small industries. Except for the summer
safaris of city people up the carriage road to the summit and of more
hardy hikers of the Long Trail, which winds along the spine of the
Green Mountains all the way from Massachusetts to the Canadian
border, the mountain slumbered until relatively recent times.

Nothing has had more to do with the chronicles of Mansfield,
or indeed with those of many other Vermont mountains, than the
age of skiing. Fred Harris, founder in 1910 of Dartmouth's Outing
Club, built Vermont's first large ski jump at Brattleboro in 1922. At
Vermont Academy in Saxton's River was held, it is said, the first
winter carnival in the United States. Only one ascent and descent
of Mansfield on skis (by way of the Toll Road) is recorded prior to
the First World War. Until 1934, when W. Douglas Burden and a
group of friends arranged with a farmer in Woodstock to operate
the United States' first rope tow with the engine of a Model T Ford,
skating was Vermont's reigning winter sport. Then came the revolution. On a winter weekend the foot of Mount Mansfield's multiple
chair and T-bar lifts now looks like the parking lot of an automobile
assembly plant. Stowe is the skiing capital of the Northeast. Big
Bromley, Burke, Jay, Mad River, Mount Snow, Pico—to name but
a few—have all come astonishingly, almost magically to life in the
empire of skiing and today the crown rests uneasily on Mansfield's
crest. For a land of forgotten cellar holes who could have forecast
such a destiny? It is as if Nature were making up for her failure to
run veins of silver through the mountains, and was now tracing them
on top.

While there is room for all the skiers in the world in a state with
as many mountains as Methuselah had years, the names of most of
them never appear on Metropolitan charts of snow conditions. Each,

however, has its place in local history and folklore and in the hearts of those who through the changing seasons watch the sun and moon rise and fall beyond them: Bloodroot, Belvidere, Haystack, Hogback, Killington, Pisgah and Equinox. So have the tidy valley of the Batten-kill, the white town of Manchester with its colonnaded inn, Herndon, summer home of Robert Todd Lincoln, and in recent decades of the Johnny Appleseed Bookshop and its poet-proprietor, Walter Hard. Remembrance of clear Octobers and painted hills flanking the highway winding south through Arlington and the pine grove up a brook that Dorothy Canfield Fisher planted back in the days of *The Bent Twig* and *Seasoned Timber* does not fade.

Breadloaf: splotches of sunlight on a stream and a tumbling road to a plateau of weathered summer buildings, long ago the refuge of that archenemy of the automobile, Joseph Battel, whose stock in trade was quiet and Morgan horses and, for his guests, long tables with dishes of oversized strawberries. Breadloaf, since 1925 the home of the first and best-reputed school for writers, a literary mountain to compete with New Hampshire's Monadnock.

For years Robert Frost lived just down the road in Ripton. Was *he* the image of Hawthorne's Great Stone Face? Certainly he was the land's and the land was his. New Hampshire?

> She's one of the two best states in the Union.
> Vermont's the other. And the two have been
> Yoke-fellows in the sap-yoke from of old
> In many marches. And they lie like wedges,
> Thick end to thin end and thin end to thick end,
> And are a figure of the way the strong
> Of mind and strong of arm should fit together . . .

The mountains?

> The Vermont mountains stretch extended straight;
> New Hampshire mountains curl up in a coil.

He would not confess a favorite, but thought Vermont "the state in a very natural state. We are [of New York, New Hampshire and Vermont] the humblest of the three." Because he was long a farmer of bare rock, "well-lost" here in the backbeyond, his poems are well-tempered, like Farmer Brown, who "bowed with grace to nature's law," and the mountain village with but 60 voters who "can't in nature grow to any more." As the people do, his poems speak sparely, with a twist, with humor, and sometimes with tender melancholy.

> If tired of trees I seek again mankind,
>   Well, I know where to hie me—in the dawn,
>   To a slope where the cattle keep the lawn.
> There amid lolling juniper recline, myself unseen, I see in white defined
>   Far off the homes of men, and farther still,
>   The graves of men on an opposing hill,
> Living or dead, whichever are to mind.

Although Robert Frost warned, with a trace of a smile, that New York is "seeping up this way," it is still possible to find in the many small towns in the comfortable valleys of Vermont and New Hampshire the kind of environment that thoughtful people are seeking: one in which there is a more basic relationship between the people and the land—the kind of environment so eloquently interpreted by Thornton Wilder in Grover's Corners, New Hampshire, the not-so-imaginary scene of *Our Town.*

For well over a century creative people, both native and adopted, have filled their pages and canvases with a testimony of affection for a country decreed by geography to be the antithesis of bigness and richness in most matters except that of the heart. Even before the industrial revolution began to widen the gulf between city and country living, Thoreau sensed the tranquillity still characteristic of much of the northland when he ascended the Concord and Merrimack rivers in 1839.

> These humble dwellings homely and sincere, in which a hearth was still the essential part, were more pleasing to our eyes than palaces or castles would have been. . . . I have not read of any Arcadian life which surpasses the actual luxury and serenity of these New England dwellings.

Rowland Robinson fairly breathed affection for the quiet hills in his nineteenth-century portrayals of the people and surroundings of Ferrisburg, Vermont. Writing about the Montpelier home of his grandfather, Daniel P. Thompson (author of *The Green Mountain Boys,* which went through fifty editions from 1839 to 1860 and lays claim to being the "original" historical novel as we know it today), Charles Miner Thompson recalled stone steps and a path past a black-cherry tree to "a white and green Greek temple of wood with fine Ionic columns." He remembered

> a square cool room facing green meadow-land, the placid river and the sharply rising hills beyond. It was a charming view and oh, so bathed in quietness. The singing of bobolinks in the early summer, and in rich July the swish of scythes through the grass and the ring of the whetstone on the blades were the harshest sounds you heard.

This same strong feeling for place is to be found in *Williamstown Branch*, an evocation of turn-of-the-century Vermont by Robert L. Duffus, a senior editor of the *New York Times*. "There is no more Yankee than Polynesian in me," remarked Bernard DeVoto a few years ago, "but when I go to Vermont I feel that I am traveling toward my own place."

And there was the eloquent testimonial of Augustus Saint-Gaudens, who chose Cornish, New Hampshire, on the Connecticut River in the shadow of Vermont's Mount Ascutney as his home. Persuaded by a friend that there were "plenty of Lincoln-shaped men" in New Hampshire, he arrived in 1885 to spend his first summer. It rather intrigued him to find that he was partly in Vermont, for his view was of the Vermont hills and his post office was across the river in Windsor. At first he found his house a little forbidding, "like an austere, upright New England farmer with a new set of false teeth," in the words of a friend. "No," corrected another friend, "it strikes me as being more like some recalcitrant New England old maid struggling in the arms of a Greek faun."

The life and scenery so enchanted him that he bought the house. He had found the remark about the Lincoln-shaped men in the hills to be true. In a century-old barn converted into a studio he had earnestly started work on sketches for a standing Lincoln and a seated Lincoln. It was three years, however, before he spent his first winter in New Hampshire.

> . . . I was deeply impressed and delighted by its exileration and brilliancy, its unexpected joyousness. . . . I was as happy as a child. I threw myself into northern life and reveled in it as keenly as I did in the dancing in the moonlight of Lispenard Street when I was a boy; especially when, skating once more after thirty-five years and playing hockey like a boy, I was knocked down twice, receiving a

magnificent black eye the first time and a swelled and cut forehead the second.

Saint-Gaudens spent the last seven years of his life in Cornish. Although they were richly happy ones they were marred by the tragic fire which burned the larger of his two studios. It consumed most of four years' work: his almost-finished seated Lincoln and a number of bas-reliefs, paintings by Winslow Homer, treasured letters from his friend Robert Louis Stevenson, and the records and sketches of two decades. Resolutely starting work again in the other studio he created during the last years much of the work for which he became famous, such as the memorial to the wife of Henry Adams in Washington's Rock Creek Cemetery. In the days before his death on August 3, 1907, he lay watching the sun go down behind Mount Ascutney. "It's very beautiful," he told his son, "but I want to go further away."

2

In a landscape with as many faces as a cut-glass bowl, the lakes, like the mountains and river valleys, have their own very different traditions. Of New Hampshire's 1,301 bodies of water the history of Winnepesaukee, the largest, is as old as that of the redmen who came to the Weirs to fish; but it really came to life, as did Vermont's Champlain, Memphremagog and the other larger lakes, in the era of the steamboat. For a century high life and low passed over their decks. John Greenleaf Whittier, ranging Vermont and New Hampshire in pursuit of material for his verse, did not overlook Winnepesaukee. "A Legend of the Lake" begins:

> Should you go to Centre Harbor
> As haply you sometime may,
> Sailing up the Winnepesaukee
> From the hills of Alton Bay.

Among the Winnepesaukee steamboats there was the *Lady of the Lake* and the long-lived *Mount Washington,* whose side wheels churned among the lake's 274 islands for 63 years. When the *Lady of the Lake* was built in Lakeport in 1848 it was clear to a local character named Rance ("Sinner") Busiel that a boatman without a steamboat was forever doomed in the wash of the paddle wheels. Although he did not have the money to build or run a steamboat, he distributed handbills advertising a moonlight excursion of the new steamer *Daisy*, Captain Rance Busiel, at the low fare of 50 cents. And sure enough when the crowd appeared at the dock on the appointed evening, there was the freshly painted *Daisy*, black smoke coming from her funnel! Surrendering their money and merrily trooping aboard, the people enjoyed the trip, although their progress seemed very slow in the darkness. If it had not been for a renegade in the crew, the *Daisy's* first excursion might not have been her last. He reported that Busiel was a charlatan and the *Daisy* an engineless barge with wheels slung over the side and a dummy smokestack propped up on deck. Motive power had been applied by four men turning the paddle wheels with two large hand cranks in the hold. The smoke issuing from her funnel had come from a pile of oily rags in a pan below decks which Sinner had ignited to prove that he was getting up steam. The secret was out! The next morning the *Daisy* disappeared and so did Sinner; it was some time before his face was seen again in Lake Village.

Vermont's equivalent of 20-mile-long Winnepesaukee is 30-mile Memphremagog, which it shares with Quebec, as it did its steamers to the end of their era. One of them, built in 1849, was very much a local enterprise, for her hull and superstructure of oak, tamarack, rock maple, Norway and white pine all came from local shores. Memphremagog's best-loved paddle boat, also called *Lady of the Lake*, sailed her land-locked route for nearly fifty years. Her first captain had the wonderful name of Handyside, and the day she was launched in 1869 was a proud one for the sequestered town of Newport at the lake's southern end. The Memphremagog House was overflowing with guests who helped the natives cheer Captain Handyside, resplendent in gold lace, to his first landing.

But of course the boating traditions of Winnepesaukee and Memphremagog are vignettes as compared with those of Champlain, the diadem of New England lakes. The commerce in goods between New York and Montreal that developed on this 114-mile boulevard of water, connected by canals with the Hudson and St. Lawrence, has been described—but not the flow of people. Nathaniel Hawthorne was struck by this in his wanderings through the north-country early in the 1830's. Stopping at Orwell with its white tavern, two stores and wharf, he was interested that such a miniature diorama of a port could have such a good run of trade, foreign as well as domestic.

I delighted in it, among other reasons, on account of the continued succession of travellers who spent an idle quarter of an hour in waiting for the ferry boat, affording me just enough time to make their acquaintance, penetrate their mysteries, and be rid of them, without the risk of tediousness on either side.

Burlington, with its "painted lighthouse on a small green island, the wharves and warehouses with sloops and schooners moored alongside, or at anchor, or spreading their canvas to the wind, and boats rowing from point to point," reminded him of some fishing town on the seacoast.

Nothing struck me more in Burlington than the great number of Irish emigrants. They have filled the British Provinces to the brim, and still continue to ascend the St. Lawrence in infinite tribes overflowing by every outlet to the States . . . the men exhibit a lazy strength and careless merriment, as if they had fed well hitherto, and meant to feast better hereafter; the women strode about, uncovered in the open air, with far plumper waists and bonnier limbs as well as bolder faces, than our shy and slender females; and their progeny, which was innumerable, had the reddest and roundest cheeks of any children in America.

Hawthorne admired the town square with its white houses, brick stores, its church, courthouse and bank.

One brick building, designated in large letters as the customs house, reminded us that this inland village is a port of entry, largely concerned in foreign trade, and holding daily intercourse with the British empire. In this border country the Canadian bank notes circulated as freely as our own, and British and American coins are jumbled into the same pocket, the effigies of the King of England being made to kiss those of the Goddess of Liberty.

He found the people to be even more heterogeneous than the coins, more so, in fact, than those of any other place he knew. There were

merchants from Montreal, British officers from the volunteer garrisons, French Canadians, wandering Irish, Scotchmen of a better class, gentlemen of the south on a pleasure tour, country squires on business; and a great throng of Green Mountain Boys, with their horse-wagons and ox-teams, true Yankees in aspect, and looking more superlatively so, by contrast with such a variety of foreigners.

While at the pier he had seen one of the stately conveyances responsible for all this bustle, a steamboat which "dashed away for Plattsburgh, leaving a trail of smoky breath behind, and breaking the glassy surface of the lake before her."

The Champlain side-wheelers grew bigger by the decade, and more luxurious until in 1903 the largest of them, *Vermont III*, 268 feet long, with 63 staterooms, a hall carpeted in green, a dining room on the main deck aft, and a barbershop with pink-marble sinks, slid off the ways at Shelburne Harbor. Like the larger of her predecessors she served in what was advertised as the finest inland water trip in America: from Montreal to New York by way of Champlain, Lake George and the Hudson River. Trains carried boat passengers from Montreal to Plattsburg, and from the head of Lake George to the Albany piers of the Hudson River Day Line; for the canals could not accommodate large ships. At Ticonderoga a small train wound from the dock of the Champlain steamers at Montcalm Landing to the Lake George terminal at Baldwin in the upper part of the town. The *Vermont's* companion steamers were the *Chateaugay*, *Reindeer*, *Maquam* and the last of the fleet, the 220-foot *Ticonderoga*, launched at Shelburne in 1906 for service from Westport to St. Albans Bay and intermediate landings.

Certainly the most nostalgic memories of campers at such summer colonies as Thompson's Point and Cedar Beach were the days before good roads and reliable cars, when the *Ticonderoga* swept grandly in each morning to carry commuters to work in Burlington, and returned them in the evening. At half past six in the morning the *Ti* left Westport.

> When you heard her tooting for the Point [recalled Jessie S. Gibbs] you knew it was breakfast time. In the later afternoon her friendly salute at Essex told you it was time to get supper on the table. And that grand, roaring blast as she came by the bluff and prepared to make her wide and majestic circle of the reefs preparatory to the Point Landing, was the signal for the entire colony to rush to the dock.

The first citizen of the Point was sportsman Dick Irving, great-grandnephew of the creator of Ichabod Crane. He weighed over 300 pounds ("Stant Williams' scales aren't big enough to weigh me") and his reputation for storytelling did justice to that of his illustrious forebear. There was the time President Roosevelt visited the Point cottage of Leslie M. Shaw, secretary of the treasury, and the tipsy gentleman leading the welcoming twilight procession shouted: "Hooray for Cleveland!"

On a magnificent morning in July, 1910, aboard the *Armenia White* on New Hampshire's Lake Sunapee, the captain, Frank Woodsum, signaled for his engineer to come to the pilothouse.

"As I entered the door," recalled the engineer, "the Captain said: 'Do you see what I see there at the dock?' I took the glasses and looked, and there at the landing stood the first Model T Ford we had seen in Sunapee. Captain Frank, arms folded, and steering the boat with feet and knees, as he so often did, said solemnly: 'There, my boy, is the end of the steamboat.' He was right."

The long reign of steam on Lake Champlain (144 years) did not end, however, until 1953, when the *Ticonderoga* returned to winter quarters for the last time. In one of history's most astonishing enterprises, early in 1955, the J. Watson Webbs had the three-deck side-wheeler hauled overland nearly two miles on new-laid railroad tracks to the grounds of the heralded Shelburne Museum. And there, after a million miles of service on Lake Champlain, she rests among many other meaningful symbols of the American spirit.

There are 750 square miles of fresh water in Vermont and New Hampshire. There is also a spray of salt. No citizens on or off New Hampshire's 18-mile seacoast ever knew more of brine, tide and ocean fog than Oscar Laighton, author of *Ninety Years at the Isles of Shoals*, a book as memorable as it is little known.

When Laighton was a baby a young writer named Richard Henry Dana came to talk about the sea with his father, then keeper of the light on tiny White Island. Mrs. Laighton went to Portsmouth once a year to buy piece goods for her children's clothing. From their older sister, Celia, Oscar and his brother heard stories of "trees higher than our lighthouse, horses that pulled carts and were steered with tackle rove through their mouths . . . stores with great jars of candy, locomotives that screamed and people rushing in every direction. My brother and I would feel some doubt about all this."

In 1834 Oscar's father bought Appledore, Smutty Nose, Malaga and the Cedar Islands from Captain Sam Haley (who had found under a flat stone on Smutty Nose silver bars worth $3,000, which he spent to repair the sea wall and build a wharf). In 1847 Laighton decided to give up his lighthouse and build a summer hotel on Appledore, ten miles from the mainland. To the children its 300 acres of wild roses, bay and huckleberry bushes seemed as big as a continent after the bare two acres and 90-foot tower of White Island. His first morning on Appledore (he was eight years old) Oscar remembered seeing a flock of sheep grazing on the flank of the hill "and gulls flying by, pink with sunrise." He remembered exploring Smutty Nose and finding the graves of the Haley family. Captain Sam, whose father operated a ropewalk for making fishlines and cordage, told often of the northeaster that drove a Spanish ship on Smutty Nose and of the fourteen dead sailors tossed up on the rocks. Oscar's sister, Celia, wrote their epitaph years later.

> Fifty long years ago these sailors died:
> (None know how many sleep beneath the waves.)
> Fourteen gray headstones, rising side by side,
> Point out their nameless graves.

In his sixteen years Oscar had never once been off the islands. He was overwhelmed with a desire to see Portsmouth despite his father's warning about the wicked world of the mainland.

> . . . I could not get the adventure out of my mind, and getting up early one morning in June, I secured a loaf of bread from my mother's pantry and set sail in the whale boat, bound for the unknown continent of the United States! . . . The sun was just rising in dazzling splendor as I passed Blue Beach Point. There was a fair wind from the southwest, and I was running free with sheets started, the boat making a delicious murmer from the glancing water under her lee bow. . . . I held my course until I made the red buoy, off Kitts Rock; then, leaving Whale's Back Light to starboard, stood in for Four Point Light. This I rounded and kept to the westward by the Newcastle shore till I came to Pull-and-be-damned Point (so-called because it was impossible to row by it when the tide is running

strongly). Ahead was Fort Washington on Pierce's Island, and the Narrows with the city of Portsmouth coming into view. It was then about high water in the river, and I sailed to a lumber wharf and made my boat fast alongside a schooner tied up there. After I had lowered my sails and made things snug, I took a look up the wharf and saw my first horse. The critter was fast fore and aft to a lumber wagon, and showing all the earmarks of a Bengal tiger. I kept aboard my boat until he was driven off and noticed that the method of steering him was just as Sister had told me. . . .

At the end of Daniel Street I came to the big open square called "The Parade" where I saw crowds of people, horses, carriages and countless stores and dwellings. It was all new and wonderful, but I began to feel lonesome and started back to my boat, keeping an eye to windward and dodging people on the sidewalk. At last I reached the landing, and, there being no horse on the wharf, I jumped aboard my boat and got sail on her. . . . I reached home at half past two that afternoon, and found that Mother had been worried, but had saved a good dinner for me. Father only said, "Did you have a pleasant trip, Sonny?"

There was so much doing on Appledore that Oscar forgot his wanderlust. Since the 1600's the islands had harbored fleets of fishing boats, sometimes, he remembered, as many as 300 at once, their decks fairly dancing with mackerel. The sails of these vessels made a constantly moving backdrop to the island that his father had brought spectacularly to life with his hotel. In 1859 he added a wing with 40 more rooms and a dance hall, but in time even this proved inadequate. After his death in 1866 the brothers added to their already vast establishment a dining room to seat 500 people, another wing with 50 more rooms (the porch was now 500 feet long) and a steamboat called the *Appledore* with a capacity of 150. "When the steamer was part way over the Captain would blow the whistle once for every 10 passengers so we would know how many were on the boat before she arrived. Old Colonel Bailey hitched up a yarn that if there were ten blasts of the whistle we would run and put an extra bucket of water in the chowder!"

Visitors' paintings covered the walls of their 100-foot office of black walnut, a gathering place each evening, it seemed to Oscar, for the elite of the world. Among the honored guests were Hawthorne, James Russell Lowell, Whittier and William Morris Hunt.

A special cottage built for Celia, who had gained notice as a poet, was the scene of many pleasant gatherings of the literati. A number of friends had leased land to build cottages and during the latter quarter of the century Appledore came to look like a village. It was considered the finest hotel on or off the coast. Many, like Wentworth-by-the-Sea, were modeled after it. Fifty pretty waitresses in lace caps had all they could attend to in the dining room, while in the lounge "the hum of conversation was like intermission in a big theater."

Almost every season Oscar Laighton would fall in love with some beautiful guest. ("When I was 18 I became so crazy about a young lady at our house that when she departed I found a pair of old shoes she had left and kept them under my pillow every night for years. Seems strange! If they were removed, I could not sleep a wink until I replaced them.") Yet he never married.

In 1894 Celia died, and in 1899, his brother. Because of improved transportation ashore and the competing hotels of Hampton Beach and other such resorts, Appledore began to lose money and had to be sold. Eventually taken over by a syndicate, it burned to the ground during the first year of the First World War, and all the cottages with it. But by this time Oscar Laighton was an old man running a motorboat among the Isles of Shoals and had nothing except his memories to lose.

XV

ECONOMIC SORROWS
AND POLITICAL PLEASURES

While Vermont and New Hampshire have aptly been called twin states, they are not identical. Their differences, however, are not as easily counted as their similarities. Vermont is thought of as rural and New Hampshire as industrial, yet Vermont has considerable industry and New Hampshire has hundreds of square miles of rural countryside.

The marble tunnels under Proctor, the tunnels of talc under the hills of Waterbury and Johnson, the great geometric pits of granite in Barre, the sprawling electronics and machine-tool factories in the cities, the corridors of clacking shuttles and looms in many valley towns—these and many others are so intimately a part of the Green Mountain economy that it could not run without them. Industry has had much to do with bonding the elements of Vermont's present-day character.

When the Central Vermont, the Rutland, and other railroads hopefully advanced up and down the valleys in the mid-1800's it was not Yankees, generally speaking, but boatloads of Irishmen, arriving via the St. Lawrence and Lake Champlain, who laid the tracks. On New England roofs there may be as much slate mined in Fair Haven by Welshmen and Poles, as by Yankees. Barre, the so-called granite capital of the world, is an amalgam of Italians, Scots, Finns, French, Irish and even Spanish, Swiss, Austrians and Scandinavians. In front of the machines of the textile mills that have resisted the temptation to go south one more likely hears a babble of French Canadian than a Yankee twang. These other nationalities have helped the Yankees who remained fill the vacuum behind the tens of thousands who went west. The first-generation immigrants gravitated toward industry, although French Canadians have taken over hundreds of farms in northern Vermont and have done very well by the land, while the Irish have entered business and the professions. Perhaps as much as two thirds of Vermont's population, however, is still what might be called native stock.

Because it is too far away from markets and sources of raw materials the Green Mountain State does not attract heavy industry. (It is thus spared the social and economic ills of great smoking cities.) The moving out of textiles has caused readjustments that the moving in of diversified light industries has made somewhat less painful. The

279

products of these firms weigh relatively little so that distance from raw materials and from markets is not so critical. What manufacturers of electronics and certain other specialized products, such as hosiery, do seek are stable communities of industrious people. They have found small hill towns comfortable, and vice versa, because often there are just enough people to accommodate a single factory without disrupting the community. Frequently one of these new firms moves into the defunct plant of a native business. From this it should not be implied that home-grown industries, such as woodworking, are not still an important part of the diverse industrial kaleidoscope. Many of them still thrive after generations under the same native ownership.

If any general statement is to be made about Vermont industry, it is that no general statement *can* be made. It does seem likely that industry will never get the upper hand of the landscape, so long as people drink fresh milk and seek the hills and lakes for their vacations. Although Vermont remains a farming state, the auctioneer's gavel has hammered away at the 20-cow hill farm until it is becoming a rarity. Yet increasing production from the larger herds of lowland farms maintains the state's reputation as the milk shed for greater Boston and New York. It acquired this status by way of a century and a half of trial and error with almost every crop and animal that would grow in the hills and be sold for a profit. Vermont's cheese is still famous, as are its maple-sugar bushes and apple orchards. But it is torrents of milk that pay off bank loans for milking parlors and the other expensive trappings of the modern dairy, with enough left to keep some five thousand families on their land. A few impoverished hill farmers cling to the soil, preferring to stay poor than give up the old homestead and struggle with the uncertainties of a different and perhaps less independent life. There is no denying the poverty of a few backwater communities, or the inbreeding and the high rate of suicide that such marginal areas seem to engender. Vermont is not just a green paradise as many tourists "oohing" and "ahing" over the foliage, the tranquil villages, and the quaint independence of the people seem to think. Its problems, both social and economic, arise in part from the expensive maintenance of a forward-looking state government by fewer people (450,000) than there are in a single large metropolitan city. The fact that they succeed at all is attributed to their resourcefulness and to the consummate pride they take in their 9,564 square miles of mountains, valleys and lakes.

Fortunately, Vermonters' unhurried life is one that ever-larger numbers of outlanders want to share, for without tourism, as without industry and farming, the state economy would founder. The mere mention of inland lakes like Willoughby, Morey, Fairlee, Dunmore, Bomoseen, Hortonia, St. Catherine, conjures up visions of the wigwams of thousands of young squaws and braves from the cities, of modest summer cottages, family-style inns and guest houses, and state parks under canopies of pines where today's nomads can pitch their tents or set up their trailers. The fall foliage tour has augmented the traditional summer vacation. An avalanche of skiers descends in December and melts gradually away in March.

Although tourists are also important to New Hampshire, industry reigns there, and because it does well over 300,000 of its 750,000 people are classified as urban dwellers. The Merrimack cities of Manchester and Nashua, with 87,000 and 55,000 people, respectively, continue to dominate the industrial scene; but it is far different from what it was a few decades ago. On November 15, 1936, Francis Brown wrote in the *New York Times* about a city of the dead.

> The grilled gates are locked and the fallen leaves swirl beyond them in the mill yard which the weeds have occupied. In places grass has overgrown the railway sidings, while around the newer buildings on the river's right bank the shrubbery is already tangled and unkempt. Paint peels from exposed woodwork. Electric lights are broken. On the clock tower the hands stand obstinately at 8.

Amoskeag, the colossus of the textile world, had collapsed. Fifteen thousand people were out of work. New Hampshire's largest city was in a state of semiparalysis. The stroke was inevitable—so claimed the management, reporting the rising pressure of debt. Or was it senseless fratricide, as the labor unions charged?

During the early days before the Civil War the preponderance of Amoskeag's huge task force was from the hills. Then foreigners by the thousands poured in. During one week in April of 1869, 2,300 French Canadians passed through St. Albans on the cars of the Central

Vermont Railroad, the majority en route to the Merrimack's assorted mills. By 1890 there were 40,000 Canadians in New Hampshire but these were just the vanguard of those to come. There were 15,000 Irish and lesser numbers of Germans, Norwegians and Swedes. Of the names of 360 workers added to Amoskeag payrolls in December of 1912, only 8 per cent were American. Half the others were French and the rest were Irish, Greek, Polish, English, German, Scottish, Swedish, Lithuanian and Russian. The company liked foreigners because for $1.50 a day they would work from 6:40 in the morning until 6:00 at night, and because they were inclined not to join unions.

In order to keep labor organizers away from their 45 acres of buildings and their 15,500 workers, who wove 147,000 miles of cloth each year, the management evolved a paternal program with every possible employee benefit except significant increases in pay. It offered medical care, clothing, fuel, interest-free mortgages on homes, stock-ownership, correspondence courses, recreational facilities and social programs. But in 1922 the plant was shut down in a strike for a 48-hour week. It turned out disastrously for the employees, since their union had to ask the company under what terms they might return. Although they went back to a 54-hour week, the company decided that its welfare program did not pay and canceled it. The following year Amoskeag followed the lead of other textile companies in raising wages 12½ per cent, but in 1924 it reduced them 10 per cent and, in the face of a $4,100,000 loss (before dividends), increased the work load.

In 1927 the trustees began to liquidate the company by withdrawing $8,000,000 from its cash reserves. The all-powerful treasurer, F. C. Dumaine, explained that this was necessary to forestall raids by Wall Street speculators on the company's surplus! To many it seemed that the management was sending one of only two lifeboats ashore with the strongbox, leaving all hands on board to go down with the ship—all hands, that is, except the bondholders. But there was no question that Amoskeag was sinking. In 1880 New England had 80 per cent of all the spindles in the cotton industry. Only 30 per cent remained in 1935, the year before Treasurer Dumaine and the bondholders took to the remaining lifeboat.

In justice to the management, the large losses of the depression years must be considered, the walkout of the employees in 1933, the national textile strike in 1934, and finally the flood of 1936. Since 1929 the officers had bought new machinery and had tried to make operating economies. For a time, during years of the National Recovery Act, business looked good (perhaps falsely so), but the Textile Code reduced weekly working hours to 40, on a 54-hour-a-week pay scale. Toward the end the employees agreed to a reduction, but it was too late.

There were inquiries by a governor's committee and by a federal court, which charged the trustees with putting their winnings aside and playing safe. A Congressional investigator declared that the Amoskeag Manufacturing Company (a holding concern) and a hand-picked bondholders' protective committee were guilty of "sheer manipulation." In the final analysis it seems to have been a matter of ethics. It is the prerogative of bondholders to save themselves, but not over the dead body of a community of 82,000 dependent people, at least not without a consecrated effort to remedy their plight.

What possible hope could there be for Manchester? Little or none whatever, it seemed to the thousands concerned during the threadbare fall and winter of 1936. But what wonders they achieved. Within ten years energetic citizens' committees had filled the brick caverns along the Merrimack with over a hundred assorted businesses and industries. Today Manchester is better off than as if the great monolith of the textile world had continued in business, for the livelihood of the people does not depend upon a single group of nonresident trustees around a polished table. There is strength in diversity. The new Manchester, large as it is, has much more in common with its environment.

Under the dull-sounding title of *Investigation of Closing of Nashua, N.H., Mills and Operations of Textron, Incorporated* is to be found drama worthy of Gotham, and valuable instruction in high finance as it is fought in the tax jungles today. It is a biography of Royall Little, whom Emil Rieve (general president, Textile Workers' Union of America) calls a "capitalist, but in the field of finance, rather than the field of production." It is the story of the Nashua Manufacturing Company, organized in 1823, with Daniel Webster as one of the incorporators, a company whose noted label of Indian Head cloth survived every catastrophe until 1948 when its assets served to nourish the far-flung empire of Textron, Incorporated.

If there is a lesson in the demise of Amoskeag and Nashua Manufacturing it is that any northcountry concern that wants to stay independent had better not be too rich or too poor. If too rich it is in danger of being plucked off the vine by city capitalists and having the juice squeezed out of it. If it has debt it is likely to be bought merely for the carry-over of its losses as a tax benefit for a large company in a high income bracket. Of course some native concerns that otherwise would have gone out of business have been saved by the very bigness that has ruined their neighbors. By becoming part of a larger enterprise with much better marketing facilities they have prospered as never before. But such companies are in danger of losing the character they had when locally owned, for the decisions are made in big cities, often without regard for local interests and welfare.

Although Vermont is one of the very few states with no metropolitan areas, industry accounts for over half its income. Manufacturing is modest in scale and widely dispersed because the cities and towns are. International Business Machines' giant plant in Essex Junction and Burlington's General Electric are exceptions. The contrast in New Hampshire, one of the most urban states with its concentration of people and industry in the flatlands of the southeast, could hardly be greater. This area, part of the seaboard megalopolis, belongs not to the hill country but to Boston.

The migration continues toward New Hampshire's fifteen cities with populations of over 7,000. Despite the drifting to the south of textiles, they still hold a commanding place in the state's economy. The manufacturing of machinery also is important, as are shoes and leather products, electronics and paper. The Portsmouth Navy Yard faces an uncertain future. New Hampshire industry has survived various economic cataclysms with surprising vigor and is responsible today for the modest growth of the state's population— while Vermont has gained more slowly. Presumably the moral of this is that if Vermont wants to grow it should have more industry. It could use more, comfortably, but if it had as much as New Hampshire its character might change and that, to its tens of thousands of admirers, would be a loss hard to calculate.

One industry that both states still share is lumbering. The forested north smells of wood pulp. Every year untold miles of paper towels roll out of the Brown Company in the border country of Berlin. Beecher Falls, Vermont, which makes maple furniture, actually straddles the Canadian border. (The Line, as it is called, used to run right through the hotel barroom so that during prohibition anyone who wanted a drink had merely to step over a row of brass tacks into Canada.)

There is still an aura of the frontier in the Northeast Kingdom. One reason for this, wrote Stewart Holbrook, its native spokesman, is all the false-front buildings in Colebrook, West Stewartstown, Canaan and Pittsburg, the last stand of old-time logging.

> The frontier lingered in our region because it was remote and so sparsely populated that no railroad ever reached it until just before the turn of the century. . . . If our fathers wanted to travel . . . they could hitch up and drive twenty or forty miles to North Stratford, New Hampshire, where the Grand Trunk came in from Portland and left for Montreal, its thundering Moguls moaning through the wilderness called Hegan Woods and emitting blasts that could be heard, on a still cold night, in Lemington, even in Colebrook.

In the days not so long ago "when two thousand men were cutting spruce around First, Second and Third Lakes . . . the bells of tote-teams could be heard at all hours of the day and night from First Lake Dam to Scott's Bog." The Connecticut Lakes are now reservoirs for hydroelectric stations downriver "and the whole region round about is a reservoir for fish and game that are taken by down-country sports who board at professional camps set in second-growth among stumps made in the roaring days of Jigger Johnson, Big Jim La Voie and 'Phonse Roby."

2

As it turned out, Winston Churchill did not need the fortune he inherited from his father. After his graduation from West Point he served as an editor of the *Army and Navy Journal* and *Cosmopolitan* magazine, but the achievements that brought him critical acclaim and wealth were the novels he wrote at Harlakenden House, his river estate in Cornish, New Hampshire. To read *Coniston* is to learn (from a native of Missouri) almost all any layman need know about New Hampshire politics in the early 1900's. The book is a faithful portrayal of New England character and it is strange that Churchill is not better known today.

> Never, since the days of Pompadour and Du Barry, until American politics were invented, has a state been ruled from such a place as Number 7 in the Pelican House—familiarly known as the Throne Room. In this historic cabinet there were five chairs, a marble-topped table, a pitcher of iced water, a bureau, a box of cigars and a Bible, a chandelier with all the gas jets burning, and a bed, whereon sat such dignitaries as obtained an audience—railroad presidents, governors and ex-governors and prospective governors, the Speaker, the President of the Senate, Bijah Bixby, Peleg Hardington, mighty chiefs from the North Country, and lieutenants from other parts of the state. . . .
>
> "All Gaul," said Mr. Merrill—he was speaking to a literary man —"all Gaul is divided into five railroads."

The reason *Coniston* is so sound politically, quite apart from its literary merits, is because its author very nearly won the governorship of New Hampshire on the Progressive-Republican ticket in 1906. He and such other reformers as ex-Senator William Chandler threw so much sand into the Republican machine that Robert P. Bass, their candidate in 1910, won the governorship. In the face of charges that he was a wealthy man buying his way into the State House, Bass replied that at least it was his own money he was spending in the campaign and not that of the Boston and Maine Railroad. The influence of the Progressive-Republicans was such that the legislature adopted two of their favorite reforms: that senators be elected directly by the people instead of by the assembly and that railroads be prohibited from giving passes to any state representatives or public official. Through such tactics the railroads had for years been getting what they wanted and were the foremost influence in New Hampshire politics.

The Democrats won for the first time in 1912, because of the split on the national scene between Roosevelt and Taft and because the local Republicans were divided. In 1916 Woodrow Wilson carried the state by 63 votes. Possibly because the air in the hills was rare and fine for Democrats, Wilson chose the home of Winston Churchill in Cornish as his summer White House in 1913 and 1915.

Unlike New Hampshire, which again went Democratic in the national elections of 1936, 1940 and 1944, Vermont never elected a Democrat to state or national office from the time the Republican party was founded until, in 1958, owing to a three-way split in the Republican primaries, a Democrat won an unexpired term in the House of Representatives. The first Democrat to be elected governor, Phillip H. Hoff, served longer (three terms) than any other in the state's history. An outlander with liberal views, he was succeeded by Republican Deane C. Davis, a typical Vermonter with a generally, though not exclusively, conservative outlook. To classify the durable George D. Aiken, senior Republican in the U.S. Senate (senior also in integrity) as exclusively liberal, would be to deny him his birthright of independence too strong to be classified. One mystery, seemingly unfathomable, is why this independence took so long to find expression in a two-party system. The answer may be that in recent decades, at least, the state Republican edifice has been roomy enough to accommodate diverging views.

It was after the exodus to the West and the great upheaval of the War Between the States that Green Mountain politics settled serenely into its tryst with the party of Lincoln. For decades it seemed that the easiest way to the governorship was to become president of a railroad or be thought well of by the Vermont Fish and Game Club. This organization's most historic meeting was held on Friday, September 6, 1901, at the picturesque stone homestead of Lieutenant Governor Nelson W. Fisk on Isle La Motte. A reception for Theodore Roosevelt had been given that morning at the Van Ness House in Burlington and the vice-president was then driven to the wharves where, with Winston Churchill and other notables, he steamed to Isle La Motte in the yacht of Colonel W. Seward Webb. A thousand people were present for the ceremonies to be held on Fisk's lawn, but just before the reception the telephone company called to report that President McKinley had been shot by an anarchist in the Temple of Music in Buffalo.

The Fisk homestead burned and the Vermont Fish and Game Club no longer exists. The course of state Republican politics, once charted by railroad presidents, by the marble governors of Proctor, by the so-called kingmaker of the National Life Insurance Company, Fred Howland, and more recently by the Farm Bureau and the utilities, is now quite completely in the hands of the rank and file. It is not possible to say whether it is "conservative" or "liberal." It is dangerous to brand Vermonters as conservative because they have always adhered to the Republican party and believe in paying as they go—or, for that matter, to identify as liberals those who favor the spending programs of a paternal government. (If such a philosophy harnesses future generations with debt, the liberals may turn out to have been conservatives, or reactionaries, and vice versa.) It is a matter of semantics. Certainly these labels, as they are popularly understood, cannot be attached with any certainty to the average Vermont senator or congressman.

The heritage of independence goes back to Ethan Allen and the days when the state was a republic with the most democratic constitution in America. It not only outlawed slavery but did not require a voter to own property. During the federal period, when Congressman Matthew Lyon was arrested by the minions of John Adams for alleged violation of the Alien-Sedition Acts, Vermonters re-elected him to a second term while he was serving his sentence in the Vergennes jail. For decades this same stubborn free spirit found expression, within the state's borders, in the unwritten Mountain Rule: that no governor could come from the same side of the mountains as his predecessor. The legislature spurned federal largess after the flood of 1929, and again in 1936 when the New Deal offered to build a parkway along the spine of the Green Mountains. The representatives at Montpelier appropriated thousands to fight federal seizure of lands (for flood control) without their permission. Recently this most Republican of states beat down attempts to keep the Communist party off the ballot and to remove what minorities considered offensive textbooks. But it has been reluctant to lift the "Blue Laws." Although Vermont now permits Sunday movies and the sale of liquor (if a town so votes), no one can be served standing up, bars must close at midnight, and outdoor liquor advertisements are prohibited. With a longing glance at the tax receipts flowing into Concord from New Hampshire's race track at Rockingham Park, the Vermont legislature emasculated a bill to permit horse racing on the grounds that it would lead to corruption, political and otherwise.

The watchful eye of the racing commission and statehouse on the

Pownal track caused its manager to comment ruefully in Montpelier that Pownal is known in racing circles as "the church." William Allen White once refused to believe there was no graft in Vermont, but eventually conceded the assertion to be true on the grounds there is so little money in the state that everyone knows where every dollar is. Calvinism, lingering in the small towns which for generations dominated the legislature, hasn't encouraged graft in Montpelier. Perhaps the government remains relatively pure because it is still small enough to be manageable, as are the towns and cities sprinkled almost evenly over the landscape.

While the composition of the Senate has always been based on county population, membership to the House, until it was reapportioned in 1964, consisted of one representative from every town or city regardless of size. As more outlanders come into the state, as further adjustments in reapportionment are perhaps made, as the towns further relinquish their autonomy by becoming "bedroom" communities serving larger centers; as the social programs of a paternal federalism continue to erode Vermont's vaunted independence and self-reliance, the historic image of the state may change decisively.

Democrats have been busy with their pails in the Republican sugar bush and have gained seats in both houses. The catalyst for putting a Democrat in the governor's chair is a split in the Republican primary. This allows the swing vote, composed of independents and recent arrivals, or "suntanners," many of whom are liberals, to reinforce the traditionally Democratic Catholic and labor vote. Composed of the large seepage of French Canadians into the northern counties, the Irish in the cities, and smaller ethnic groups, much of the Catholic vote, however, is conservative. Nor do the French and Irish see eye-to-eye. A supreme effort is therefore required for the Democrats to muster a united front. Although the Republican legislative majority sits rather uneasily these days, it is likely to remain in control for the foreseeable future.

Whatever its composition the Vermont House of Representatives is likely to remain one of the most interesting forums in America, and one of the most frustrating, as lobbyists, emerging red-faced and shaken from the defeat of their bills, have found out through the years. As Duane Lockard writes in *New England State Politics:*

"Groups appear to form, disperse, and reform with ever changing composition depending upon the question before the House." Although many of the representatives do not have a college education, the reading and thinking they have done through the winters and the wisdom they have gained through their long struggles with the land more than make up for it. Unless it is the town meeting there can be no fresher expression of the grass roots or any more nearly akin to the America of the rural nineteenth century. It is true that the steely-eyed enemies of federal handouts are becoming rarer in the legislature these days, for Yankees find it hard to turn their backs on Santa Claus, particularly if no strings are attached. Revenue sharing is gladly accepted. If there were another flood, Vermont would accept federal money for reconstruction. Why not? All the other states do. This may come as a shock to admirers of the frugal and self-sufficient Vermont of yore, and so may the fact that the state government has become expensive and topheavy. Recommendations of a Little Hoover Commission for streamlining state government were carried out by its chairman, Deane Davis, as governor ten years later. But Parkinson's Law applies in Vermont as elsewhere.

The political scene in New Hampshire is quite different. One reason is that over half the people are city dwellers, more are immigrants, more are Democrats. As in Vermont, however, the small towns have managed to control the state government and, with several exceptions, to elect a phalanx of Republican governors. As in Vermont, the governors, although of the same party, have differed widely in their outlook. (John G. Winant, Vermont-born Sherman Adams, and H. Styles Bridges plowed deeply in the larger American landscape, but at right angles to each other.) Unlike Vermont, city Democrats have had strong enough pluralities, as has been said, to carry the state in several national elections. There is no lieutenant governor in New Hampshire, but a cabinet-like council helps run the executive branch. With 400-odd members, the New Hampshire House of Representatives is a formidable body, the largest of any state in the Union. In 1965 the constitution was amended to provide that members of both House and Senate be elected roughly according to population. Previously any town with 600 people was entitled to a representative in the House, but approximately 1200 city people were necessary to elect one.

Senate membership formerly depended upon the amount of direct taxes the various districts paid—a vestige of New Hampshire's royal government. In Revolutionary days only those who paid a tax or served in the militia could vote. The first state constitution required representatives and senators to have property worth £300 and £400, respectively. The districts or counties paying the most taxes were privileged to elect the most representatives and senators. Since the seacoast county of Rockingham was the richest and supplied five of the state's twelve senators, control of the government, much to the annoyance of inland communities, remained with the seacoast gentry. The government's early troubles with the Connecticut River towns, bent on secession, and with Dartmouth College arose from the lopsided coastal majorities in the legislature. Because the seacoast gentry rightly considered Dartmouth responsible for much of the trouble with the river towns and for voting reforms that these towns forced upon the government in the Constitutional Convention of 1782, college presidents, professors and instructors were forced temporarily to join Catholics on the list of the disenfranchised. Had it not been for Daniel Webster's victorious defense of the privately chartered college before the Supreme Court in 1818, control of Dartmouth would have gone to the state government.

There are curious parallels between New Hampshire's present problems and those of a century and a half ago. Now it is the Rockingham Race Track that rides high in the government. Drawing crowds of factory workers from industrial southeastern New Hampshire and northeastern Massachusetts, the track is a garden for bookies who place bets amounting to tens of millions a year. The track employs some thirty to forty members of the legislature and in various ways, tangible and intangible, exerts influence in Concord. New Hampshire has no state income tax while Vermont has the highest in the union. The importance of a concentrated industrial population yielding its savings to the state by way of a prosperous race track is presumably established!

It is clear that governments, too, are products of heredity and environment and that the slightest variation in either produces altogether different consequences. While the Twin States have much in common, in many ways they are strangers.

XVI

LITANY IN EVERGREEN

It was Governor Frank W. Rollins who first proposed that the wandering sons of New Hampshire be lured back, if only briefly, in an annual celebration to be known as Old Home Week. Thousands answered the invitations of no less than 65 local committees and on Saturday evening, August 26, 1899, welcoming fires blazed on mountain and hill from the Connecticut to the sea. Old Glory flew above every second doorway, and the grass of village greens was flattened under an army of lunch baskets. There were pie-eating contests and balloon ascensions. "Pyrotechnic programs" followed the speeches of the local boys who had made good, while the brass and woodwinds blew themselves out behind the Japanese lanterns on octagonal bandstands.

So successful was this first observance that New Hampshire enacted a law making Old Home Week official. Vermont chose August 16, the anniversary of the Battle of Bennington, as the climax of its week of nostalgia and 45 towns paid homage to the good old days in 1901. While the vitality has gone out of Old Home Week as an annual observance, it is very much alive as a concept in the era of automation and nuclear physics.

In introducing the first issue of *Yankee*, Robb Sagendorf, publisher of *The Farmer's Almanac*, wrote that certain values that helped make America what it is are in danger, even in the land where they are held in highest esteem, of being smothered up in an era almost godlessly standardized and mechanized. "Coming out of his fields, his forests, his shop [the Yankee] is hungry and he is faint and he finds the dwellers of the tents offering him more miles to the gallon, more energy hours to the dollar, more religion per program." Chain stores and neon-lighted gas stations are invading his main street. Slowly but inexorably his institutions are becoming standardized, his government, nationalized. His individuality, even the accents of his speech, are being diluted in streams of national releases and national hookups. It is an atmosphere in which little is sacred except novelty and in which the heritage of the past seems meaningless. Sinclair Lewis' advice, to guard this heritage and to live by it no matter what the rest of the country does, is not easy to follow under such circumstances.

There are about as many signs that the northcountry may not

be able to keep the faith as there are that it can and will. Certainly it cannot and should not remain in a state of nature but it can and should use every stratagem to resist the pressures that war against its physical beauty and the individuality of its people. It is heartening to report not only that the northcountry Yankee as a type is far from extinct, but that he continues even to dent the national consciousness and conscience. Lest it be forgotten it was Vermont's Senator Ralph Flanders who helped free the country of the shocking paralysis of the McCarthy hearings by handing the senator from Wisconsin the note placing him in contempt of the United States Senate. Handily surviving McCarthy's charge that he was "a senile old man," Flanders explained to a friend: "I figured I was expendable."

Certainly it would be hard to find a better example of one kind of Yankee resourcefulness than the struggles of a few men to put the almost-defunct mountain town of Weston back on the map with a summer theater, the Vermont Guild of Old Time Crafts and Industries, and the widely known Vermont Country Store. The key to the identification of its proprietor, Vrest Orton, as a controversial-minded, card-carrying Vermonter are the peppery vignettes and editorials in *The Voice of the Mountains* (his mail-order catalogue) on such subjects as "The Right to Fail." Amplifying the wise remark of a Princeton University friend who commented that young people today no longer have the right to fail, Orton writes:

> . . . I believe that we have deprived many of our young folk of this classic American right to fail by bolstering them up with all manner of guarantee and subsidy. Naturally it is the desire of every parent to do everything possible for his children, but sometimes, it seems to me, we go too far, and by various methods arrange matters so the young-ones *can't* possibly fail. And then if, perchance, they do fail, we immediately spring into the breech and with our mature powers try to fix things so the kids won't get hurt as the result of their failure.

In *This Country Life* Samuel Ogden, who chose to settle in and labor for the rehabilitation of the town of Landgrove, Vermont, seeks further answers for the disquiet of today's youth.

> The more small tasks of daily living are performed mechanically, or by outsiders for hire, the less there is any homelife. And what is

more, if there is no real homelife the small tasks of daily living become more and more burdensome to those who perform them. So a vicious circle is set up wherein, because of outside distractions and cheap excitements and amusements, less time is devoted to the making of a home; and the less homelike the habitation becomes, the less interest any member of the family has in being there.

New Hampshire's most heart-warming example of a man who turned his back on suburbia to seek the rewards of a quiet place is George Woodbury. In *John Goffe's Legacy* he writes of his fulfillment in rebuilding the mill of his pioneer ancestor, and making it into a one-man milking-stool factory.

> What makes this mill distinctive is that in such a long span of time it has neither expanded into a great industrial complex, nor has it perished altogether. In a frantically changing world there is distinction in something—anything—that has managed to remain stationary. More than this, the mill and the land surrounding it has been the well-loved home of eight consecutive generations of the first founders.

New Hampshire and Vermont have been forerunners in recognizing the almost psychological need of people, liberated from physical labor by machines, to make things with their hands. New Hampshire's Arts and Crafts Commission, set up in 1931 by Governor Winant, grew out of the efforts of a small group of people in Center Sandwich to collect homemade objects such as rugs, baskets, furniture and wrought-iron utensils and to offer them for sale. By 1940 the 30-odd home industries composing the League of New Hampshire Arts and Crafts were thriving. The movement yearly gains momentum and is now a significant factor in the economies of both states. There is also widespread nonprofessional interest in painting and in music, as anyone who attends the regional exhibits of the southern or northern Vermont artists and the concerts of the pioneer Vermont Symphony Orchestra is well aware.

The danger of overcommercialization and the false emphasis on what is sometimes called by the natives "the artsy-craftsy" group is always present. A distinction is to be made between the sincere craftsmen and the people who come in station wagons wearing over-size glasses and peasant costumes to cavort among the "natives" and depart before Labor Day with a repertoire of stories about the quaint characters they have met. The outlanders who are truly welcome in the hillcountry are those who understand and want to share a particular way of life. Dorothy Canfield Fisher has written that Vermonters "having been forced to build up a scheme of life in which cash is not so important . . . esteem highly certain human qualities even though they do not conduce to the making of large incomes." The thousands of outlanders who do understand and who have chosen to work in Vermont, to spend vacations or to retire there, have enjoyed the happiest relationships with their adopted communities and have done them no end of good. Often they are professional or business people of the highest caliber, as, for example, the unpretentious and little-known summer colony at Greensboro of Princeton professors and business executives. No one has even tried to count the number of corporation presidents, scientists and authors who are living quietly up the road in remodeled farmhouses.

The deeper we go into the atomic area and the more complex and impersonal the megalopolis becomes, the more the denizens of suburbia thirst for the way of life, the human values, the natural surroundings still so abundantly present in the northcountry. And, the faster they stream in to buy land and to build year-round houses, or second homes. Or buy land now and build later, or buy and build in the hope of selling to the new thousands who may be coming. A tidal wave is thus in the making. This is the dilemma for native and newcomer: at what point do seekers inundate the life and surroundings they seek? To what extent should they be aided, restrained, or rebuffed in their search? Does a farmer sell the ancestral acres to a developer for more money than he's seen in his whole life? Should various state agencies have the right to step in and narrow his options in the name of conservation, open spaces, and the public good? If so, to what extent? How is he compensated?

Vermont has been a pioneer among the states in facing this dilemma with a broad program of conservation and planning. And not a moment too soon in southern counties, literally awash with speculators and developers. It is as late for southeastern New Hampshire to take action as it is for New Jersey or Florida, but much of the high country in central and northern reaches of both states is largely intact. Not having suffered city real-estate pressures to tear down, to rebuild, and to modernize, towns have thus far succeeded, in large measure unwittingly, in preserving the character of their countryside. The charm of the white country village is that of simplicity. There are few gems of architecture but ever so many buildings with an elegant plainness that derives from pleasing proportions and understatement in decoration. The notable exception is, of course, Portsmouth, which is just now taking steps to guard its priceless architectural heritage (although not in time to prevent an insensitive former governor from tearing down the superb Storer-Cutter mansion and putting up a cement-block bowling alley). Among its many remaining showpieces are the Wentworth-Gardner House and the Macphaedris-Warner House whose brick came from Holland and whose stairway walls are still decorated with the original murals. The 32-room mansion of Governor Benning Wentworth with its curious gables still stands at Little Harbor, and the late Georgian mansion built by Governor John Langdon in 1784. The tidewater region is a handbook of American architecture from the mid-seventeenth century through the Federal and Greek Revival periods.

Less pretentious, but built by owners and artisans who cared, the dwellings and churches of the inland communities in some ways are more interesting than the captains' walks and embellished cornices of Portsmouth. The houses of the small Vermont town of Castleton were designed and built by a home-grown architect, or "house-joiner," as Thomas Dake called himself. Imagination and ingenuity in making the most of the simple embellishments the people he worked for could afford, are responsible for the charm of these dwellings. The wood, brick and stone structures of North Chester, Woodstock, Newfane, and Craftsbury Common, of Orford, Norwich, Lyme, Walpole and Hancock, among many other towns, are studies in character and integrity. There is no more utter contrast to the Gothic cathedrals of Europe than the New England church or meetinghouse, yet who will deny its importance as an original art form? The vanishing covered bridge, designed purely as a functional structure, is just as pleasing aesthetically. All of which is to affirm that there is much in rural Vermont and New Hampshire to interest even the critical Englishman who sets so much store by an unspoiled countryside.

Is Vermont, which John Gunther has written is the most impregnably Yankee of all states, really unspoiled (or is this a myth inspired by the gospel according to fanatics)? The answer is largely yes, particularly in the north, which, as Walter Hard has remarked, has not yet been "summerized." To judge whether this is true one must visit some town off the traveled routes. The village of Morrisville is not on the highway to Montreal; it is not even on the road from Burlington to St. Johnsbury, but is off by itself between Hyde Park and Stowe. It is on a railroad, the St. Johnsbury and Lamoille County (formerly the Portland and Ogdensburg and then the St. Johnsbury and Lake Champlain), one of the immortal branch lines that once fancied itself as being a vital transcontinental link from Portland to the West. Having given up its passenger service it now subsists on talc, granite, wooden boxes, Christmas trees, and other local products. It is not possible to say how many trains there are a day at present. They run whenever they are needed, and are dispatched either east or west from the main office at Morrisville.

Morrisville (pop. 2,000) has six churches, an academy, and a foundry. It houses an overflow of skiers from Stowe and its hospital cares for dozens of bone cases from Mount Mansfield each year. One of the main reasons it is thrifty looking and progressive is its municipally owned light plant, which has been in business since 1895 and sells power to adjacent communities. The power in the light plant, as well as in the Morrisville Historical Society and other community enterprises, is Willard K. Sanders, who conducts business out of a roll-top desk in full view of a gallery of town dignitaries framed on the wall. The Consolidated Edison Company would do well to follow Sanders' example of submitting to the public an annual report that tells not only how much money the plant takes in and spends during the year, but what is going on in its sphere of influence. Of course too much is going on in New York and that is why it would not be possible for Consolidated Edison to produce such a report.

Little that is interesting escapes Sanders' attention and the result is a document that has wide circulation, not necessarily because it recounts the Water and Light Department's struggles to prosperity through hurricane, drought and flood, but because it is so entertaining. Understatement, the essence of Yankee humor (as well as architecture) is such a scarce commodity elsewhere in the United States that precious examples of it are forever being smuggled out of the Green Mountains and, like pressed flowers, carefully stored away. As for Sanders' reports—the light and water business is their main concern, but he does not hesitate to throw all precedent to the winds, even in his opening paragraphs. "This report will differ from the majority of periodicals published this past year in two respects: it will make no reference to the research of Dr. Kinsey, nor will it relate how a prominent radio personality outwitted the United States Navy." Before he gets down to business he has most likely taken a sly swipe at Montpelier or Madison Avenue.

> During the past few years I have tried to determine which of the millions of kilowatt-hours which are delivered to our customers has done the most for humanity and could be determined the "Kilowatt-Hour of the Year." Such a determination would require exhaustive research; one might save a life at the hospital, another might have been consumed in bringing us a "commercial" of more or less value on television, like one, for example, which appears several times each day and which has run for two years with but a single change; the word "stumick" has become "stomach." (Do you realize that every time "puttering Pete puts in a patio," or any other one-minute commercial run, two kilowatt-hours are consumed over our entire system to bring that message?)

Generally speaking, it is history that interests Sanders most and he looks fondly back to the not-so-good days when frugal customers "had but one light wired in their houses, this being equipped with 50 feet or so of cord so that the light could be carried from room to room as needed, thus reducing the flat rate charged for wiring the entire house." Those were the days of knob-and-tube wiring "when there were more pennies in the fuse boxes than there were fuses, in which case the motto on the penny, 'In God We Trust,' had a particular application." On April 15, 1895, the Hotel Randall was wired, "a drop cord depending from a rosette in each room and carbon lamps shedding their jaundiced glow over the flowered wallpaper; all for the sum of $97.75, according to our records. In 1906 they purchased a Simplex flat iron for $4.00. . . . Many interesting things could be told of the happenings within these walls, but they do not come within the scope of this report."

Since Morrisville early furnished Stowe with power it was all the straining generators could do to supply the trolley which ran from the mountain resort to Waterbury.

... it was not unusual for the Mount Mansfield Railroad, particularly when heavily loaded or bucking snow-drifts, to bring these generators to a near stop or to trip out the circuit breaker on a switchboard before they reached the top of Shutesville Hill, or broke through the hard-packed crust on the right of way. If the current breakers didn't trip, the lights went out, or nearly out, all over the Village until the generator came back to normal speed. By watching the variation of the light one could easily trace the "Toonerville Trolley" through its entire distance from Stowe to Waterbury, and when at last it achieved its final destination the lights would settle down to approximately normal voltage and frequency.

When Sanders joined the department service calls were made to Elmore by sleigh and a livery stable horse.

Our first duty upon getting well outside the Village was to stop the horse (no difficult task), get out of the sleigh and make up a bushel or two of snowballs and pile them in the "boot" of the sleigh. Once the horse was again coaxed into motion, the skillful application of snowballs to that portion of the horse nearest the sleigh from time to time, would keep him in some semblance of motion.

In discussing what is known in power circles as the "load factor" ("It costs just as much to run the plant whether it is loaded to its full capacity, or running practically idle"), and the doubtful value to the Morrisville system of power from the St. Lawrence development, Sanders is off again in the horse latitudes.

... supposing that you feared that your horse might become disabled and you wanted to have another horse in reserve, and that you contracted with your livery stable owner to reserve a horse for your use whenever you wanted it. If he was a Vermont livery stable owner, he wouldn't agree to it unless you agreed to use his horse a certain number of hours per day, or pay for it when you didn't use it; in fact he might tell you that you would have to use his horse all that you could (which wouldn't be much if he was like some livery stable horses I have seen) and keep your own horse in reserve. This would be a horse of a different color; you would then be paying the high rental price for the use of the livery horse while your own horse would remain in the barn most of the time, eating his head off and dreaming whatever horses dream, as your cost per mile soared.

Your own horse-per-mile costs would be prohibitive and your own load-factor (horse-factor) would be nearly zero. This is precisely the condition that appears likely to affect us in connection with St. Lawrence power on the presently proposed basis.

In cleaning out the racks which keep the debris from the reservoir from getting into the turbines, Mr. Sanders reports finding dead deer, particularly at the approach of hunting season when apparently "the animals become amphibious. The strange thing is that these deer are invariably without horns or hind quarters."

Concerning finances and bill collections Sanders finds "something about mail from the Water and Light Department that discourages opening. . . . What a waste of money it would be if we should decide to enclose a dollar bill in each envelope!"

> In this same connection, we have an instance in which service had been discontinued for non-payment in a rural area, the meter removed and the meter-socket sealed. Rumors reached us that lights and television were still being used at this location without benefit of either clergy or meter so we investigated. True, such a connection had been contrived (we will not divulge the modus-operandi for obvious reasons) and free service obtained. We might add that this amateur engineer is currently being lodged in durance vile at the expense of the State.

Sanders is not one to comply, at least not without comment, with bureaucratic directives from Montpelier.

> Early in 1940 the Public Service Commission issued an order requiring all Class B companies, including this department, to conform to a certain uniform system of accounts. . . . We can think of only one thing which was omitted, this being a record of the length of the shadows cast by the several thousand poles in our system, which laid end to end might reach somewhere.

It was a long time before the Water and Light Department could afford a two-way radio system between the office and its trucks, an obvious saving of time and money in making service calls, emergency and otherwise. When finally the equipment was ordered and the antenna was being installed on the roof of the office, it was not fifteen minutes before a self-appointed guardian of the public treasure declared that a television antenna was being installed for the entertainment of the Light Department. Sanders reported that this beat by an hour his estimate of the time when such an announcement would be made.

There is an old church near Lake Elmore whose steeple, struck by lightning, was replaced with a more practical though less imposing one. Its interior, however, remains the same "with its well-thumbed and dog-eared Bible . . . its pulpit chairs on a raised platform at the far end, together with other chairs clustered about an ancient and wheezy reed organ . . . the floor slightly heaved by the repeated frosts of winter, the wood-chunk stove with yards of stove-pipe winding up to the chimney hole high in the back wall, the arched windows, the swinging leather-covered doors at its entrance." The church, writes Sanders, still radiates the sense of use to which it was dedicated and on a summer Sunday with the sun streaming through the windows it is a true sanctuary of peace. The kilowatt that he likes most to contemplate—his Kilowatt-Hour of the Year—"is the single one which was used in the old church at Lake Elmore this past year, and to what better use could it be put than in the worship of God?"

Most certainly Vermont and New Hampshire are keeping the faith as a land where education has always been highly prized. It was Vermont's Senator Justin Morrill who in 1862 was responsible for the Land Grant College Act placing higher education within the reach of those who otherwise could not afford it. The state in which the first medical school was founded, and the first teachers' college, continues its wide experiments in education. The so-called Vermont Plan, of bringing Harlem children into rural homes for two weeks during the summer, was begun in 1944 by A. Ritchie Low, a minister from Johnson. It was also during the Second World War that Dorothy Thompson, a resident of Barnard, conceived of the Vermont Farm Volunteers, a successful organization offering young city dwellers board, room and pay for seasonal employment on undermanned Green Mountain farms.

Bennington College, whose curriculum is not based upon the usually prescribed courses and credits, but upon mastery of a given field in the arts, has been a daring and successful innovator even in so-called progressive circles. Bennington's International Summer School, sponsored by the United States Department of State and the

Institute of International Education, gives students from all over the world a view of American life. Clearly evident in the program of Plainfield's Goddard College, which believes in learning through doing, is the influence of Vermonter John Dewey. Putney is widely known for its Experiment in International Living. On a southern Vermont hilltop the Marlboro School seeks to develop talented young musicians by offering them the opportunity to study chamber music with such virtuosos as Rudolf Serkin (a resident of nearby Guilford).

The University of Vermont, chartered in 1791, continues to expand the facilities of its associated schools of medicine, agriculture and engineering and at the same time provide for its growing enrollment in liberal arts. The Lane Series, administered by the university through a benefactor, brings outstanding concert and stage attractions to Burlington each year. By no means suffering from its proximity, only 38 miles to the south, Middlebury College supplements its liberal arts course with a well-attended summer language school and the Breadloaf School of English. As if these institutions were not enough for a state small in size and population, there is Norwich, the reputable old military university at Northfield, which has been enormously invigorated by the momentum of the World War II tank commander, Major General Ernest Harmon. Norwich was founded in 1820 in the Connecticut River town of the same name by the son of a Vermont farmer, Alden Partridge, who had first served two years as superintendent of West Point. He is given credit for being the first exemplifier in America of the elective system in a liberal education; at the same time of a citizenry well prepared to take up arms so that they would be in the position of "awing-down their would-be foes." This thesis apparently still holds in the atomic era when, although it is considered too dangerous to fight, it is also considered too dangerous not to prepare.

The mention of these universities does not take into account sectarian colleges like St. Michael's or such Goodbye-Mr.-Chips secondary schools as Vermont Academy, which thrive in their small-town relationships. And what of New Hampshire's noted preparatory school at Exeter and Concord's recherché St. Paul's? While Granite State educators do not seem to have been as interested as Vermonters in improvising, they do have, other than the University of New Hampshire at Durham, Dartmouth to their credit—and Dartmouth has been dominant in the northcountry since the colonies became a republic. In recent decades, during the presidencies of Ernest M. Hopkins, John Sloan Dickey, and John G. Kemeny, it has taken seven-league strides, lately with a year-round academic schedule, and the revitilization of the associated schools of medicine, engineering, and business. But the liberal arts college still predominates. An extraordinary feature of the multi-million dollar building program which anticipated the 200th anniversary of the founding year, 1769, is Dartmouth's Hopkins Center, a complex of theaters and studios calculated to make the student more aware of the lasting values of the arts during his most impressionable years. The flight from urban life emphasizes Dartmouth's setting in a village on a plateau above the Connecticut, free in its vivid association with the seasons from the "snares and divertissements" of the city visualized by Founder Eleazar Wheelock.

Ex-President Hopkins believed these intangibles to have been the most important influence in his life. In a letter to a sociology professor during the Second World War he wrote that he and Chief Justice Hughes once compared their backgrounds and found them to be almost the same and that

> The greatest single blessing that could come to a boy was to be born into a country minister's family and to grow up under the circumstances which attached economically, mentally and spiritually to a country parsonage.
>
> The life that I lived in subsequent villages—Dunbarton, Hopkinton, and Franklin, New Hampshire, Georgetown and Uxbridge, Massachusetts, and Perkinsville, Vermont—was as far removed from anything which is existent as family life in these days as can be imagined. From earliest times that I can remember I was responsible for taking care of the horse, keeping the varnish on the buggy clean and bright, and driving around the countryside while my father made pastoral calls, attended funerals, or, best of all, exchanged pulpits with pastors in neighboring villages. Our home life was a pattern practically unknown at the present time—up and around soon after sunrise in summer and long before sunrise in winter, breakfast, morning prayers, school, and then home in the late afternoon for chores. . . .
>
> Probably the greatest formative influence in my life was the evenings, when after supper dishes were cleared up, a big hanging

lamp over the dining room table was lit and there was general understanding in the family that everybody was to read, though later in
the evening any questions that any one of us had would be taken
up and discussed seriously.

This is the atmosphere which has enabled a country thin in population and relatively poor in most resources, except human ones, to
have produced such an inordinately large number of effective men—
men like the fighting doctor from Winchester, New Hampshire,
Major General Leonard Wood, who became Army Chief of Staff
before the First World War by way of service with Theodore Roosevelt's Rough Riders, the governorship of Cuba and participation,
with Walter Reed, in the conquest of yellow fever. It was a Vermonter, Admiral Charles E. Clark, who sailed the *Oregon* around the
Horn under forced draft to Santiago; and Henry T. Mayo, the son of
a Lake Champlain steamboat captain, who rose to the command of
the United States Atlantic Fleet during the First World War.

In *Democracy Fights*, Philip N. Guyol tells of the astonishing in-
filtration by New Hampshire natives into the military and naval
hierarchy during the Second World War. The list includes one admiral, a vice-admiral, seven rear admirals, a lieutenant general, three
major generals, seven brigadiers, the commanders of the WAVES
and the Marine Corps Women's Reserve. The ranking officer of this
group was Thomas C. Kinkaid, commander of the North Pacific
Fleet, a native of Hanover. The name of Vice-Admiral Forrest P.
Sherman of Merrimack is synonymous with victory in the Gilberts,
the Marshalls and the Marianas. Secretaries of the Navy Frank Knox
and John L. Sullivan were both from New Hampshire. Vannevar
Bush, from East Jaffrey, New Hampshire, president of the Carnegie
Institution in Washington, became chairman of the National De-
fense Research Committee. Warren R. Austin of Burlington was the
United States' first ambassador to the United Nations. William D.
Hassett of Northfield served as secretary to both wartime presidents.

Not many years ago no less than four of the executive officers of
the American Telephone and Telegraph Company were Vermonters,
the president of the Association of American Railroads, the lieutenant
governor of Nova Scotia, and the literary editor of *Time*. Learned
Hand, the grandson of Augustus Cincinnatus Hand of Hand's Cove,
Shoreham (where Ethan Allen gathered the Green Mountain Boys

for their assault on Fort Ticonderoga), was acknowledged to be the nation's greatest living jurist, although he did not sit on the Supreme Court. It seems fitting that the first issue of the magazine *American Heritage* was produced in a state which was the birthplace of the first internationally-known American Shakespearian critic (Henry Norman Hudson, 1814-1886, from Cornwall, Vermont) and of Colonel Frank Haskell, author of *The Battle of Gettysburg*, acknowledged to be one of the foremost books on the Civil War. The impress upon the literary scene of editors like George Harvey, from Peacham, president of Harper & Brothers from 1900 to 1915, has been deep and permanent. Scribner's incomparable Maxwell Perkins, discoverer and alter ego of Thomas Wolfe, F. Scott Fitzgerald and Ring Lardner, wrote of his Vermont heritage:

> We were always taught that, in a community like Windsor, the truly important men were the school teacher, the newspaper editor and the clergyman. The doctor, too, was more respected than the business man. These people were supposed to have made a sacrifice because they cared more to serve their professions, and what they meant, than for money.

Something of the universal character of the Boy Scout movement, which began with a troop in Barre, and of Rotary, founded by Paul Harris of Wallingford, is suggested by the present imprint of the old Tuttle Publishing Company: "Rutland, Vermont and Tokyo, Japan" —and by a well-weathered sign in London which reads: "B. F. Stevens and Brown—Vermont Gallery." Benjamin Franklin Stevens spent his early life in Vermont, and there acquired his taste for scholarship from his father, Henry; but it was in London that he became so well established and known as a seller and collector of rare books. Yankees are not necessarily silent, like Calvin Coolidge (although he could talk his head off when the spirit moved him), and they are certainly not stay-at-homes.

In *Faces in the Crowd* David Riesman wonders if the northcountry will continue to produce such men, since the younger generation stands relatively idle—without the old necessities. A great majority of the trail blazers came off the farms or out of the small towns. The farms these days are dwindling rapidly in number. Without an avenue to the great stream of interstate commerce the small towns are hav-

ing to struggle for a place in the sun. Their people will find it hard
to maintain their traditional independence if they become enmeshed
in the cogs of a kind of rural suburbia; but unless they gear themselves to the complex economic apparatus of the twentieth century
they cannot subsist. That is the problem. Doubtless it will be in the
heart of the Green Mountains, suggests Fred Lewis Pattee, "that
centuries from now will be discovered the last specimens of the old
Yankee Puritan stock, then long supposed to be extinct, just as even
now one finds specimens of the aboriginal celts in the mountains of
Wales and Cornwall."

Meanwhile it is well to repeat for the whole northcountry the
prayer ascribed to the Rev. Samuel Peters, who, long before the Revolution, as he looked out over a vast primeval landscape, declared: "We
have met here on the rock Etam standing on Mount Pisgah . . . to
dedicate and consecrate this extensive wilderness . . . and give it a
new name worthy of the Athenians and ancient Spartans; which new
name is 'Verd-Mont' in token that her mountains and hills shall be
ever green and shall never die."

BIBLIOGRAPHY

ADAMS, JAMES TRUSLOW. *New England in the Republic, 1776-1850.* Boston: Little, Brown & Company, 1926.
———, *The Founding of New England.* Vol. 1. Boston: Little, Brown & Company, 1927.
ADAMS, NATHANIEL. *Annals of Portsmouth.* Portsmouth: C. Norris, 1825.
ALDRICH, THOMAS BAILEY. *An Old Town by the Sea.* Boston and New York: Houghton Mifflin Company, 1893.
ALLEN, ETHAN. *A Brief Narrative of the Proceedings of the Government of New York* . . . Hartford, 1774.
———, *Narrative of the Captivity of Col. Ethan Allen Containing His Voyages & Travels.* Albany: Pratt & Clark, 1814.
———, *Reason, the Only Oracle of Man* . . . Boston: J. P. Mendium, 1854.
ALLEN, ETHAN and IRA. *Biographical Sketches and Documents.* Montpelier, Vt.: Vermont Historical Society, 1947.
ANDREWS, EDWARD DEMING. *The People Called Shakers.* New York: Oxford University Press, 1953.
AUGUR, HELEN. *Passage to Glory.* New York: Doubleday & Company, 1946.

BACHELDER, N. J. (Secretary). *Report of Old Home Week in New Hampshire August 26 to September 1, 1899.* Manchester, N. H.: Arthur E Clarke, 1900.
BACON, EDWIN N. *The Connecticut River and the Valley of the Connecticut.* New York: G. P. Putnam's Sons, 1906.
BALL, DR. B. L. *Three Days on the White Mountains.* Boston: Lockwood, Brooks & Company, 1877.
BASS, GOV. ROBERT P. *Address as Chairman of the First New Hampshire*

Convention of the Progressive Party. Concord: Ruemely Press, 1912.

———, *On the Present National Political Situation*. Manchester, N.H., 1912.

BATES, ERNEST SUTHERLAND, and DITTEMORE, JOHN V. *Mary Baker Eddy*. New York: Alfred A. Knopf, 1932.

BEANE, S. C. "Captain Alden Partridge," *The Granite Monthly*, Vol. 12, Nos. 3 and 4 (March, April), 1889.

BEASLEY, NORMAN. *The Cross and the Crown, the History of Christian Science*. New York: Duell, Sloan & Pearce, 1952.

BELKNAP, JEREMY. *The History of New Hampshire*. 3 Vols. J. P. Mann & J. K. Remick, 1812.

Biographical Sketches of Vermonters. 2 Vols. Montpelier: Vermont Historical Society, 1947.

BISHOP, MORRIS. *Champlain, The Life of Fortitude*. New York: Alfred A. Knopf, 1948.

BLAISDELL, PAUL H. *Three Centuries on Winnipesaukee*. Concord, N.H., 1936.

BOND, F. FRASER. *Mr. Miller of "The Times."* New York: Charles Scribner's Sons, 1931.

BORGMANN, CARL W. *"U. V. M.," the University of the State of Vermont! 1791*. The Newcomen Society in North America, 1956.

BOUCHER, ROLAND R. *The Shakers in New Hampshire*. A thesis submitted to the University of New Hampshire in partial fulfillment of the requirements for the degree Master of Arts. Durham: University of New Hampshire, 1947.

BOWLES, ELLA SHANNON. *New Hampshire: Its History, Settlement and Provincial Period*. Concord: New Hampshire State Board of Education, 1938.

BREWSTER, CHARLES W. *Rambles about Portsmouth*. 2 Vols. Portsmouth, N.H.: Lewis W. Brewster, 1873.

BRIGGS, NICHOLAS A. "Forty Years A Shaker," *The Granite Monthly*, Vol. 52, No. 12 (December, 1920); Vol. 53, Nos. 1, 2, and 3 (January, February and March), 1921.

BRODIE, FAWN M. *No Man Knows My History*. New York: Alfred A. Knopf, 1945.

BROOKS, VAN WYCK. *The Flowering of New England 1815-1865*. New York: E. P. Dutton & Co., 1936.

BROWN, FRANCIS. *Raymond of the Times*. New York: W. W. Norton & Company, 1951.

———, "A New England Chapter. (The Vast Plant of Manchester, Abandoned . . .)," *New York Times*, Nov. 15, 1936. Sect. VIII, p. 6.

BROWN, ROLLO WALTER. "Mrs. MacDowell and Her Colony," *The Atlantic*, Vol. 184, No. 1 (July, 1949).

BROWNE, GEORGE WALDO. *The Amoskeag Manufacturing Co.* Manchester: Amoskeag Manufacturing Co., 1915.

BURGOYNE, Gen. JOHN. *Orderly Book of Lieut. Gen. John Burgoyne from His Entry into the State of New York until His Surrender at Saratoga, 16th Oct. 1777.* Albany, N.Y.: J. Munsell, 1860.

BURGUM, EDWIN G. *The Concord Coach.* Pamphlet. Concord: New Hampshire Historical Society.

BURROUGHS, STEPHEN. *Memoirs of the Notorious Stephen Burroughs of New Hampshire.* New York: The Dial Press, 1924.

CABOT, THEODORA. "Young Reformers Climb Mount Washington," *New England Quarterly*, Vol. VI, No. 21 (March 1933).

CARTER, JAMES ELMER. *Jeffersonian Democracy and the Congregational Clergy of Vermont, 1800-1815.* A Thesis Submitted to the Graduate College as a Partial Fulfillment of the Requirements for the Degree of Master of Arts, University of Vermont, 1953.

CHANDLER, WILLIAM E. Speech Against Railroad Domination and in Favor of Progressive and Insurgent Republicanism; at Laconia, N.H., Aug. 17, 1910.

CHANNING, WILLIAM ELLERY. *The Wanderer.* Boston: James R. Osgood & Company, 1871.

CHAPPELL, GEORGE S. *Colonial Architecture in Vermont.* In the White Pine Series of Architectural Monographs, Vol. 4, No. 6 (December, 1918).

CHENEY, G. A. "Winston Churchill and Harlakenden House," *The Granite Monthly*, Vol. 33, No. 3 (September, 1902).

CHRISTMAN, HENRY. *Tin Horns and Calico.* New York: Henry Holt & Company, 1945.

CHURCHILL, WINSTON. *Coniston.* New York: Macmillan & Co., Ltd., 1906.

CLARK, ADELBERT. "Mount Washington," *The Granite Monthly*, Vol. 27, No. 5 (November, 1899).

CLARKE, ARTHUR E. *Report of Old Home Week in New Hampshire, 1899.* Arthur E. Clarke, 1900.

CLEMENT, JOHN P. "What Happened at Hubbardton," *Vermont School Journal*, Vol. 14, No. 4 (April, 1948).

CONGDON, HERBERT WHEATON. *Old Vermont Houses.* New York: Alfred A. Knopf, 1946.

————, "Dake of Castleton," *Vermont Quarterly*, New Series, Vol. 17, Nos. 2-3 (April-July, 1949).

COOLIDGE, GUY OMERON. "The French Occupation of the Champlain Valley from 1609 to 1759." *Proceedings of the Vermont Historical Society*, New Series, Vol. 6, No. 3 (1938).

COX, SIDNEY. *Robert Frost*. New York: Henry Holt & Company, 1929.

CRANE, CHARLES EDWARD. *Let Me Show You Vermont*. New York: Alfred A. Knopf, 1937.

CRAWFORD, LUCY. *The History of the White Mountains*. Portland: F. A. & A. F. Gerrish, 1845.

CREAMER, DANIEL, and GOULTER, CHARLES W. *Labor and the Shut-Down of the Amoskeag Textile Mills*. Work Projects Administration, National Research Project, Report No. L-5. Philadelphia, 1939.

CROCKETT, WALTER HILL. *Vermont: The Green Mountain State*. 4 Vols. New York: The Century History Company, 1921.

————, *A History of Lake Champlain, 1606-1936*. Burlington: Hobart J. Shanley, 1909.

CUNEO, JOHN R. *Robert Rogers of the Rangers*. New York: Oxford University Press, 1959.

CURRIER, JOHN M. "Lumbering on the Connecticut River between 1840 and 1850," *The Granite Monthly*, Vol. 26, No. 2 (February, 1894).

CURTIS, GEORGE TICKNOR. *Life of Daniel Webster*. 2 Vols. New York: D. Appleton & Company, 1872.

DAKIN, EDWIN FRANDEN. *Mrs. Eddy*. New York: Charles Scribner's Sons, 1929.

DWIGHT, TIMOTHY. *Travels in New England and New York*. 4 Vols. New Haven: Timothy Dwight, 1821 and 1822.

DYER, JOSEPH. *A Compendious Narrative Elucidating the Character, Disposition and Conduct of Mary Dyer* . . . Concord: Isaac Hill, 1818.

DYER, MARY M. *The Rise and Progress of the Serpent from the Garden of Eden, to the Present Day: with a Disclosure of Shakerism* . . . Concord, N.H., 1847.

————, *A Brief Statement of the Sufferings of Mary Dyer* . . . Boston: William S. Spear, 1818.

EATON, WALTER PRITCHARD. "Making Our Traditions Work for Us," *Yankee*, Vol. 4, No. 2 (February, 1938).

ELKINS, HERVEY. *Fifteen Years in the Senior Order of Shakers*. Hanover: Dartmouth Press, 1853.

Essays in the Social and Economic History of Vermont. Montpelier: Vermont Historical Society, 1943.

FASSETT, JAMES H. *Colonial Life in New Hampshire.* Boston, New York: Ginn & Company, 1899.

FENN, G. MANVILLE. *Memoir of Benjamin Franklin Stevens.* London: Chiswick Press, 1903.

FISHER, DOROTHY CANFIELD. "Vermont Summer Homes," *Vermont Life,* Vol. 3, No. 3 (1949).

FISKE, JOHN. *The Beginnings of New England.* Boston & New York: Houghton Mifflin Company, 1892.

FLEXNER, JAMES THOMAS. *The Traitor and the Spy.* New York: Harcourt, Brace & Company, 1953.

FLITCROFT, JOHN E. *The Novelist of Vermont.* Cambridge: Harvard University Press, 1929.

FORBES, CHARLES S. "President McKinley in Vermont," *The Vermonter,* Vol. 3, No. 10 (October, 1902).

———, "President Roosevelt," *The Vermonter,* Vol. 7, No. 4 (November, 1901).

———, "The President in Vermont," *The Vermonter,* Vol. 8, No. 3 (October, 1902).

FOX, DIXON RYAN. *Yankees and Yorkers.* New York: University Press, 1900.

FRENCH, ALLEN. *The Taking of Ticonderoga in 1775: The British Story.* Cambridge: Harvard University Press, 1928.

FROST, ROBERT. *Collected Poems of Robert Frost.* New York: Henry Holt & Company, 1939.

FUESS, CLAUDE MOORE. *Daniel Webster.* 2 Vols. Boston: Little Brown & Company, 1930.

FULLER, LOUIS. "Parker Pillsbury: An Anti-Slavery Apostle," *New England Quarterly,* Vol. 19, No. 3 (September, 1946).

GABRIEL, RALPH H. "Mary Baker Eddy, The Truth and the Tradition" (By Ernest Sutherland Bates and John V. Dittemore), Book Review in *New England Quarterly,* Vol. 6, No. 1 (March, 1933).

GIBBS, JESSIE S. *Thompson's Point.* Pamphlet. Burlington, Vt.

GOLDTHWAIT, JAMES WALTER. *The Geology of New Hampshire.* Concord: Rumford Press, 1925.

GORDON, CAPTAIN GEORGE A. "The Defense of Fort Number Four," *The Granite Monthly,* Vol. 40, Nos. 4 & 5 (April and May, 1908).

GRAHAM, JOHN A. *A Descriptive Sketch of the Present State of Vermont.* London: Henry Fry, 1797.

GREELEY, HORACE. *Recollections of a Busy Life.* New York: J. B. Ford & Co., 1868.

GUNTHER, JOHN. *Inside U.S.A.* New York: Harper & Brothers, 1947.

GUYOL, PHILLIP N. *Democracy Fights, A History of New Hampshire in World War II.* Hanover: Dartmouth Publications, 1951.

HALL, HILAND. *The History of Vermont.* Albany: Joel Munsell, 1868.

HAMMOND, OTIS G. *Some Things about New Hampshire.* Concord: New Hampshire Historical Society, 1930.

Hands That Built New Hampshire. Compiled by workers of the Writers' Program of the Works Projects Administration of New Hampshire. Brattleboro, Vt.: Stephen Daye Press, 1940.

HARRIS, A. B. "Among the Shakers," *The Granite Monthly*, Vol. 1, No. 1 (April, 1877).

HART, ALBERT B. *Salmon Portland Chase.* Boston and New York: Houghton Mifflin Company, 1899.

HASKETT, WILLIAM J. *Shakerism Unmasked . . .* Pittsfield: E. H. Walkley, 1828.

HAYES, JOHN L. *A Reminiscence of the Free-Soil Movement in New Hampshire, 1845.* Cambridge: John Wilson & Son, 1885.

HAYES, LYMAN S. *The Connecticut River Valley in Southern Vermont and New Hampshire.* Rutland, Vt.: The Tuttle Company, 1929.

HEMENWAY, ABBY MARIA. *The Vermont Historical Gazetteer.* 5 Vols. Burlington, Vt.: 1868-1891.

HOLBROOK, STEWART H. *The Yankee Exodus.* New York: Macmillan Company, 1950.

———, "The Wildest Portion of Vermont," *Vermont Life*, Vol. 8, No. 2 (1953-1954).

HOPKINS, ERNEST MARTIN. *Letter to Professor John Mecklin.* Offices of Administration, Dartmouth College, March 1, 1943.

HOPWOOD, G. R. *An Experiment in a Platonic Society: The Perfectionist Communities of John Humphrey Noyes.* Thesis Submitted to the Graduate Council in Partial Fulfillment of the Requirements for the Degree of Master of Arts. Burlington: University of Vermont, 1951.

HOWE, HENRY F. *Prologue to New England.* New York: Farrar & Rinehart, 1943.

HOWELLS, JOHN MEAD. *The Architectural Heritage of the Merrimack.* New York: Architectural Book Publishing Company, 1941.

————, *The Architectural Heritage of the Piscataqua.* New York: Architectural Book Publishing Company, 1937.

HUBBARD, GUY. "The Influence of Early Windsor Industries Upon the Mechanical Arts," Vermont Historical Society Proceedings, 1921-1923.

HUDEN, JOHN. *Indian Place Names in Vermont.* Burlington, Vt., 1957.

HUGUENIN, CHARLES A. "Ethan Allen, Parolee on Long Island," *Vermont History,* Vol. 15, No. 2 (April, 1957).

HUNGERFORD, EDWARD. *Daniel Willard Rides the Line.* New York: G. P. Putnam's Sons, 1938.

HUNTINGTON, JOSHUA H. *Mount Washington in Winter.* Boston: Chick & Andrews, 1871.

JENNINGS, WALTER W. *The American Embargo—1807-1809.* University of Iowa Studies, Vol. 8, No. 1. Iowa City: University of Iowa, 1929.

JOHNSON, CLIFTON. "The Passing of the Shakers," *Old-Time New England,* Vol. 25, Nos. 1 and 2 (July and October, 1934).

JOHNSON, Mrs. MIRIAM. *A Narrative of the Captivity of Mrs. Johnson . . .* Windsor, Vt.: Thomas M. Pomroy, 1814.

JONES, MATT BUSHNELL. *Vermont in the Making—1750-1777.* Cambridge: Harvard University Press, 1939.

KALIJARVI, THORSTEN V. *The Government of New Hampshire.* Durham, N.H.: The Record Press, 1939.

KALM, PETER. *Travels in North America.* Edited by Adolph B. Benson. New York: Wilson-Erickson, 1937.

KENDALL, EDWARD AUGUSTUS. *Travels through the Northern Parts of the United States in the Years 1807-1808.* Vol. 3. New York: I. Riley, 1809.

KILBOURNE, FREDERICK W. *Chronicles of the White Mountains.* Boston and New York: Houghton Mifflin Company, 1916.

KIPLING, RUDYARD. *Letters of Travel, 1892-1913.* New York: Doubleday, Page & Company, 1920.

————, *Something of Myself.* New York: Doubleday, Doran & Company, 1937.

LAIGHTON, OSCAR. *Ninety Years at the Isles of Shoals.* Boston: The Beacon Press, 1930.

LAMB, WALLACE E. *The Lake Champlain and Lake George Valleys.* 3 Vols. New York: The American Historical Company, 1940.

LATHEM, EDWARD CONNERY. "Daniel Webster's College Days," *Dartmouth Alumni Magazine*, Vol. 45, No. 1 (October, 1952).

LATHROP, GEORGE PARSONS (Editor). *The Complete Works of Nathaniel Hawthorne*. Boston: Houghton Mifflin Company, 1883.

LEVITT, EMILY S. "Vermonters Who Helped Establish the City of Beloit, Wisconsin," *Vermont History*, Vol. 25, No. 4 (1957).

LEYDA, JAY (Editor). *The Indispensible Melville*. New York: The Book Society, 1952.

LINDSAY, IRA. *Tradition Looks Forward, The University of Vermont: A History, 1791-1904*. Burlington: University of Vermont, 1954.

LINSLEY, D. C. *Morgan Horses: A Premium Essay on the Origin, History, and Characteristics of this Remarkable American Breed of Horses* . . . New York: C. M. Saxton & Company, 1856.

LOCKARD, DUANE. *New England State Politics*. Princeton, N.J.: Princeton University Press, 1959.

LONGFELLOW, HENRY WADSWORTH. *The Complete Works of* . . . Boston and New York: Houghton Mifflin Company, 1893.

LUDLUM, DAVID M. *Social Ferment in Vermont, 1791-1850*. Montpelier: Vermont Historical Society, 1948.

McCALLUM, JAMES DOW. *Eleazar Wheelock, Founder of Dartmouth College*. Manuscript Series No. 4. Hanover, N.H.: Dartmouth College Publications, 1939.

MacDOWELL, MARIAN. *The First Twenty Years of the MacDowell Colony*. Peterborough, N.H.: Transcript Printing Company, 1951.

MARSH, CAROLINE. *Life and Letters of George Perkins Marsh*. New York: Charles Scribner's Sons, 1888.

MARSHALL, GERTRUDE WEEKS. *Indian Stream Republic and the Indian Stream War*. Groveton, N.H., 1935.

MARTINEAU, HARRIET. *Retrospect of Western Travel*. Vol. 3. London: Saunders & Otley, 1838.

MAYO, LAWRENCE SHAW. *John Langdon of New Hampshire*. Concord, N.H.; The Rumford Press, 1937.

———, *John Wentworth*. Cambridge: Harvard University Press, 1921.

———. "The History of the Legend of Chocorua," *New England Quarterly*, Vol. 19, No. 3 (September, 1946).

MELCHER, MARGUERITE FELLOWS. *The Shaker Adventure*. Princeton: Princeton University Press, 1941.

METCALF, H. H. "The Story of the Isles of Shoals," *The Granite Monthly*, Vol. 46, No. 8 (August, 1914).

MILLER, PERRY. *The Transcendentalists*. Cambridge: Harvard University Press, 1951.

MILMINE, GEORGINE. *The Life of Mary Baker G. Eddy and the History of Christian Science*. New York: Doubleday, Page & Company, 1909.

MILTON, GEORGE FORT. *The Eve of Conflict: Stephen A. Douglas and the Needless War*. Boston: Houghton Mifflin Company, 1934.

MONAHAN, ROBERT S. *Mount Washington Reoccupied*. Brattleboro, Vt.: Stephen Daye Press, 1933.

MUNSON, GORHAM B. *Robert Frost*. New York: George H. Doran Company, 1927.

NASHUA MANUFACTURING COMPANY. Investigation of Closing of Nashua, N.H., Mills and Operations of Textron, Incorporated. (Hearings before a Subcommittee of the Committee on Interstate and Foreign Commerce, United States Senate, 80th Congress, 2d Session; held at Nashua, N.H., Sept. 22, 23, and 24, 1948, and at Boston, Mass., Oct. 26, 27, 28, Nov. 8, 9, 10, 22, 23, 24, Dec. 7 and 8, 1948. Parts 1 and 2. Washington: Government Printing Office, 1948 and 1949.

NEWTON, EARLE. *The Vermont Story*. Montpelier: Vermont Historical Society, 1949.

NICKERSON, HOFFMAN. *The Turning Point of the Revolution*. Boston and New York: Houghton Mifflin Company, 1928.

NORDHOFF, CHARLES. *The Communistic Societies of the United States*. New York: Harper & Brothers, 1875.

NOYES, NATHANIEL. *Incidents in White Mountain History*. Boston: Nathaniel Noyes, 1857.

NUTTING, HELEN CUSHING. *Monadnock Records of 3 Centuries*. New York: Stratford Press, 1925.

O'CALLAGHAN, REVEREND JEREMIAH. *Usury, funds and banks; also forestalling traffick and monopoly; and so forth*. Burlington, Vt., 1834.

OGDEN, SAMUEL R. *This Country Life*. New York: A. S. Barnes, 1946.

O'HARA, JOHN E. *Erie's Junior Partner, the Economic and Social Effects of the Champlain Canal upon the Champlain Valley*. New York: Columbia University Press, 1957.

ORTON, VREST. "The Weston Revival," *Vermont Life*, Vol. 1, No. 1 (1946).

———. *The Voice of the Mountains*. Weston, Vt.: 1958.

O'SHEA, BERNARD G. "Volunteer Farmers," *Vermont Life*, Vol. 5, No. 4 (Summer, 1951).

PAGE, ELWIN L. *Abraham Lincoln in New Hampshire*. Boston and New York: Houghton Mifflin Company, 1929.

PALMER, PETER S. *History of Lake Champlain from Its First Exploration by the French in 1609 to the Close of the Year 1814*. Albany: J. Munsell, 1866.

PARKMAN, FRANCIS. *Montcalm and Wolfe*. Vol. 2. Boston: Little, Brown and Company, 1937.

——. *Pioneers of France in the New World*. Boston: Little, Brown and Company, 1870.

PARTON, JAMES. "Daniel Webster," *North American Review*, Vol. CIV. Boston: Ticknor and Fields, 1867.

PATTEE, FRED LEWIS. *Penn State Yankee*. State College: Pennsylvania State College, 1953.

PEARSON, EDMUND. *The Autobiography of a Criminal: Henry Tufts*. New York: Duffield & Company, 1930.

PEATTIE, RODERICK (Editor). *The Friendly Mountains*. New York: Vanguard Press, 1942.

PEEL, ROBERT. *Christian Science: Its Encounter with American Culture*. New York: Henry Holt & Company, 1958.

PELL, JOHN. *Ethan Allen*. Boston and New York: Houghton Mifflin Company, 1929.

PENROSE, CHARLES, JR. *They Live on a Rock in the Sea! The Isles of Shoals in Colonial Days*. Princeton University Press: Newcomen Society in North America, 1957.

PERKINS, THE REVD. NATHAN. *A Narrative of a Tour Through the State of Vermont from April 27 to June 12, 1789*. Woodstock, Vt.: Elm Tree Press, 1920.

PERRY, BLISS. *The Heart of Emerson's Journals*. Boston and New York: Houghton Mifflin Company, 1926.

PETERS, REV. SAMUEL. *A History of the Rev. Hugh Peters*. New York, 1807.

PICARD, SAMUEL T. *Life and Letters of John Greenleaf Whittier*. 2 Vols. Boston and New York: Houghton Mifflin Company, 1894.

Platform of the Progressive Party of New Hampshire. Adopted by the Delegates in Convention Assembled at Concord, September 26th, 1912. Ruemely Press, 1912.

POWELL, LYMAN P. *Mary Baker Eddy, A Life Size Portrait*. New York: Macmillan Company, 1930.

PREBLE, GEORGE HENRY. *History of the United States Navy-Yard, Portsmouth, New Hampshire*. Washington: Government Printing Office, 1892.

RAZEE, GEORGE W. *The Story of Abbot-Downing and Their Concord Coach.* Thesis. Department of History, Dartmouth College, 1949.

RIESMAN, DAVID. *Faces in the Crowd.* New Haven: Yale University Press, 1952.

ROBERTS, REV. GUY. *The Profile and How It Was Saved.* Pamphlet. Littleton, N.H.: Courier Printing Company, 1917.

ROBINSON, EDWIN ARLINGTON. "The Peterborough Idea," *North American Review,* Vol. CCIV, No. 730 (September, 1916).

ROBINSON, ROWLAND E. *In New England Fields and Woods.* Rutland, Vt.: Charles E. Tuttle Company.

ROGERS, MARY COCHRANE. Glimpses of an Old Social Capital. Boston, 1923.

ROGERS, ROBERT. *Journals of Robert Rogers* . . . Albany: Joel Munsell's Sons, 1883.

ROZWENC, EDWIN C. "The Group Basis of Vermont Farm Politics, 1870-1945," *Vermont History,* Vol. 25, No. 3 (October, 1957).

Rural Vermont: A Program for the Future, The Vermont Commission on Country Life. Burlington: Free Press Printing Company, 1931.

SAINT-GAUDENS, HOMER. *The Reminiscences of Augustus Saint-Gaudens.* 2 Vols. New York: Century Company, 1913.

SALTONSTALL, WILLIAM G. *Ports of Piscataqua.* Cambridge: Harvard University Press, 1941.

SANDERS, WILLARD K. *Annual Reports of the Water and Light Department, 1941-1957.* Morrisville, Vt.

———. *The Morrisville Water and Light Department, 1895-1951.* Morrisville, Vt.

SCOTT, KENNETH. "Counterfeiting in Colonial New Hampshire," *Historical New Hampshire,* Vol. 13, (December, 1957).

SHAKERS (Overseers of The Enfield and Canterbury, New Hampshire, Colonies). *A Remonstrance Against the Testimony and Application of Mary Dyer* . . . Concord: Isaac Hill, 1818.

SHOWERMAN, GRANT. *The Indian Stream Republic and Luther Parker.* In Collections of the New Hampshire Historical Society. Vol. 11. Concord, N.H.: New Hampshire Historical Society, 1915.

SHY, JOHN W. *James Abercromby and the Campaign of 1758.* A Thesis submitted to the Graduate College of the University of Vermont in Partial Fulfillment of Requirements for the degree of Master of Arts. Burlington, 1957.

SILLIMAN, BENJAMIN. *Remarks Made on a Short Tour between Hartford and Quebec in the Autumn of 1819.* New Haven: S. Converse, 1820.

SMITH, GORDON M. *Artists in the White Mountains.* Pamphlet. Manchester, N.H.: Currier Gallery of Art, 1955.

Some Account of the Shakers at Canterbury. In Collections, Topographical, Historical and Biographical, Relating Principally to New Hampshire. Edited by J. Farmer and J. B. Moore. Vol. 1. Concord: Hill & Moore, 1822.

SPARKS, JARED. *The Life of John Ledyard, The American Traveller . . .* Cambridge: Hilliard & Brown, 1829.

———. *The Life and Treason of Benedict Arnold.* Boston: Hilliard, Gray & Company, 1835.

SQUIRES, JAMES DUANE. *The Granite State of the United States.* 2 Vols. New York: American Historical Company, 1956.

STACKPOLE. EVERETT S. *History of New Hampshire.* 5 Vols. New York: American Historical Society, 1916.

STARK, CALEB. *Memoir and Official Correspondence of General John Stark.* Concord: Edson C. Eastman, 1877.

STARK, GENERAL GEORGE. "Frederick G. Stark and the Merrimack River Canals," *The Granite Monthly,* Vol. 9, Nos. 1 and 2 (January and February, 1886).

STEARNS, BERTHA-MONICA. "Two Forgotten Reformers," in *New England Quarterly,* Vol. 6, No. 21 (March, 1933).

STEIN, BENJAMIN C., JR. "Vermont Plan," *Vermont Life,* Vol. 3, No. 3 (1949).

STILWELL, LEWIS D. *Migration from Vermont.* Montpelier: Vermont Historical Society, 1948.

STONE, ARTHUR F. *The Vermont of Today.* 4 Vols. New York: Lewis Historical Publishing Company, 1929.

SWIFT, LINDSAY. *William Lloyd Garrison.* Philadelphia: George W. Jacobs & Company, 1911.

TARBELL, EDMUND CHARLES II. *William Badger (1752 to 1830) Master Shipbuilder of Maine.* Princeton University Press: Newcomen Society in North America, 1955.

THERIAULT, GEORGE F. *The Setting.* Manuscript. Department of Sociology, Dartmouth College.

THOMPSON, CHARLES MINER. *Independent Vermont.* Boston: Houghton Mifflin Company, 1942.

THOMPSON, SARAH GOODWIN. *The Formation of the Republican Party in Vermont, 1854 to 1860.* Thesis Submitted to the Graduate

Council in Partial Fulfillment of the Requirements for the degree of Master of Arts, University of Vermont. Burlington, 1952.

THOMPSON, ZADOCK. *History of the Vermont* . . . Burlington: Chauncey Goodrich, 1842.

THOREAU, HENRY DAVID. *Excursions*. Boston: Tichnor & Fields, 1864.

———. *A Week on the Concord and Merrimack Rivers*. Boston and New York: Houghton Mifflin Company, 1906.

TOCQUEVILLE, ALEXIS DE. *Democracy in America*. New York: Alfred A. Knopf, 1945.

TOYNBEE, ARNOLD J. *A Study of History*. New York: Oxford University Press, 1946.

TROLLOPE, ANTHONY. *North America*. New York: Harper & Brothers, 1862.

TWAIN, MARK. *Mark Twain's Letters*. New York: Harper & Brothers, 1917.

———. *Christian Science* (In Mark Twain's *Works*, Vol. XXV.) Hartford, Conn.: American Publishing Company, 1907.

TYLER, ROYALL. *The Chestnut Tree*. Brattleboro, Vt.: Driftwood Press, 1931.

UNTERMEYER, LOUIS. *An Anthology of the New England Poets from Colonial Times to the Present Day*. New York: Random House, 1948.

Upper Connecticut, The: Narratives of its Settlement and its Part in the American Revolution. Vol. 1. Montpelier: Vermont Historical Society, 1943.

UPTON, RICHARD FRANCIS. *Revolutionary New Hampshire*. Hanover: Dartmouth College Publications, 1936.

Vermont, A Guide to the Green Mountain State. American Guide Series. Works Projects Administration. Boston: Houghton Mifflin Company, 1937.

VIGILANTE, S. L. " 'Eighteen-Hundred-and-Froze-to-Death': The Cold Summer of 1816 and Westward Migration from New England," *Bulletin* of the New York Public Library, Vol. LII (September, 1948).

WAGGONER, HYATT HOWE. "Hawthorne's 'Canterbury Pilgrims': Theme and Structure," *New England Quarterly*, Vol. 22, No. 3 (September, 1939).

WATERMAN, W. R. "The Connecticut River Valley Steamboat Company," *Vermont History*, Vol. 15, No. 2 (April, 1957).

WATSON, JOHN H. "Vermont Constitution—Slavery," *Proceedings* of the Vermont Historical Society, 1919-1923.

WEBSTER, DANIEL. *An Oration Pronounced at Hanover, New Hampshire, the 4th Day of July, 1800.* Hanover: Moses Davis, 1800.

WELD, ISAAC JR. *Travels through the States of North America, and the Provinces of Upper and Lower Canada during the years 1795, 1796 and 1797.* Vol. 1. London: John Stockdale, 1800.

WEYGANDT, CORNELIUS. *The Heart of New Hampshire.* New York: G. P. Putnam's Sons, 1944.

WHEELOCK, JOHN HALL. *Editor to Author: The Letters of Maxwell E. Perkins.* New York: Charles Scribner's Son, 1950.

WHELDEN, FORD H. "It All Began in Hanover," *Dartmouth Alumni Magazine*, Vol. 43, No. 7 (April, 1951).

WILBUR, JAMES B. *Ira Allen, Founder of Vermont: 1751-1814.* Boston and New York: Houghton Mifflin Company, 1928.

WILBUR, SIBYL. *The Life of Mary Baker Eddy.* Boston: Christian Science Publishing Co., 1913.

WILGUS, WILLIAM J. *The Role of Transportation in the Development of Vermont.* Montpelier: Vermont Historical Society, 1945.

WILLEY, REV. BENJAMIN G. *Incidents in White Mountain History.* Boston: Nathaniel Noyes, 1857.

WILLIAMSON, CHILTON. *Vermont in Quandary: 1763-1825.* Montpelier: Vermont Historical Society, 1949.

WILSON, HAROLD FISHER. *The Hill Country of Northern New England.* Montpelier: Vermont Historical Society, 1947.

WILSON, JAMES HARRISON. *The Life of Charles A. Dana.* New York and London: Harper & Brothers, 1907.

WOODBURY, GEORGE. *John Goffe's Legacy.* New York: W. W. Norton & Company, 1955.

WOODWARD, FLORENCE H. *The People of Vermont, Population Patterns and Trends since 1940.* Montpelier: Vermont Development Commission, 1958.

ZWEIG, STEFAN. *Mental Healers.* London: Cassell & Company, 1933.

INDEX

73 74 75 9 8 7 6 5 4 3 2 1